WORLD COMMUNISM

Key Documentary Material

Compiled and Edited
with an Introduction by
SIDNEY HOOK
New York University

AN ANVIL ORIGINAL
under the general editorship of
LOUIS L. SNYDER

D. VAN NOSTRAND COMPANY, INC.
PRINCETON, NEW JERSEY
TORONTO   LONDON
NEW YORK

TO THOSE WHO WISH TO REMAIN UNDECEIVED

———————————————

D. VAN NOSTRAND COMPANY, INC.
120 Alexander St., Princeton, New Jersey (*Principal office*) : 24 West 40 St., New York, N.Y.
D. VAN NOSTRAND COMPANY (Canada), LTD.
25 Hollinger Rd., Toronto 16, Canada
D. VAN NOSTRAND COMPANY, LTD.
358, Kensington High Street, London, W.14, England

PRINTED IN THE UNITED STATES OF AMERICA

TABLE OF CONTENTS

Introduction 5

Part I. Communist Doctrine and Organization

1. Propositions in the Communist Theory of Organization 14
2. The State and Revolution 19
3. The Stateless Society—The Rule of Lynch Law 21
4. The Meaning of Dictatorship 22
5. The Communist Conception of Democracy 23
6. Communism and Social Democracy 25
7. The Strategy of World Revolution 27
8. The Twenty-One Conditions of Communist Orthodoxy 36
9. Theory of Fascism 43

Part II. Communist Practice

10. The Duties of the Communist Party Member 50
11. Communists and Trade Unions 53
12. Communist Propaganda and Education 58
13. The Communist Party Member Above Ground and Underground 61
14. Why Should Communists Participate in Elections? 64
15. United-Front Tactics 67
16. Aid to Revolutionary Movements 70

Part III. Communism in the U.S.S.R.

17. The Meaning of Coexistence 74
18. Can Communism Survive without World Revolution? 76
19. Defense of the Soviet Union at All Costs 79
20. The Population Bomb and Mother Heroines 82
21. Lenin's Testament 84
22. The Nazi-Soviet Pact, August 23, 1939 86
23. Before and After Hitler Struck Against His Ally 93
24. The Moscow Trials 97
25. Why Did They Confess? 107
26. Khrushchev on Stalin's Crimes 110
27. The Case of Comrade Eikhe 114

3

28. Khrushchev's "Revision" of Leninism   117
29. Soviet Anti-Semitism   122
30. The Soviet Union and the United Nations   127

PART IV. COMMUNISM IN THE UNITED STATES

31. Recognition of the Soviet Union by the United
    States   132
32. The Mechanics of Control of American Com-
    munists by the Soviet Union   134
33. Stalin and the American Communist Party   136
34. The Comrades Squabble—Father Decides   141
35. The Communist Pledge of Allegiance   146
36. How to Achieve a Soviet America   148
37. Roosevelt's March to Fascism   150
38. Self Determination for the Black Belt   152
39. The Student Movement   156
40. The Communist Party "Disaffiliates" from the
    Communist International   160
41. The Dissolution of the Communist International 162
42. The Duclos Letter Revising the Political Struc-
    ture of the Communist Party   165
43. Communists, Loyalty and War   170
44. Henry A. Wallace to Herbert A. Philbrick   174
45. The Findings of the Subversive Activities Con-
    trol Board   175

PART V. THE COMMUNIST MOVEMENT
IN OTHER COUNTRIES

46. The Communist Movement in Mexico, France
    and India   178
47. Communism, Colonialism, and the Underde-
    veloped Countries   186
48. China's "Agrarian Reformers"   190
49. Yugoslavia   201
50. Hungary   212
51. Poland   221

PART VI. FACTS AND ILLUSIONS

52. The Canadian Espionage Operation   244
53. Ideological Espionage: Harry Gold's Confes-
    sion   251
54. A Political Triptych of Comrade Khrushchev   253
LIST OF ANVIL BOOKS   256

INTRODUCTION

This volume attempts to present the theory and historical practice of the international Communist movement by means of relevant documents, most of them from authoritative official Communist sources.

Several features of the collection should be noted in order to avoid misunderstanding.

First, by the term "Communism," and its cognate expressions, is meant the official Communist movement which grew out of the Russian Revolution of October 1917 and the founding of the Soviet Union and the Communist International. There have been opposition and deviating groups of Communists within the Soviet Union and other countries, but their differences have been mainly strategic and tactical, concerned primarily with how best to implement the basic doctrines to which all subscribed. The situation is a little different with respect to the practices of Communist *states* which on certain matters have fallen out with each other; but, here too, there is common allegiance, on the whole, to Communist ideology. Communist China, Yugoslavia and the U.S.S.R. all profess loyalty in theory and practice to "Bolshevik-Leninism," which is the Communist version of Marxism. Whatever variety exists in the practices of Communist regimes—accountable in part by national differences, the period when they were established, and the methods by which they came to power—is of little significance compared to the great gulf between these regimes and societies committed to democracy. For political and tactical purposes in defense of democracy, however, these differences may be of considerable importance.

Second, with some exceptions to be noted later, the relationship between the Communist Party of the Soviet Union and the international Communist movement has been one of complete subordination of the second to the first, from the earliest days of the Bolshevik dictatorship to the present. On all major matters of policy, the needs of the Soviet Union as a state power have been primary.

The Communists throughout the world, as well as those whom they influenced and led, have been encouraged from the beginning to regard the Soviet Union as the leader in the march towards world communism, and to make its defense a consideration overriding everything else. This is especially true with respect to the needs of Soviet foreign policy, whose exigencies have determined, down to a hair, the foreign policy of organizations originally affiliated with the Third International and subsequently grouped together less formally since World War II.

Although the internal and foreign policies of the Soviet Union are to some extent related, a change in one does not necessarily give rise to a change in the other. Under Stalin, domestic conditions were radically transformed from what they were under Lenin. After Stalin's death, the intensity of terror was reduced by Khrushchev. But under all three—Lenin, Stalin and Khrushchev—the foreign policy of the Soviet Union shows an impressive consistency. Even here there have been variations, to be sure, in pace, boldness, and timing, but with respect to extending the orbit of Communist domination and penetration, all have pursued the same basic objective. The special meaning given to the doctrine of "peaceful coexistence," which, in effect, declares Communist willingness to expand without war, goes back to the days of Lenin, who first employed the notion for foreign consumption. Stalin, too, in interviews with correspondents, was wont to stress the willingness of the Soviet Union to coexist with other social systems. At the same time, in the directives to their own Communist Party members, Lenin and Stalin stressed the inescapability of armed conflict between the free and the Communist world. However, the growing military strength and increasing political triumphs of the Soviet Union, and especially the dangers of nuclear conflict which threaten the national existence of all powers, have led Khrushchev to proclaim that war is no longer inevitable in order for the inevitable world triumph of Communism to be achieved. This revision is Khrushchev's contribution to the canons of latterday Bolshevik-Leninism. Although he qualifies his revision by still urging revolutionary wars against colonial powers (other than the Soviet Union) and warning that nuclear war is always possible, the renunciation of the belief that war is necessary is of the first importance. It is one of the causes of the current rift between Communist China and the Kremlin, in which the overwhelming majority of Communist Parties of the world has faithfully followed the latter.

It is this profound interrelation between Soviet foreign policy and the political behavior of the Communist movement which accounts for the preponderance of space I have given to the program and activities of the Communist Party of the U.S.S.R.

Third, the language in which some of these documents are couched will appear puzzling to the uninitiated reader. The early documents are arresting in the frank and bold manner with which they call for the dictatorship of the proletariat under the leadership—or dictatorship—of the Communist Party and for revolutionary action, culminating in armed insurrection. In the later documents, this language disappears almost completely and is replaced by a vocabulary which, if taken literally, would involve a repudiation of basic Communist beliefs. The language of the later years, however, cannot be taken literally, but only in its historical context and with an eye on the purposes for which it is employed. Two considerations especially must be borne in mind with respect to the later documents. The first is the use of "Aesopian language"; the second, the strategy of the "Trojan Horse." These devices of propaganda and agitation were described by Lenin, the organizer, and Dimitroff, one-time head, of the Communist International, who were the first to employ these expressions from Greek mythology and to characterize them.

Lenin explains in the preface to the second edition of his pamphlet, *Imperialism,* originally written in 1916, that in order to get around the then-existing czarist censorship, he had to formulate his political judgments in Aesopean language. Once the Kerensky democratic revolution of February 1917 abolished censorship, Aesopian language was not necessary. Communists could now resort to the frank proclamation of their aims which had hitherto been restricted to their illegal literature. Indeed, in order to differentiate the Communist program from that of Social Democracy and other democratic socialist movements, this frankness was considered mandatory. In every country of the world in which the Communists were legally recognized during the 1920's and mid-1930's, they openly proclaimed their objectives, their means, their strategy and tactics. In many countries, especially the United States, this rather fearsome but honest expression of intention was regarded by most political observers as quaintly irrelevant to serious political problems, as an illustration of political psychopathology rather than of rational ideology. With the growing might of the Soviet Union, the economic depression of the West, and the evidence of Communist infiltration into key areas of social and economic life, greater attention began to be paid to the Communists' own statement of purpose. Passages like those from William Z. Foster's *Towards Soviet America, (see Document No. 34)*, together with Communist infiltration into trade unions and government convinced more and more people that Communists were not harmless heretics but really dangerous conspirators, serving the interests of a foreign power intent upon destroying democracy. In consequence, certain measures were taken, and more were proposed, to bar members of the Communist Party and those under its discipline from strategic positions of trust and confidence, on the ground that since their declared first loyalty was to the government of the Soviet Union and the cause of the Communist Party, they were unfit to serve their own government or to fill the commanding posts of trade unions and other cultural organizations of a democracy.

The Communists were not long in drawing the necessary conclusions from the heightened awareness on the part of their intended victims of what the Communist program had in store for them. They toned down, modified and reinterpreted their declarations in order to make them read as later-day translations of the classics of Western democracy and liberalism, from Jefferson to Mill. The citations of earlier programmatic documents, written in a frantic mood, were now characterized as an expression of "sectarianism," which in this context really meant the enunciation of truths out of season. Communist diehards who were unable, or unwilling, to pretend to the role of 20th-century Jeffersonians were ruthlessly purged.

Another, and perhaps more important, reason explains the shift to Aesopean language from the mid-1930's on.

In the interests of its own security, especially out of fear of Hitler (whom the Kremlin had helped to come to power by concentrating its fire against German Social-Democracy), the Soviet Union espoused the formation of National Fronts, Popular Fronts, and United Fronts. In all of these, representatives of classes and parties slated ultimately to be destroyed under the Communist dictatorship were invited to join the Communists to help withstand the imminent dangers of Fascist dictatorship. Because of the necessities of a common front under these circumstances, the view that the dictatorship of the proletariat could be carried out only by the dictatorship of the Communist Party—which was one of Lenin's chief abridgments of Marxism—had to be formally declared as irrelevant to the more pressing concern of preserving existing democracy against the Fascist onslaught. Since, in the light of historical experience, it appeared that the Communists reserved for themselves the privilege to denounce as Fascists or Social-Fascists any of their current allies in such Fronts, they naturally did not always have easy sailing. Not all who cooperated with them were dupes. Although most were deceived, a few entered into the alliance with their eyes open. The non-Communist allies in these Communist-dominated Fronts consoled themselves with the illusion that they themselves were using the Communists for their own aims. On the whole, these common or united fronts were highly successful in furthering Communist strategy until the Nazi-Soviet Pact confirmed what socialist critics and knowledgeable liberals had long maintained: that every kind of common front with the Communist Party soon develops into a transparent facade for the Communist Party, or (to use a different metaphor employed by the Communists themselves) into "a transmission belt" for Communist purposes, and, in the end, prejudices the worthy objectives in behalf of which the original Front was ostensibly set up.

The fourth feature of this collection is that it does not take at face value the claims of the Communists, as well as many of their opponents, that they are the lineal and legitimate heirs of Marx and Engels. Bolshevik-Leninism is as much a revision of the fundamental theories of Marx and Engels as is the revisionism of Edward Bernstein, the great German Social-Democratic protagonist of reformism. The entire question has been explored in another volume of the Anvil Series (No. 7: *The Ambiguous Legacy: Marx and the Marxists*), to which the reader is referred for further elaboration.

I am acutely aware of the shortcomings of this work, most of which stem from its necessary brevity. But of one thing I am confident. No one who ponders the words of the official spokesman of the Communist movement will be taken by surprise at the actions of the Soviet Union and its satellites. After the Geneva Conference in 1955, the statesmen, as well as most publicists, of the free world heralded a "thaw" in Communist social and political life. They anticipated it would be followed by strong freshets of democratic thought and feeling which in turn would prepare a broad river bed for important democratic institutional changes throughout the Communist world. They confidently predicted a less intransigent posture in foreign policy. Geneva was followed by Hungary and the decimation of the freedom fighters in 1956. In 1959, Khrushchev visits to the West and his strident claims that a Summit Conference was necessary to preserve "peaceful coexistence" were taken as evidence that the Soviet Union wished to abandon the cold war against the West. In fact, in 1960, Khrushchev torpedoed the Paris Summit Conference and threatened to atom bomb the United States if it were necessary to safeguard Cuba and the Congo from aggression.

No claim is made that the Communist ideology is the only or exclusive factor in determining Communist behavior. Other factors—including relatively chance events, the personality of Communist leaders, geography, national tradition—enter into the making of history. What is claimed is that Communist ideology is the most constant, and often the strongest, of these many factors, and that without understanding it and giving it due weight, we cannot predict Communist behavior.

The record, as grim as it is, does *not* preclude the possibility that the Communist world may renounce its program of world domination and its goal of a world Communist state. But if it does so, it must give prior evidence by deeds, and not merely by words, that it is no longer bound by the ideological commitments expressed in the documents contained in this volume; and that it has foresworn the massive campaigns of infiltration, subversion, and conspiratorial deception—unparalleled in scope and intensity by anything previously known in history—against the free world. The likelihood that it will some day do so depends upon many things. The most important among them is the defensive power of the free world to make armed aggression too costly. What Karl Marx said of Czarist Russia in the 19th century holds for Bolshevik Russia in the 20th. "The Russian bear is certainly capable of anything as long as he knows that other animals he has to deal with are capable of nothing." Almost equally important is the capacity of the institutions of the democratic world to expand their programs of welfare and civil freedom to embrace all their citizens. They should present to the uncommitted world a pattern of a culture both politically free and socially just. The resources of the free sector of civilization should be made generously available to those nations which wish to benefit from the blessings of science and technology without paying the terrible price in human degradation and suffering that the Communist leaders have imposed on their hapless peoples.

For purposes of exposition, I have presented the material under six broad, overlapping rubrics, but the reader may begin at any point of special interest without departing very far from the main Communist line.

I am indebted to Dr. Milorad Drachkovitch, Senior Staff Member of the Hoover Institution on War, Revolution and Peace, Stanford, California, for his generous assistance in collecting and translating the materials on Yugoslavia. I am profoundly indebted to Professor Louis L. Snyder, who in relation to this book has functioned not merely as an editor, but as a wise counsellor and scholar.

South Wardsboro, Vermont
September 1962

SIDNEY HOOK

Part 1

COMMUNIST DOCTRINE
AND ORGANIZATION

— 1 —

PROPOSITIONS IN THE COMMUNIST THEORY OF ORGANIZATION

A. The Communist as Professional Revolutionist

Among the important documents of the international Communist movement is Lenin's What's to Be Done?, *originally published in 1902. In it Lenin criticizes those who believe that the miserable economic conditions of the workers can be substantially improved by narrow economic trade union activity without a corresponding political organization. For him every economic struggle is potentially a political struggle. He denies, however, that the spontaneous revolt of the workingclass and allied oppressed groups against onerous living and working conditions is sufficient to develop proper political consciousness and activity. A political organization of professional revolutionists is necessary. This organization brings Communism (or Socialism, as it was called in Lenin's early days) to the workers. The organization of political discontent, leading to the ultimate overthrow of the existing social order, is the specific task of the Communist Parties of the world. Poverty by itself does* not *lead to Communism. Only a Communist Party can lead the struggle towards Communism. Note that in 1902 Lenin called himself a Social-Democrat; later a Bolshevik (see below); and only after the October Revolution of 1917 a "Communist." Despite the changes in nomenclature, however, he retained his organizational ideas. These ideas influenced the organizational structure not only of the Russian Bolshevik Party, but of all parties affiliated with the Communist International. The following selections are from pp. 233-4, 287-8, 298, 299, 335-6, 344-5 of Lenin's* Selected Works, *Vol. 1, Part I, Foreign Languages Publishing House, Moscow, 1952.*

✔   ✔   ✔

. . . We have said that *there could not yet be* Social-Democratic consciousness among the workers. It could only be brought to them from without. The history of all countries shows that the working class, exclusively by its own effort, is able to develop only trade union consciousness, i.e., the conviction that it is necessary to combine in unions, fight the employers and strive to compel the government to pass necessary labour legislation, etc. The theory of Socialism, however, grew out of the philosophic, historical and economic theories that were elaborated by the educated representatives of the propertied classes, the intellectuals. According to their social status, the founders of modern scientific Socialism, Marx and Engels, themselves belonged to the bourgeois intelligentsia. In the very same way, in Russia, the theoretical doctrine of Social-Democracy arose quite independently of the spontaneous growth of the working-class movement; it arose as a natural and inevitable outcome of the development of ideas among the revolutionary socialist intelligentsia. . . .

. . . Class political consciousness can be brought to the workers *only from without,* that is, only from outside of the economic struggle, from outside of the sphere of relations between workers and employers. The sphere from which alone it is possible to obtain this knowledge is the sphere of relationships between *all* the classes and strata and the state and the government, the sphere of the interrelationship between *all* the classes. For that reason, the reply to the question: what must be done in order to bring political knowledge to the workers? cannot be merely the one which, in the majority of cases, the practical workers, especially those who are inclined towards Economism, mostly content themselves with, i.e., "go among the workers." To bring political knowledge to the *workers* with the Social-Democrats must *go among all classes of the population,* must dispatch units of their army *in all directions.* . . .

. . . Only a party that will *organize* really *nation-wide* exposures can become the vanguard of the revolutionary forces in our time. . . .

. . . But if we have to undertake the organization of really nation-wide exposures of the government, what, then, will the over-zealous advocates of "close organic contact with the proletarian struggle" ask of us. The reply is: . . . we Social-Democrats will organize these public exposures; . . . all the questions raised by the agitation will be elucidated in a consistently Social-Democratic spirit, without any concessions to deliberate or non-deliberate distortions of Marxism; . . . this all-round political agitation will be conducted by a party which unites into one inseparable whole the pressure upon the government in the name of the whole people, the revolutionary training of the proletariat, while safeguarding its political independence, and guidance of the economic struggle of the working class, the utilization of all its spontaneous conflicts with its exploiters which rouse and bring into our camp increasing numbers of the proletariat! . . .

. . . But since you raise the question of *organizations* being wiped out and stick to that question, then I assert that it is far more difficult to wipe out a dozen wise men than a hundred fools. And this position I shall defend no matter how much you instigate the crowd against me for my "antidemocratic" views, etc. As I have already said time and again that by "wise men," in connection with organization, I mean professional revolutionaries, irrespective of whether they are trained from among students or workingmen. I assert: 1) that no revolutionary movement can endure without a stable organization of leaders that maintains continuity; 2) that the wider the masses spontaneously drawn into the struggle, forming the basis of the movement and participating in it, the more urgent the need of such an organization, and the more solid this organization must be (for it is much easier for demagogues to sidetrack the more backward sections of the masses); 3) that such an organization must consist chiefly of people professionally engaged in revolutionary activity; 4) that in an autocratic state, the more we *confine* the membership of such an organization to people who are professionally engaged in revolutionary activity and who have been professionally trained in the art of combating the political police, the more difficult will it be to wipe out such an organization, and 5) the *greater* will be the number of people of the working class and of the other classes of society who will be able to join the movement and perform active work in it. . . .

. . . In order to be fully prepared for his task, the worker-revolutionary must also become a professional revolutionary. Hence B-v is wrong when he says that since the worker spends eleven and a half hours in the factory, the brunt of all other revolutionary functions (apart from agitation) "*must necessarily* fall mainly upon the shoulders of an extremely small force of intellectuals." But this is not out of sheer "necessity." It is so because we are backward, because we do not recognize our duty to assist every capable worker to become a *professional* agitator, organizer, propagandist, literature distributor, etc., etc. In this respect, we waste our strength in a positively shameful manner; we lack the ability to husband that which should be tended and reared with special care. . . .

B. The Bolshevik Party

The following extracts explain how the Russian Communist Party acquired the name "Bolshevik" (which means "majority"), in its early years. At the Second Congress of the Russian Social-Democratic Party in London in 1903, controversy raged over whether the Party should be organized along the lines Lenin advocated in his What's to Be Done? *Lenin's faction had a narrow "majority." It subsequently called itself the Bolshevik or majority faction even when in fact it subsequently had fewer members than the Menshevik or so-called minority faction. Lenin had a shrewd sense of the importance of political semantics. The following excerpts are from "One Step Forward, Two Steps Back," pp. 410-11, 452 of the* Selected Works, *Vol. 1, Part I.*

✓ ✓ ✓

. . . The first question is that of the political significance of the division of our Party into a "majority" and a "minority" that took shape at the Second Party Congress and pushed all previous divisions among Russian Social-Democrats far into the background.

The second question is that of the significance in principle of the position taken up by the new *Iskra* on organizational questions, in so far as this position is really based on principle.

The first question concerns the starting point of the struggle in our Party, its source, its causes, and its fundamental political character. The second question concerns the ultimate outcome of the struggle, its finale, the total of principle that results from the addition of all that pertains to the realm of principle and the subtraction of all that pertains to the realm of squabbling. The answer to the first question is obtained by analyzing the struggle at the Party Congress; the answer to the second, by analyzing what is new in the principles of the new *Iskra*. Both these analyses, which constitute nine-tenths of my pamphlet, lead to the conclusion that the "majority" is the revolutionary, and the "minority" the opportunist wing of our Party; the disagreements that divide the two wings at the present moment for the most part concern not questions of program or tactics but only organizational questions; the new system of views that emerges the more clearly from the columns of the new *Iskra* the more it tries to lend profundity to its position and the more that position becomes cleared of all the committed squabbles about co-option—is opportunism in matters of organization. . . .

. . . The principal ideas which the *Iskra* strove to make the basis of the Party's organization amounted essentially to the following—two: first, the idea of centralism, which defined in principle the method of deciding all particular and detail questions of organization; second, the special function of an organ, a newspaper, for ideological leadership, an idea which took into account the temporary and special requirements of the Russian Social-Democratic working-class movement amidst conditions of political slavery, on the understanding that the *initial* base of operations for the revolutionary assault would be set up abroad. The first idea, the only correct one in principle, was to permeate the entire Rules; the second, being a particular idea necessitated by temporary circumstances of place and mode of action, took the form of a *seeming* departure from centralism in the proposal to set up *two centres*, a *Central Organ* and a *Central Committee*. Both these principal *Iskra* ideas of Party organization had been developed by me in the *Iskra* editorial (No. 4) "Where to Begin?" and in *What Is to Be Done?*

— 2 —

THE STATE AND REVOLUTION

In leading the opposition to the Kerensky Provisional Government, Lenin found it necessary to develop the theory of the state as a guide to revolutionary practice and policy. The work entitled State and Revolution *is largely exegetical and strives to make the Bolshevik program of violent overthrow of the democratic Kerensky government appear to be the inescapable consequence of Marxist theory. It contains a savage polemic against socialists like Kautsky who, in agreement with Marx in his later years, believed that a peaceful transition between capitalism and socialism was possible. The following passages are from the English edition published by the Foreign Languages Publishing House in Moscow, 1952,* Selected Works, *Vol. 2, Part I.*

The state is the product and the manifestation of the *irreconcilability* of class antagonisms. The state arises when, where, and to the extent that the class antagonisms *cannot* be objectively reconciled. And, conversely, the existence of the state proves that the class antagonisms *are* irreconcilable.

It is precisely on this most important and fundamental point that distortions of Marxism arise along two main lines.

On the one hand, the bourgeois, and particularly the petty-bourgeois, ideologists, compelled under the pressure of indisputable historical facts to admit that the state only exists where there are class antagonisms and the class struggle, "correct" Marx in such a way as to make it appear that the state is an organ for *reconciling* the classes. According to Marx, the state could neither arise nor maintain itself if a reconciliation of classes were possible. But with the petty-bourgeois and philistine professors and publicists, the state—and this frequently on the strength of benevolent references to Marx—becomes a conciliator of the classes. According to Marx, the state is an organ of class *domination,* an organ of *oppression* of one class by another; its aim is the creation of "order" which legalises and perpetuates this oppression by moderating the collisions between the classes. . . .

The replacement of the bourgeois by the proletarian state is impossible without a violent revolution. The abolition of the proletarian state, i.e., of all states, is only possible through "withering away."

On the other hand, the "Kautskyist" distortion of Marx is far more subtle. "Theoretically," there is no denying that the state is the organ of class domination, or that class antagonisms are irreconcilable. But what is forgotten or glossed over is this: if the state is the product of the irreconcilable character of class antagonisms, if it is a force standing *above* society and "increasingly separating itself from it," then it is clear that the liberation of the oppressed class is impossible not only without a violent revolution, *but also without the destruction* of the apparatus of state power, which was created by the ruling class and in which this "separation" is embodied. . . .

Again, during the *transition* from capitalism to Communism, suppression is *still* necessary; but it is the suppression of the minority of exploiters by the majority of exploited. A special apparatus, special machinery for suppression, the "state," is *still* necessary, but this is now a transitional state, no longer a state in the usual sense, for the suppression of the minority of exploiters, by the majority of the wage slaves of *yesterday,* is a matter comparatively so easy, simple and natural that it will cost far less bloodshed than the suppression of the risings of slaves, serfs or wage labourers, and will cost mankind far less. This is compatible with the diffusion of democracy among such an overwhelming majority of the population, that the need for *special machinery* of suppression will begin to disappear. The exploiters are, naturally, unable to suppress the people without a most complex machinery for performing this task; but *the people* can suppress the exploiters even with very simple "machinery," almost without any "machinery," without any special apparatus, by the simple *organisation of the armed masses* (such as the Soviets of Workers' and Soldiers' Deputies.

— 3 —

THE STATELESS SOCIETY—THE RULE OF LYNCH LAW

The actual development of the Russian Revolution belied Lenin's anticipations in many ways. The dictatorship of the proletariat in fact became the dictatorship of the minority Communist Party over the proletariat—which constituted only a minority of the entire population—and over all other classes. The organs of repression did not dissolve into "simple organizations of the armed masses." They developed new forms, including not only standing, professional armies, but the dreaded secret police which pervaded every nook and cranny of the country and was responsible only to the Political Bureau of the Communist Party. Instead of withering away as the socialized economy expanded, the state became stronger and stronger. Although "classes" have allegedly disappeared in the Soviet Union, the state still thrives.

Nothing indicates so clearly the Utopian character of Lenin's thinking, which constituted one source of his fanaticism, as his belief that some day, after communism has been established, there will be no need for police, courts, judges or any other institutions to dispense justice. The following passage describes how "excesses" will be handled. It is interesting to observe that Lenin believed that even excesses will no longer occur once economic

*poverty disappears. The possibility that there exist forms
of oppression or exploitation not rooted in economic
causes receives no attention.* (Selected Works, *Vol. 2,
Part I*).

✓   ✓   ✓

Finally, only Communism renders the state absolutely
unnecessary, for there is *no one* to be suppressed—"no
one" in the sense of a *class,* in the sense of a systematic
struggle with a definite section of the population. We are
not Utopians, and we do not in the least deny the possibility and inevitability of excesses on the part of *individual
persons,* nor the need to suppress *such* excesses. But, in
the first place, no special machinery, no special apparatus
of repression is needed for this; this will be done by the
armed people itself, as simply and as readily as any crowd
of civilised people, even in modern society, parts a pair of
combatants or does not allow a woman to be outraged.
And, secondly, we know that the fundamental social cause
of excesses which consist in violating the rules of social
life is the exploitation of the masses, their want and their
poverty. With the removal of this chief cause, excesses
will inevitably begin to *"wither away."* We do not know
how quickly and in what succession, but we know that
they will wither away. With their withering away, the
state will also *wither away.*

— 4 —

THE MEANING OF DICTATORSHIP

*The term "dictatorship" is employed by Lenin in a
most literal sense. It is essential to be clear about Lenin's
meaning, for it is a clue to what happens when the dictatorship is exercised by a political party in the name of
a class which cannot freely express its consent or dissent.*

Quotations from Lenin are from Selected Works, *Vol. 2, Part II, p. 41*f.

⚡   ⚡   ⚡

Dictatorship is rule based directly upon force and unrestricted by any laws.

The Revolutionary dictatorship of the proletariat is rule won and maintained by the use of violence by the proletariat against the bourgeoisie, rule that is unrestricted by any laws. [*from* The Proletarian Revolution]

Not a single important political or organizational question is decided by any state institution in our republic without the guiding instructions of the Central Committee of the Party. [*from* Left-Wing Communism]

Stalin makes explicit what is implied in the above sentence in his assertion that "the dictatorship of the proletariat" is essentially "the dictatorship" of the Communist Party. (Foundations of Leninism, *Moscow, 1934, Chapter VIII.*)

Here in the Soviet Union, in the land of the dictatorship of the proletariat, the fact that not a single important political or organisational question is decided by our Soviet and other mass organisations without directions from the Party must be regarded as the highest expression of the leading rôle of the Party. *In this sense* it could be said that the dictatorship of the proletariat is *in essence* the "dictatorship" of its vanguard, the "dictatorship" of its Party, as the main guiding force of the proletariat.

— 5 —

THE COMMUNIST CONCEPTION OF DEMOCRACY

The current era is marked by "the degradation of the word." One of the words whose meaning has been vio-

lently altered to fit the purposes of political propaganda is "democracy." Hitler and Mussolini called their dictatorships "democracy in a higher sense." Peron, the former dictator of Argentina, spoke of his regime as "directed democracy"; Franco speaks of "the organic democracy" of Spain. The following comment by Stalin on the Draft Constitution of 1936 indicates why Communists, who permit no freedom of speech, press, assembly and other rights of political dissent, who outlaw all opposition political parties, claim that theirs is the only "thoroughly democratic" regime in the world. The Communist Party claims its rule represents the interests of the workers, and therefore it is democratic no matter what its form. Other dictators have made the same claim that they were ruling in the interests of the people. Even if it were true, this would not make a regime democratic, as the existence of benevolent despotism shows. A democratic regime must rest on freely given consent *of the governed. Without the right of legal political opposition, consent is never free. This document is from* International Press Correspondence, *November 28, 1936, p. 139.*

✓   ✓   ✓

Finally, there is one group of critics [who] charge that the draft makes no change in the existing position in the U.S.S.R., that it leaves the dictatorship of the working class intact, does not provide for the freedom of political parties and preserves the present leading position of the Communist Party in the U.S.S.R. At the same time, this group of critics believes that the absence of freedom for parties in the U.S.S.R. is an indication of the violation of fundamental principles of democracy.

I must admit that the Draft New Constitution really does leave in force the regime of the dictatorship of the working class and also leaves unchanged the present leading position of the Communist Party in the U.S.S.R.

If our venerable critics regard this as a shortcoming of the Draft Constitution, this can only be regretted. We Bolsheviks, however, consider this as a merit of the Draft Constitution. As for the freedom of various political parties, we here adhere to somewhat different views. A party is part of a class, its vanguard section. Several parties, and consequently freedom of parties, can only exist in a society, where there are antagonistic classes whose interests are hostile and irreconcilable, where there are, say, capitalists and workers, landlords and peasants, kulaks and poor peasants, and so on. But in the U.S.S.R. there are no longer such classes as capitalists, landlords, kulaks and so on. There are only two classes in the U.S.S.R., workers and peasants, whose interests are not only not antagonistic, but on the contrary, are amicable. Consequently, in the U.S.S.R. there is no ground for the existence of several parties, nor therefore, for the existence of freedom for such parties.

In the U.S.S.R. there are grounds for only one party, the Communist Party. In the U.S.S.R. only one party can exist, the Communist Party, a party which boldly defends the interests of workers and peasants to the very end. And there can hardly be any doubts about the fact that it defends the interests of these classes not so badly.

They talk about democracy, but what is democracy? Democracy in capitalist countries where there are antagonistic classes is, in the last analysis, democracy for the strong, democracy for a propertied minority. Democracy in the U.S.S.R., on the other hand, is democracy for the toilers, is democracy for all. But from this it follows that the principles of democracy are violated, not by the draft of a new Constitution of the U.S.S.R., but by bourgeois constitutions. This is why I think that the Constitution of the U.S.S.R. is the only thoroughly democratic Constitution in the world.

— 6 —

COMMUNISM AND SOCIAL DEMOCRACY

On November 7, 1934, almost two years after Hitler's Fascist government was established in Germany, the Daily Worker *reprinted a speech of Stalin's delivered to celebrate the 10th anniversary of the Bolshevik Revolution.*

Among other things Stalin indicates the Communist conception of the nature and role of Social-Democracy. In 1935 at the Seventh Congress of the Communist International, fearful of Hitler's intentions towards the Soviet Union, the Kremlin reversed its course and offered a united front to the Social-Democrats whose death it had consistently proclaimed and advocated. The following paragraph is from the conclusion. Its study is specially recommended to those who draw a simple equation between socialism and Communism.

＊   ＊   ＊

Between social democracy and Marxism there lies today an abyss. From now on the only bearer and stronghold of Marxism is Leninism, Communism.

The October Revolution has separated social democracy from Marxism and driven it into the camp of the immediate defenders of capitalism against the first proletarian dictatorship in the world. When the social democratic leaders abuse the "Soviet regime" and laud parliamentary "democracy," they thereby wish to say that they are fighting and will fight for the re-establishment of capitalist conditions in the Soviet Union, for the maintenance of capitalist slavery in the "civilized" States. Present day social democracy is an ideological support of capitalism. Lenin was indisputably right when he said that the present social democratic politicians "will, in the civil war of the proletariat against the bourgeoisie, inevitably side with the Versaillaise against the Communards."

One cannot put an end to capitalism without putting an end to social democracy within the labor movement. Consequently, the era of the death of capitalism is at the same time the era of the death of social democracy in the labor movement.

The era of the rule of the Second International and of social democracy in the labor movement is at an end.

There has commenced the era of the rule of Leninism and the rule of the Third International.

THE STRATEGY OF
WORLD REVOLUTION

The first Congress of the Communist International was held in Moscow in March, 1919. It consisted mostly of members of the Russian Communist Party, some of whom were appointed to represent Communist groups of other countries. The second Congress was held during July and August, 1920, in Moscow. It was better attended. Reliable knowledge concerning the Communist movement was not easily obtainable among socialist and labor groups in Europe. On the strength of their own interpretation of the Communist program, and their overriding interests in peace, some of these groups evinced a sympathetic interest in what the Russian Communists were doing. Of the little that was known in the West about the Communist program, few took Communist revolutionary pronouncements literally. Most socialists assumed that the call for civil war, armed insurrection, revolutionary dictatorship and terror reflected the special local conditions of backward Russia, which had never known the free political institutions of Western Europe and America.

With a commendable frankness, which was not abandoned until the Seventh Congress, the Russian leaders of the Third International laid down the political line which was to be followed by all Communist Parties without exception. The reader will find in the following passages, excerpted from the underground publications of the American Communist Party (issued in the name of The Contemporary Publishing Society), the basic strategy which is to control Communist tactics in the struggle for the conquest of political power. These expressed principles have never been recalled, although additions have been made from time to time. No Communist is more authoritative than Lenin, the author of these theses. They will be found in his Collected Works. English edition, Moscow, Vol. IX.

The Fundamental Tasks of the Communist International

THESES ADOPTED BY THE SECOND CONGRESS

1. A characteristic feature of the present moment in the development of the international Communist movement is the fact that in all the capitalist countries the best representatives of the revolutionary proletariat have completely understood the fundamental principles of the Communist International, namely, the dictatorship of the proletariat and the power of the Soviets; and with a loyal enthusiasm have placed themselves on the side of the Communist International. A still more important and great step forward is the unlimited sympathy with these principles manifested by the wider masses not only of the proletariat of the towns, but also by the advanced portion of the agrarian workers.

On the other hand two mistakes or weaknesses in the extraordinarily rapidly increasing international Communist movement have shown themselves. One very serious weakness directly dangerous to the success of the cause of the liberation of the proletariat consists in the fact that some of the old leaders and old parties of the Second International—partly half-unconsciously yielding to the wishes and pressure of the masses, partly consciously deceiving them in order to preserve their former role of agents and supporters of the bourgeoisie inside the Labor movement—are declaring their conditional or even unconditional affiliation to the Third International, while remaining, in reality, in the whole practice of their party and political work, on the level of the Second International. Such a state of things is absolutely inadmissible, because it demoralizes the masses, hinders the development of a strong Communist Party, and lowers their respect for the Third International by threatening repetition of such betrayals as that of the Hungarian Social-Democrats, who had rapidly assumed the disguise of Communists. The second much less important mistake, which is, for the most part, a malady inherent in the party growth of the movement, is the tendency to be extremely "left," which leads to an erroneous valuation of the role and duties of the party in respect to the class and to the mass, and of the obligation of the revolutionary Communists to work in the bourgeois parliaments and reactionary labor unions.

The duty of the Communists is not to gloss over any of the weaknesses of their movement, but to criticize them openly, in order to get rid of them promptly and radically. To this end it is necessary, 1) to establish concretely, especially on the basis of the already acquired practical experience, the meaning of the term: "Dictatorship of the Proletariat" and "Soviet Power," and, 2) to point out what could and should be in all countries the immediate and systematic preparatory work to realizing these formulas; and, 3) to indicate the ways and means of curing our movement of its defects.

2. The victory of Socialism over Capitalism—as the first step to Communism—demands the accomplishment of the three following tasks by the proletariat, as the only really revolutionary class:

The first task is to lay low the exploiters, and above all the bourgeoisie as their chief economic and political representative; to defeat them completely; to crush their resistance; to render impossible any attempts on their part to reimpose the yoke of capitalism and wage-slavery.

The second is to inspire and lead in the footsteps of the revolutionary advance guard of the proletariat, its Communist party—not only the whole proletariat or the great majority, but the entire mass of workers and those exploited by capital; to enlighten, organize, instruct, and discipline them during the course of the bold and mercilessly firm struggle against the exploiters; to wrench this enormous majority of the population in all the capitalist countries out of their state of dependence on the bourgeoisies; to instill in them, through practical experience, confidence in the leading role of the proletariat and its revolutionary advance guard. The third is to neutralize or render harmless the inevitable fluctuations between the bourgeoisie and the proletariat, between bourgeois democracy and Soviet Power, on the part of that rather numerous class in all advanced countries—although constituting a minority of the population—the small owners and proprietors in agriculture, industry, commerce, and the corresponding layers of intellectuals, employees, and so on.

The first and second tasks are independent ones, demanding each of them their special methods of action in respect to the exploiters and to the exploited. The third task results from the two first, demanding only a skilful, timely, supple combination of the methods of the first and second kind, depending on the concrete circumstances of each separate case of fluctuation.

3. Under the circumstances which have been created in the whole world, and especially in the most advanced, most powerful, most enlightened and freest capitalist countries by militarist imperialism—oppression of colonies and weaker nations, the universal imperialist slaughter, the "peace" of Versailles—*to admit the idea of a voluntary submission of the capitalists to the will of the majority of the exploited, of a peaceful, reformist passage to Socialism, is not only to give proof of an extreme petty bourgeois stupidity, but it is a direct deception of the workmen, a disguisal of capitalist wage-slavery, a concealment of the truth.* [*Editor's italics*] This truth is that the bourgeoisie, the most enlightened and democratic portion of the bourgeoisie, is even now not stopping at deceit and crime, at the slaughter of millions of workmen and peasants, in order to retain the right of private ownership over the means of production. Only a violent defeat of the bourgeoisie, the confiscation of its property, the annihilation of the entire bourgeois governmental apparatus, parliamentary, judicial, military, bureaucratic, administrative, municipal, etc., even the individual exile or internment of the most stubborn and dangerous exploiters, the establishment of a strict control over them for the repression of all inevitable attempts at resistance and restoration of capitalist slavery—only such measures will be able to guarantee the complete submission of the whole class of exploiters.

On the other hand, it is the same disguising of capitalism and bourgeois democracy, the same deceiving of the workmen, when the old parties and old leaders of the Second International admit the idea that the majority of the workers and exploited will be able to acquire a clear Socialist consciousness, firm Socialist convictions and character under the conditions of capitalist enslavement, under the yoke of the bourgeoisie, which assumes an endless variety of forms—the more refined and at the same time the more cruel and pitiless, the more cultured the given capitalist nation. In reality it is only when the advance guard of the proletariat, supported by the whole class as the only revolutionary one, or a majority of the same, will have overthrown the exploiters, crushed them, freed all the exploited from their position of slaves, improved their conditions of life immediately at the expense of the expropriated capitalists—only after that, and during the very course of the acute class struggle, it will be possible to bring about the enlightenment, education and organization of the widest masses of workers and exploited around the proletariat, under its influence and direction; to cure them of their egotism, their non-solidarity, their vices and weaknesses engendered by private ownership, and to transform them into free workers.

4. For victory over capitalism a correct correlation between the leading Communist Party—the revolutionary class, the proletariat—and the masses, i.e., the whole mass of workers and exploited, is essential. If the Communist Party is really the advance guard of the revolutionary class, if it includes the best representatives of the class, if it consists of perfectly conscious and loyal Communists, enlightened by experience gained in the stubborn revolutionary struggle—if it can be bound indissolubly with the entire life of its class, and through the latter with the whole mass of the exploited, and if it can inspire full confidence in this class and this mass, only then is it capable of leading the proletariat in the pitiless, decisive, and final struggle against all the forces of capitalism. On the other hand, only under the leadership of such a Party will the proletariat be able to employ all the forces of its revolutionary onslaught, nullifying the inevitable apathy and partial resistance of the insignificant minority of the demoralized labor aristocracy, the old trade-union and guild leaders, etc. Only then will the proletariat be able to display its power which is immeasurably greater than its share in the population, by reason of the economic organization of capitalist society itself. Lastly, only when practically freed from the yoke of the bourgeoisie and the bourgeois governing apparatus, only after acquiring the possibility of freely (from all capitalist exploitation) organizing into its own Soviets, will the mass—i.e., the total of all the workers and exploited—employ for the first time

in history all the initiative and energy of tens of millions of people, formerly crushed by capitalism. Only when the Soviets will become the only State apparatus, will effectual participation in the administration be realized for the entire mass of the exploited, who, even under the most cultured and free bourgeois democracy, remain practically excluded from participation in the administration. Only in the Soviets does the mass really begin to study, not out of books, but out of its own practical experience, the work of Socialist construction, the creation of a new social discipline, a free union of free workers.

6. The conquest of political power by the proletariat does not put a stop to its class struggle against the bourgeoisie; on the contrary, it makes the struggle especially broad, acute, and pitiless. All the groups, parties, leaders of the Labor movement, fully or partially on the side of reformism, the "center," and so on, turn inevitably, during the most acute periods of the struggle, either to the side of the bourgeoisie or to that of the wavering ones, and the most dangerous are added to the number of the unreliable friends of the vanquished proletariat. Therefore the preparation of the dictatorship of the proletariat demands not only an increased struggle against all reformists and "centrist" tendencies, but a modification of the nature of this struggle.

The struggle should not be limited to an explanation of the fallacy of such tendencies, but it should stubbornly and mercilessly denounce any leader in the Labor movement who may be manifesting such tendencies, otherwise the proletariat will not know whom it must trust in the most decisive struggle against the bourgeoisie. The struggle is such, that the slightest hesitation or weakness in the denunciation of those who show themselves to be reformists or "centrists," means a direct increase of the danger that the power of the proletariat may be overthrown by the bourgeoisie, which will on the morrow utilize in favor of the counter-revolution all that which to short-sighted people appears only as a "theoretical difference of opinion" to-day.

7. In particular one cannot stop at the usual doctrinaire refutation of all "collaboration" between the proletariat and the bourgeoisie:

The simple defense of "liberty and equality," under the

condition of preserving the right of private ownership of the means of production, becomes transformed under the conditions of the dictatorship of the proletariat—which will never be able to suppress completely all private ownership—into a "collaboration" with the bourgeoisie, which undermines directly the power of the working class. The dictatorship of the proletariat means the strengthening and defense, by means of the ruling power of the State, of the "non-liberty" of the exploiter to continue his work of oppression and exploitation, the "inequality" of the proprietor (i.e., of the person who has taken for himself personally the means of production created by public labor and the proletariat). That which before the victory of the proletariat seems but a theoretical difference of opinion on the question of "democracy," becomes inevitably on the morrow of the victory, a question which can only be decided by force of arms. Consequently, without a radical modification of the whole nature of the struggle against the "centrists" and "defenders of democracy," even a preliminary preparation of the mass for the realization of a dictatorship of the proletariat is impossible.

8. The dictatorship of the proletariat is the most decisive and revolutionary form of class struggle between the proletariat and the bourgeoisie. Such a struggle can be successful only when the revolutionary advance guard of the proletariat leads the majority. The preparation of the dictatorship of the proletariat demands, therefore, not only the elucidation of the bourgeois nature of all reformism, all defense of "democracy," with the preservation of the right to the ownership of the means of production; not only the denunciation of such tendencies, which in practice mean the defense of the bourgeoisie inside the Labor movement—but it demands also the replacing of the old leaders by Communists in all kinds of proletarian organizations, not only political, but industrial, co-operative, educational, etc. The more lasting, complete, and solid the rule of the bourgeois democracy has been in any country, the more has it been possible for the bourgeoisie to appoint as labor leaders men who have been educated by it, imbued with its views and prejudices and very frequently directly or indirectly bribed by it. It is necessary to remove all these representatives of the Labor aristoc-

racy, all such "bourgeois" workmen, from their posts and replace them by even inexperienced workers, so long as these are in unity with the exploited masses, and enjoy the latter's confidence in the struggle against the exploiters. The dictatorship of the proletariat will demand the appointment of such inexperienced workmen to the most responsible State functions, otherwise the rule of the Labor government will be powerless and it will not have the support of the masses.

9. The dictatorship of the proletariat is the most complete realization of a leadership over all workers and exploited, who have been oppressed, beaten down, crushed, intimidated, dispersed, deceived by the class of capitalists, on the part of the only class prepared for such a leading role by the whole history of capitalism. Therefore the preparation of the dictatorship of the proletariat must begin immediately and in all places by means of the following methods among others:

In every organization, union, association—beginning with the proletarian ones at first, and afterwards in all those of the non-proletarian workers and exploited masses (political, professional, military, co-operative, educational, sporting, etc., etc.) must be formed groups or nuclei of Communists—mostly open ones, but also secret ones which become necessary in each case when the arrest or exile of their members or the dispersal of their organization is threatened; and these nuclei, in close contact with one another and with the central Party, exchanging experiences, carrying on the work of propaganda, campaign, organization, adapting themselves to all the branches of social life, to all the various forms and subdivisions of the working masses, must systematically train themselves, the Party, the class, and the masses by such multiform work. [Editor's Italics]

At the same time it is most important to work out practically the necessary methods on the one hand in respect to the "leaders" or responsible representatives, who are very frequently hopelessly infected with petty bourgeois and imperialist prejudices; on the other hand, in respect to the masses, who, especially after the imperialist slaughter, are mostly inclined to listen to and accept the doctrine of the necessity of leadership of the proletariat as the only way out of capitalistic enslavement. The masses must be approached with patience and caution, and with an understanding of the peculiarities, the special psychology of each layer, each profession of these masses.

10. In particular one of the groups or nuclei of the Communists deserves the exclusive attention and care of the party, namely, the parliamentary faction, i.e., the group of members of the Party who are members of bourgeois representative institutions (first of all state institutions, then local, municipal, and others). . . . such a tribune has a special importance in the eyes of the wider circles of the backward or prejudiced working masses; therefore, from this very tribune, the Communists must carry on their work of propaganda, agitation, organization, explaining to the masses why the dissolution of the bourgeois parliament (Constituent Assembly) by the national Congress of Soviets was a legitimate proceeding at the time in Russia (as it will be in all countries in due time). . . .

11. One of the chief causes of difficulty in the revolutionary Labor movement in the advanced capitalist countries lies in the fact that owing to colonial dominions and super-dividends of a financial capital, etc., capital has been able to attract a comparatively more solid and broader group of a small minority of the labor aristocracy. The latter enjoy better conditions of pay and are most of all impregnated with the spirit of professional narrow-mindedness, bourgeois and imperialist prejudices. This is the true social "support" of the Second International reformists and centrists, and at the present moment almost the chief social support of the bourgeoisie.

Not even preliminary preparation of the proletariat for the overthrow of the bourgeoisie is possible without an immediate, systematic, widely organized and open struggle against the group which undoubtedly—as experience has already proved—will furnish plenty of men for the White Guards of the bourgeoisie after the victory of the proletariat. All the parties adhering to the Third International must at all costs put into practice the mottoes: "deeper into the masses," "in closer contact with the masses," understanding by the word "masses" the entire mass of workers and those exploited by capitalism, especially the less organized and enlightened, the most oppressed and less adaptable to organization. . . .

12. *For all countries, even for most free "legal" and "peaceful" ones in the sense of a lesser acuteness in the class struggle, the period has arrived, when it has become absolutely necessary for every Communist party to join systematically lawful and unlawful work, lawful and unlawful organization.* [*Editor's italics*] . . . It is especially necessary to carry on unlawful work in the army, navy, and police, as, after the imperialist slaughter, all the governments in the world are becoming afraid of the national armies, open to all peasants and workingmen, and they are setting up in secret all kinds of select military organizations recruited from the bourgeoisie and especially provided with improved technical equipment.

On the other hand, it is also necessary, in all cases without exception, not to limit oneself to unlawful work, but to carry on also lawful work overcoming all difficulties, founding a lawful press and lawful organizations under the most diverse, and in case of need, frequently changing names. This is now being done by the illegal Communist parties in Finland, in part in Germany, Poland, Latvia, etc. It is thus that the I.W.W. in America should act, as well as all the lawful Communist parties at present, in case prosecutors start prosecutions on the basis of resolutions of the congresses of the Communist International, etc.

— 8 —

THE TWENTY-ONE CONDITIONS OF COMMUNIST ORTHODOXY

The following conditions were laid down by the Communist International as rules governing acceptance of applications of all groups and parties seeking affiliation. They played a decisive role in splitting the labor and so-

cialist movement of the West, which in many countries regarded Communist rhetoric as mere phrasemongery and naïvely assumed that common action for common gains would be sufficient to insure organizational unity. These conditions indicated that the Communist International, directed by the Kremlin, took the business of armed insurrection seriously. That is why, among other reasons, it demanded the expulsion from any organization seeking affiliation, of all democratic, reformist leaders, particularly those who interpreted the phrase "the dictatorship of the proletariat" as broadly synonymous with "workers' democracy" and therefore refused to establish a "dictatorship of the Communist Party" over the proletariat. The tone in which these conditions were formulated, demanding "unconditional and peremptory" obedience, is eloquent evidence of the para-military spirit which characterizes the Communist movement. The document, here reprinted from the same source as No. 7, made some sections of the democratic socialist and labor movement aware of the threat which Communism—as a movement organized by, and in behalf of, the Soviet Union—posed to the traditional ideals of freedom and justice associated with socialism.

The Second Congress of the Communist International rules that the conditions for joining the Communist International shall be as follows:

1. The general propaganda and agitation should bear a really Communist character, and should correspond to the programme and decisions of the Third International. The entire party press should be edited by reliable Communists who have proved their loyalty to the cause of the Proletarian revolution. The dictatorship of the proletariat should not be spoken of simply as a current hackneyed formula, it should be advocated in such a way that its necessity should be apparent to every rank-and-file working man and woman, to each soldier and peasant, and should emanate from everyday facts systematically recorded by our press day by day.

All periodicals and other publications, as well as all party publications and editions, are subject to the control of the presidium of the party, independently of whether the party is legal or illegal. The editors should in no way be given an opportunity to abuse their autonomy and carry on a policy not fully corresponding to the policy of the party.

Wherever the followers of the Third International have access, and whatever means of propaganda are at their disposal, whether the columns of newspapers, popular meetings, labor unions or co-operatives,—it is indispensable for them not only to denounce the bourgeoisie, but also its assistants and agents—reformists of every color and shade.

2. Every organization desiring to join the Communist International shall be bound systematically and regularly to remove from all the responsible posts in the labor movement (Party organizations, editors, labor unions, parliamentary factions, co-operatives, municipalities, etc.), all reformists and followers of the "centre," and to have them replaced by Communists, even at the cost of replacing at the beginning "experienced" men by rank-and-file working men.

3. The class struggle in almost every country of Europe and America is entering the phase of civil war. Under such conditions the Communists can have no confidence in bourgeois laws. They should create everywhere a parallel illegal apparatus, which at the decisive moment should do its duty by the party, and in every way possible assist the resolution. In every country where in consequence of martial law or of other exceptional laws, the Communists are unable to carry on their work lawfully, a combination of lawful and unlawful work is absolutely necessary.

4. A persistent and systematic propaganda and agitation is necessary in the army, where Communist groups should be formed in every military organization. Wherever, owing to repressive legislation, agitation becomes impossible, it is necessary to carry on such agitation illegally. But refusal to carry on or participate in such work should be considered equal to treason to the revolutionary cause, and incompatible with affiliation with the Third International.

5. A systematic and regular propaganda is necessary in the rural districts. The working class can gain no victory unless it possesses the sympathy and support of at least part of the rural workers and of the poor peasants,

and unless other sections of the population are equally utilized. Communist work in the rural districts is acquiring a predominant importance during the present period. It should be carried on through Communist workingmen of both city and country who have connections with the rural districts. To refuse to do this work, or to transfer such work to untrustworthy half reformists, is equal to renouncing the proletarian revolution.

6. Every party desirous of affiliating with the Third International should renounce not only avowed social patriotism, but also the falsehood and the hypocrisy of social pacifism; it should systematically demonstrate to the workers that without a revolutionary overthrow of capitalism no international arbitration, no talk of disarmament, no democratic reorganization of the League of Nations will be capable of saving mankind from new Imperialist wars.

7. Parties desirous of joining the Communist International must recognize the necessity of a complete and absolute rupture with reformism and the policy of the "centrists," and must advocate this rupture amongst the widest circles of the party membership, without which condition a consistent Communist policy is impossible. The Communist International demands unconditionally and peremptorily that such rupture be brought about with the least possibly delay. The Communist International cannot reconcile itself to the fact that such avowed reformists as for instance Turati, Modigliani, Kautsky, Hillquit, Longuet, Macdonald and others should be entitled to consider themselves members of the Third International. This would make the Third International resemble the Second International.

8. In the Colonial question and that of the oppressed nationalities there is necessary an especially distinct and clear line of conduct of the parties of countries where the bourgeoisie possesses such colonies or oppresses other nationalities. Every party desirous of belonging to the Third International should be bound to denounce without any reserve all the methods of "its own" imperialists in the colonies, supporting not only in words but practically a movement of liberation in the colonies. It should demand the expulsion of its own Imperialists from such colonies, and cultivate among the workingmen of its own

country a truly fraternal attitude towards the working population of the colonies and oppressed nationalities, and carry on a systematic agitation in its own army against every kind of oppression of the colonial population.

9. Every party desirous of belonging to the Communist International should be bound to carry on systematic and persistent Communist work in the labor unions, co-operatives and other labor organizations of the masses. It is necessary to form Communist groups within the organizations, which by persistent and lasting work should win over labor unions to Communism. These groups should constantly denounce the treachery of the social patriots and of the fluctuations of the "centre." These Communist groups should be completely subordinated to the party in general.

10. Any party belonging to the Communist International is bound to carry on a stubborn struggle against the Amsterdam "International" of the yellow labor unions. It should propagate insistently amongst the organized workers the necessity of a rupture with the yellow Amsterdam International. It should support by all means in its power the International Unification of Red Labor Unions, adhering to the Communist International, which is now beginning.

11. Parties desirous of joining the Third International shall be bound to inspect the personnel of their parliamentary factions, to remove all unreliable elements therefrom, to control such factions, not only verbally but in reality, to subordinate them to the Central Committee of the party, and to demand from each proletarian Communist that he devote his entire activity to the interests of real revolutionary propaganda.

12. All parties belonging to the Communist International should be formed on the basis of the principle of democratic centralization. At the present time of acute civil war the Communist Party will be able fully to do its duty only when it is organized in a sufficiently thorough way when it possesses an iron discipline, and when its party centre enjoys the confidence of the members of the party, who are to endow this centre with complete power, authority and ample rights.

13. The Communist parties of those countries where the Communist activity is legal, should make a clearance of their members from time to time, as well as those of

the party organizations, in order systematically to free the party from the petty bourgeois elements which penetrate into it.

14. Each party desirous of affiliating with the Communist International should be obliged to render every possible assistance to the Soviet Republics in their struggle against all counter-revolutionary forces. The Communist parties should carry on a precise and definite propaganda to induce the workers to refuse to transport any kind of military equipment intended for fighting against the Soviet Republics, and should also by legal or illegal means carry on a propaganda amongst the troops sent against the workers' republics, etc.

15. All those parties which up to the present moment have stood upon the old social and democratic programmes should, within the shortest time possible, draw up a new Communist programme in conformity with the special conditions of their country, and in accordance with the resolutions of the Communist International. As a rule the programme of each party belonging to the Communist International should be confirmed by the next congress of the Communist International or its Executive Committee. In the event of the failure of the programme of any party being confirmed by the Executive Committee of the Communist International, the said party shall be entitled to appeal to the Congress of the Communist International.

16. All the resolutions of the congresses of the Communist International, as well as the resolutions of the Executive Committee are binding for all parties joining the Communist International. The Communist International, operating under the conditions of most acute civil warfare, should be centralized in a better manner than the Second International. At the same time, the Communist International and the Executive Committee are naturally bound in every form of their activity to consider the variety of conditions under which the different parties have to work and struggle, and generally binding resolutions should be passed only on such questions upon which such resolutions are possible.

17. In connection with the above, all parties desiring to join the Communist International should alter their name. Each party desirous of joining the Communist International should bear the following name: Communist

Party of such and such a country, section of the Third Communist International. The question of the renaming of a party is not only a formal one, but is a political question of great importance. The Communist International has declared a decisive war against the entire bourgeois world, and all the yellow Social Democratic parties. It is indispensable that every rank-and-file worker should be able clearly to distinguish between the Communist parties and the old official "Social Democratic" or "Socialist" parties, which have betrayed the cause of the working class.

18. All the leading organs of the press of every party are bound to publish all the most important documents of the Executive Committee of the Communist International.

19. All those parties which have joined the Communist International, as well as those which have expressed a desire to do so, are obliged in as short a space of time as possible, and in no case later than four months after the Second Congress of the Communist International, to convene an Extraordinary Congress in order to discuss these conditions. In addition to this, the Central Committees of these parties should take care to acquaint all the local organizations with the regulations of the Second Congress.

20. All those parties which at the present time are willing to join the Third International, but have so far not changed their tactics in any radical manner, should, prior to their joining the Third International, take care that not less than two-thirds of their committee members and of all their central institutions should be composed of comrades who have made an open and definite declaration prior to the convening of the Second Congress, as to their desire that the party should affiliate with the Third International. Exclusions are permitted only with the confirmation of the Executive Committee of the Third International. . . .

21. Those members of the party who reject the conditions and the theses of the Third International, are liable to be excluded from the party.

This applies principally to the delegates at the Special Congresses of the party [called to consider the question of affiliation].

THEORY OF FASCISM

The rise of Fascism was and is an historical phenomenon difficult to explain in terms of orthodox Marxist-Leninist theory. The combination of economic distress and exacerbated nationalism generated in Germany and Italy a mass movement which turned against socialism. The base of this movement was drawn from impoverished members of the lower middle class, students, and unemployed factory and agricultural workers. When the Fascists came to power in Germany they exercised an absolute dictatorship over all sectors of society, including industry. The Communist view interpreted Fascism as the dictatorship of finance capital despite the fact that in some countries, such as Argentina under Peron, there was little finance capital and the workers were among the chief beneficiaries of his rule; while in Germany, finance capitalism was denounced in the Nazi decalogue as dominated by "international Jewry." The bitter attacks on parliamentary democracy in Italy and Germany by Communists carrying out directives to discredit the democratic process, contributed substantially to Fascist success. The Communist line in Germany was determined by the expectation that the Fascists would prepare the way for the Communists to come to power by their inability to solve their domestic problems ("Nach Hitler kommen Wir"— "After Hitler, we will take over"—*was one of their slogans) and failing that, they would embroil the democratic countries into war, which would result in a common ruin of both sides and leave the Soviet Union to inherit Europe.*

Hitler's accession to power was marked by a reign of terror against all liberal, democratic and working-class parties. By measures that were hardly popular with finance capitalists (like Thyssen, who fled to save his life), the Nazis were able to improve economic conditions somewhat. The Communists who had previously regarded the Socialist Parties as twins of the Fascists now blamed them for the victory of the Fascist groups and berated them for not rising against the Fascists. The Communists themselves made no attempt to organize open resistance to Hitler, although they attacked the Socialists ("twins of the Fascists") for not doing so. The only armed resistance to Fascist takeover of power was made by the Socialists of Austria at a time when the Communists were denouncing them as the chief supporters and covert allies of Fascism.

As late as May 1, 1933, months after Hitler had come to power and inaugurated his reign of terror, the Communist International in its May Day proclamation asserted that the German Social Democrats were still the chief enemy of the German working class. By 1935 Hitler had smashed the Communist Party and consolidated his power by reorganizing the Reichswehr. The Soviet Union feared that Hitler would now follow the time table laid down in his Mein Kampf and attack Communist Russia before turning on the West. It therefore ordered Communist Parties to execute an about turn and work with the Social Democrats, whom they had formerly excoriated as traitors. Thus was ushered in the era of the Popular Front, through which the Communists hoped to capture the leadership of the democratic opposition to Fascism and, by means of Trojan Horse tactics after Fascism was defeated, seize political power and institute the Communist dictatorship. The Popular Front strategy largely succeeded. Many sincere individuals and groups, in their fear of Fascism, flocked to the front organizations set up by the Communist Party. Unfortified by any knowledge of Communist ideology, they took Communist professions on their face value. From this foolish dream they were rudely awakened by the Stalin-Hitler Pact of 1939, in which "the Fascist beasts" of yesterday lay down with the Communist guardians of the welfare of the workers—including the German workers whom the Fascist beasts were devouring. "Fascism," according to Molotov in 1940, "was merely a matter of taste." In 1941, however, Fascism once more became a matter of life and death. (See Document No. 23.)

The following excerpts are from Dimitroff's speech before the Seventh Congress of the Communist International

(Working Class Unity—Bulwark Against Fascism, *New York, 1935*), *in which the traditional Communist analysis of Fascism is repeated, the Social-Democrats are condemned again, and the new strategy of the Popular Front is outlined.*

✦   ✦   ✦

Comrades, as was correctly described by the Thirteenth Plenum of the Executive Committee of the Communist International, fascism in power is *the open terrorist dictatorship of the most reactionary, most chauvinistic and most imperialist elements of finance capital.*

The most reactionary variety of fascism is the *German type* of fascism. It has the effrontery to call itself National-Socialism, though having nothing in common with socialism. Hitler fascism is not only bourgeois nationalism, it is bestial chauvinism. It is a government system of political banditry, a system of provocation and torture practised upon the working class and the revolutionary elements of the peasantry, the petty bourgeoisie and the intelligentsia. It is medieval barbarity and bestiality, it is unbridled aggression in relation to other nations and countries.

German fascism is acting as *the spearhead of international counter-revolution*, as *the chief incendiary of imperialist war*, as *the initiator of a crusade against the Soviet Union, the great fatherland of the toilers of the whole world.*

Fascism is not a form of state power "standing above both classes—the proletariat and the bourgeoisie," as Otto Bauer, for instance, has asserted. It is not "the revolt of the petty bourgeoisie which has captured the machinery of the state," as the British Socialist Brailsford declares. No, fascism is not super-class government, nor government of the petty bourgeoisie or the lumpen-proletariat over finance capital. Fascism is the power of finance capital itself. It is the organization of terrorist vengeance against the working class and the revolutionary section of the peasantry and intelligentsia. In foreign policy, fascism is chauvinism in its crudest form, fomenting the bestial hatred of other nations.

This, the true character of fascism, must be particularly stressed; because in a number of countries fascism, under cover of social demagogy, has managed to gain the following of the petty-bourgeois masses who have been driven out of their course by the crisis, and even of certain sections of the most backward strata of the proletariat. These would never have supported fascism if they had understood its real class character and its true nature. . . .

The Social-Democratic leaders glossed over and concealed from the masses the true class nature of fascism, and did not call them to the struggle against the increasingly reactionary measures of the bourgeoisie. They bear great *historical responsibility* for the fact that, at the decisive moment of the fascist offensive, a large section of the toiling masses of Germany and a number of other fascist countries failed to recognize in fascism the most bloodthirsty monster of finance, their most vicious enemy, and that these masses were not prepared to resist it.

What is the source of the influence enjoyed by fascism over the masses? Fascism is able to attract the masses because it demagogically appeals to their *most urgent needs and demands*. Fascism not only inflames prejudices that are deeply ingrained in the masses, but also plays on the better sentiments of the masses, on their sense of justice, and sometimes even on their revolutionary traditions. Why do the German fascists, those lackeys of the big bourgeoisie and mortal enemies of socialism, represent themselves to the masses as "socialists," and depict their accession to power as a "revolution"? Because they try to exploit the faith in revolution, the urge towards socialism, which live in the hearts of the broad masses of the toilers of Germany.

Fascism acts in the interests of the extreme imperialists, but it presents itself to the masses in the guise of champion of an ill-treated nation, and appeals to outraged national sentiments, as German fascism did, for instance, when it won the support of the masses by the slogan "Against the Versailles Treaty!"

Fascism aims at the most unbridled exploitation of the masses, but it appeals to them with the most artful anticapitalist demagogy, taking advantage of the profound hatred entertained by the toilers for the piratical bourgeoisie, the banks, trusts and the financial magnates, and advancing slogans which at the given moment are most

alluring to the politically immature masses. In Germany
—"The general welfare is higher than the welfare of the
individual"; In Italy—"Our state is not a capitalist, but a
corporate state"; in Japan—"For Japan, without exploitation"; in the United States—"Share the Wealth," and so
forth. . . .

But whatever the masks which fascism adopts, whatever the forms in which it presents itself, whatever the
ways of which it comes to power—

*Fascism is a most ferocious attack by capital on the
toiling masses;*

*Fascism is unbridled chauvinism and annexationist
war;*

Fascism is rabid reaction and counter-revolution;

*Fascism is the most vicious enemy of the working class
and of all the toilers!* . . .

Whether the victory of fascism can be prevented
depends *in the first place* on the militant activity displayed
by the working class itself, on whether its forces are
welded into a single militant army combatting the offensive of capitalism and fascism. Having established its
fighting unity, the proletariat would paralyze the influence
of fascism over the peasantry, the petty bourgeoisie of the
towns, the youth and the intelligentsia, and would be able
to neutralize one section and win over another section.

Second, it depends on the existence of a strong revolutionary party, correctly leading the struggle of the toilers
against fascism. A party which systematically calls on the
workers to retreat in the face of fascism and permits the
fascist bourgeoisie to strengthen its positions will inevitably lead the workers to defeat.

Third, it depends on whether a correct policy is pursued by the working class towards the peasantry and the
petty-bourgeois masses of the towns. These masses must
be taken as they are, and not as we should like to have
them. It is only in the process of the struggle that they
will overcome their doubts and vacillations. It is only
provided we adopt a patient attitude towards their inevitable vacillations, it is only with the political help of the
proletariat that they will be able to rise to a higher level of
revolutionary consciousness and activity.

Fourth, it depends on whether the revolutionary proletariat exercises vigilance and takes action at the proper time. It must not allow fascism to catch it unawares, it must not surrender the initiative to fascism, it must inflict decisive blows on the latter before it can gather its forces, it must not allow fascism to consolidate its position, it must repel fascism wherever and whenever it manifests itself, it must not allow fascism to gain new positions, all of which the French proletariat is doing so successfully.

These are the main conditions for preventing the growth of fascism and its accession to power.

Comrades, millions of workers and toilers of the capitalist countries ask the question: How can fascism be prevented from coming to power and how can fascism be overthrown after being victorious? To this the Communist International replies: *The first thing that must be done, the thing with which to commence, is to form a united front, to establish unity of action of the workers in every factory, in every district, in every region, in every country, all over the world. Unity of action of the proletariat on a national and international scale is the mighty weapon which renders the working class capable not only of successful defense but also of successful counter-offensive against fascism against the class enemy.*

Ours has been a Congress of a *new tactical orientation for the Communist International.* . . .

The Congress has taken a firm decision that the united front tactics must be applied *in a new way*.

Part II

COMMUNIST PRACTICE

THE DUTIES OF THE COMMUNIST PARTY MEMBER

As distinct from other political parties, the Communist Party requires more from its members than acceptance of doctrine or program or payment of dues or attendance at party meetings. It demands "the participation of each member in the daily work of the Party." The daily work of the party is multifarious and conducted on all levels, both legal and illegal. The specific character of the work an individual Communist Party member must do depends on where he works, his background, talents and other relevant considerations as determined by his superiors in the Party hierarchy. This does not mean that all Communist Party members are active in illegal work, although they are all regarded as potentially serviceable in this field.

What is striking about the instructions printed below is the scope of the activities Communist Party members must engage in and the detailed techniques of their operation. Anyone who has had some experience with fractions of the Communist Party in trade unions, professional associations, clubs, etc. will recognize some of the specific procedures here suggested.

Not every member of the Communist Party is a good and faithful Communist who will carry out his instructions to the letter at whatever cost to himself. But the Communist Party continuously purges its own unreliable or inactive members. There is a fair presumption, therefore, whose strength depends upon the position of the member and his years of service and other factors, that the Communist Party "control commission" has determined how reliable the individual member is. No one can be an inactive member of the party except individuals who are assigned to play the role of "sleepers" in sensitive and strategic positions in non-communist organizations until such time as the hour for their activity strikes. The following extracts are from the "Theses on Tactics" adopted at the Third Congress of the Communist International in 1921. Theses and Resolutions Adopted at the Third World Congress of the Communist International, Contemporary Publishing Association, New York, 1921, pp. 49ff.

✓   ✓   ✓

The Communist Party must be a training school for revolutionary Marxism. The organic ties between the different parts of the organization and the membership become joined through daily common work in the party organization. . . .

The acceptance of a Communist program is only the expression of the will to become a Communist. If the Communist activity is lacking and the passivity of the mass of members still remains, then the party does not fulfill even the least part of the pledge it had taken upon itself in accepting the Communist program. For the first condition for an earnest carrying out of the program is the participation of all the members in the constant daily work of the Party. . . .

A Communist Party must strive to have only really active members, and to demand from every rank and file party worker that he should place his whole strength and time, in so far as he can himself dispose of it, under existing conditions, at the disposal of his Party and devote his best forces to these services.

Membership in the Communist Party entails naturally, besides communist convictions—formal registration, first as a candidate, then as a member; likewise, the regular payment of the established dues, the subscription to the Party paper, etc. But the most important is the participation of each member in the daily work of the Party.

For the purpose of carrying on the Party work every Party member must as a rule be also a member of a smaller working group: a committee, a commission, a board group, faction, or nucleus. Only in this way can the Party work be properly distributed, directed and carried on. . . .

The fractions must carefully prepare the participatiom of the communists in conferences and meetings of the trade union organizations. For instance, they must elaborate proposals, select lectures and counsel and put up as candidates for election, capable, experienced and energetic comrades.

The Communist organizations must, through their fractions, also make careful preparations in connection with all workers' meetings, election meetings, demonstrations, political festivals and such like, arranged by the hostile organizations. Wherever Communists convene their own workers' meetings, they must endeavor to have considerable groups of communists distributed among the audience, and they must make all due preparations for the assurance of satisfactory propaganda results.

Communists must also learn how to draw unorganized and backward workers permanently into the ranks of the Party. With the help of our nuclei and fractions we must induce the workers to join the trade unions and to read our Party organs. Other organizations, as for instance, educational boards, study circles, sporting clubs, dramatic societies, co-operative societies, consumers' associations, war-victims' organizations, etc., may be used as intermediaries between us and the workers. Where the Communist Party is working illegally, such workers' unions may be formed outside of the Party through the initiative of Party members and with the consent and under the control of the leading Party organs (unions of sympathizers).

Communist youths and women's organizations may also be helpful in rousing the interest of the many politically indifferent proletarians, and in drawing them eventually into the Communist Party, through the intermediary of their educational courses, reading circles, excursions, festivals, Sunday rambles, etc., distribution of leaflets, increasing the circulation of the Party organ, etc. Through participation in the general movement, the workers will free themselves from their petty bourgeois inclinations. . . .

The methods of propaganda in the armies and navies of capitalist states must be adapted to the peculiar conditions in each country. Anti-militarist agitation of a pacifist nature is extremely detrimental, and only assists the bourgeois in its efforts to disarm the proletariat. The proletariat

rejects on principle and combats with the utmost energy,
every kind of military institution of the bourgeois State,
and of the bourgeois class in general. Nevertheless, it
utilizes these institutions (army, rifle clubs, citizen guard
organizations, etc.) for the purpose of giving the workers
military training for the revolutionary battles to come.
Intensive agitation must therefore be directed not against
the military training of the youth and workers, but against
the militaristic regime, and the domination of the officers.
Every possibility of providing the workers with weapons
should most eagerly be taken advantage of.

— 11 —

COMMUNISTS AND TRADE UNIONS

*The infiltration and capture of trade unions and other
mass organizations are among the top priorities of the
Communist Party. When this subversion is successful, the
organization acts like a political or industrial arm of the
Communist Party in preparing for the seizure of power.
In the nature of the case, the legitimate interests of the
workers in these organizations, who are not Communists,
are completely subordinated to the policies of the Communist Party and ultimately of the Soviet Union. For
example, a strike will not be called in a factory manu-
facturing equipment which is scheduled for export to the
Soviet Union if the union is controlled by the Communist
Party, no matter how bad economic conditions are. On
the other hand, depending upon the exigencies of the
foreign policy of the Soviet Union, the Communist Party
will call strikes needlessly and exacerbate conditions at
the expense of the workers.*

*This Communist policy in trade unions naturally leads
to efforts by legitimate trade unions to exclude active
Communists from trade unions or to prevent them from*

becoming officials and thus subverting the ends of the organization to those of the Communist Party. Here as elsewhere Lenin teaches (and his precepts have been faithfully carried out by Communist Parties everywhere) that Communists must resort to any kind of deception to continue their work. The logic of the situation— which is quite general for all situations in which Communists seek to infiltrate in order to carry out their political purposes—is something like this: "You must permit us," they say, "to bore from within until we capture the organization. We shall then settle accounts with those who disagree with or oppose us. If you refuse to permit us to work openly, we will do it by stealth and with any means whatsoever. We are blameless for this strategy of deceit because by refusing to submit to our plans for your ultimate liquidation, you compel us to act in this way. We are really only defending ourselves against you!" The quotations below are from Lenin's Selected Works, Vol. 2, Part II, pp. 373ff.

The trade unions were a tremendous progressive step for the working class at the beginning of the development of capitalism, inasmuch as they represented a transition from the disunity and helplessness of the workers to the *rudiments* of class organisation. When the *highest* form of proletarian class organisation began to arise, *viz.*, the *revolutionary party of the proletariat* (which will not deserve the name until it learns to bind the leaders with the class and the masses into one single indissoluble whole), the trade unions inevitably began to reveal *certain* reactionary features, a certain craft narrowness, a certain tendency to be non-political, a certain inertness, etc. But the development of the proletariat did not, and could not, proceed anywhere in the world otherwise than through the trade unions, through their interaction with the party of the working class. The conquest of political power by the proletariat is a gigantic forward step for the proletariat as a class, and the Party must more than ever, and not merely in the old way but in a new way, educate and guide the trade unions, at the same time not forgetting that they are and will long remain an indispensable "school of Communism" and a preparatory school for training the proletarians to exercise their dictatorship, an indispensable organisation of the workers for the gradual transfer of the management of the whole economic life of the country to the working *class* (and not to the separate trades), and later to all the toilers. . . .

. . . You must be capable of every sacrifice, of overcoming the greatest obstacles in order to carry on agitation and propaganda systematically, perseveringly, persistently and patiently precisely in those institutions, societies and associations—even the most reactionary—in which proletarian or semi-proletarian masses are to be found. And the trade unions and workers' cooperatives (the latter at least sometimes) are precisely the organisations where the masses are to be found. . . .

. . . There can be no doubt that those gentlemen, the "leaders" of opportunism, will resort to every trick of bourgeois diplomacy, to the aid of bourgeois governments, the priests, the police and the courts, to prevent Communists joining the trade unions, to force them out by every means, to make their work in the trade unions as unpleasant as possible, to insult, bait and persecute them. We must be able to withstand all this, to agree to any sacrifice, and even—if need be—to resort to all sorts of stratagems, artifices, illegal methods, to evasions and subterfuges, only so as to get into the trade unions, to remain in them, and to carry on Communist work within them at all costs.

We have previously seen how important, according to Lenin, the penetration and control of the trade union movement is to the strategy of Communist political warfare. The following passages from the Theses of the Second Congress of the Third International show that Lenin's point of view on this (as on all other) questions became the official Communist position to be followed everywhere. The history of the trade union movement in almost all countries since 1920 testifies to the readiness and fanaticism with which the Communists in trade unions sought to implement their party directives. But they were seldom in subsequent years to be so outspoken and frank in declaring, as they did in 1920, that "the Communists must particularly subordinate the factory committees and the Unions to the Communist Party."

The duty of the Communists consists in inspiring the labor unions and the factory committee with a spirit of determined struggle, and the consciousness and knowledge of the best methods of such a struggle—the spirit of Communism. In execution of this duty the Communists must practically subordinate the factory committees and the unions to the Communist Party, and thus create a proletarian mass organ, a basis for a powerful centralized party of the proletariat, embracing all the organizations of the proletarian struggle, leading them all to one aim, to the victory of the working class, through the dictatorship of the proletariat to Communism. The Communists converting the labor unions and factory committees into powerful weapons of the revolution, prepare these mass organizations for the great task which they will have after the establishment of the dictatorship of the proletariat, for the task of being the instrument of the reorganization of economic life on a Socialistic basis. The labor unions, developed as industrial unions and supported by the factory committees as their factory organizations, will then make the working masses acquainted with their tasks of production; they will educate the most experienced workingmen to become leaders of the factories to control the technical specialists, and, together with the representatives of the Workers' State, will lay down the plan of the Socialist economic policy, and carry it out. . . .

Bearing in mind the rush of the enormous working masses into the trade unions, and also the objective revolutionary character of the economic struggle which those masses are carrying on in spite of the trade union bureaucracy, the Communists must join such unions in all countries, in order to make of them efficient organs of the struggle for the suppression of capitalism and for Communism. They must initiate the forming of trade unions where these do not exist. All voluntary withdrawal from the industrial movement, every artificial attempt to organize special unions, without being compelled thereto by exceptional acts of violence on the part of the trade union bureaucracy, such as expulsion of separate revolutionary local branches of the unions by the opportunist officials, or by their narrow-minded aristocratic policy, which prohibits the unskilled workers from entering into the organization, represents a great danger to the Communist movement. It threatens to hand over the most advanced, the most conscious workers, to the opportunist leaders, playing into the hands of the bourgeoisie. . . . The luke-warmness of the working masses, their ideological indecision, their tendency to yield to the arguments of opportunist leaders, can be overcome only during the process of the evergrowing struggle, by degrees as the wider masses of the proletariat learn to understand, by experience, by their victories and defeats, that objectively it is already impossible to obtain human conditions of life on the basis of capitalist methods of management. . . .

Placing the object and the essence of labor organizations before them, the Communists ought not to hesitate before a split in such organizations, if a refusal to split would mean abandoning revolutionary work in the trade unions, and giving up the attempt to make of them an instrument of revolutionary struggle, the attempt to organize the most exploited part of the proletariat. But even if such a split should be necessary, it must be carried into effect only at a time when the Communists have succeeded by the incessant warfare against the opportunist leaders and their tactics, by their most active participation in the economic struggle, in persuading the wider masses of workmen that the split is occurring not because of the remote and as yet incomprehensible aims of the revolution, but on account of the concrete, immediate interests of the working class in the development of its economic struggle. The Communists in case a necessity for a split arises, must continuously and attentively discuss the question as to whether a split might not lead to their isolation from the working mass.

COMMUNIST PROPAGANDA
AND EDUCATION

Communist Parties throughout the world recruit members on the basis of a multiplicity of appeals. The motivations which impel individuals to join the Communist Party are extremely varied and cannot be reduced plausibly to one class or type. But once they are inducted into the Party, members are subjected to an intensive course of indoctrination in which the program, objectives, strategy and tactics are explained to them. Whatever the personal circumstances may be which account for their joining, they can hardly plead ignorance of the revolutionary character of the organization. It has sometimes been argued that individuals who join the Communist Party under the illusion that it is merely an organization for social uplift remain disabused, that one cannot safely assume that they are aware of its conspiratorial character. Although it is abstractly possible that some individuals can remain in a state of somnambulistic self-deception, the following passages indicate how unlikely this is. They describe the intensive training given in the principles of Marxist-Leninism to all members of the Communist Party. "Leninism," declares Stalin, "is Marxism in the epoch of imperialism and proletarian revolution. To put it more concisely: Leninism is the theory and the tactics of the proletarian revolution in general, and the theory and tactics of the proletarian dictatorship in particular." Subjected to the course of Marxist-Leninist study prescribed for all party members, no literate person can fail to become aware of the nature of the party he has joined. The excerpts are from "Propaganda Theses of the Fifth World Congress of the Communist International," Inprecorr, August 29, 1924.

✓　　　✓　　　✓

Every Party member must be required to become acquainted with a certain minimum of political and theoretical knowledge at least to such a degree that the masses of the Party members will be able to answer the questions of the non-communist workers on the programme, the aims, and the tactical principles of the Communist Party, and to combat the most flagrant petty-bourgeois and social democratic prejudices of the working class. The Party must control the manner in which the members carry out this duty. . . .

Party education must be so organised as to absorb, in some form or other, all the members of the Party. The Parties must see to it that each one of their members obtains at least a thorough knowledge of elementary Marxist-Leninist propaganda. . . .

Every department of the communist educational institutions and propaganda organs must be directed towards practical and definite aims, and must be composed of students of a similar level of education. When forming classes, drawing up programmes and selecting methods, the guiding principle for all propaganda institutions must be to train the students for a definite form of party work and for the solution of definite and practical questions.

Each department of the educational propaganda institutions must represent an independent whole, having definite tasks to fulfil. It must not be regarded merely as a stepping stone to higher education.

In order to benefit as many Party members as possible (in spite of the paucity of intellectual and material means), the two forms of education should be adopted in the Marxist-Leninist propaganda institutions, viz. party-schools and self-education.

In connection with the former, the two poles of the Party-school system should be:

a) Central Party schools.

b) An extensive system of Party classes (Evening courses, series of lectures, Sunday Schools, etc.).

The central Party schools must bring together for shorter or longer periods (according to the financial resources of the Party) advanced Party workers (and eventually members of Parties of the same language groups) well versed in the principles of Marxism and Leninism. The aim of these central schools must be to systematise, extend and render more profound the student's knowledge of Marxism and Leninism, and thus train fully qualified party workers and new and strong bodies of propagandists for the development of our propagandist activities.

The principal aim of the elementary evening classes (Sunday schools) must be to impart elementary political knowledge to our Party members by teaching the first principles of Marxian-Leninist theory and method. The curriculum of these classes must be based on the programme of the Communist International. These classes must aim at making Party members fit to take up active party work and to carry on individual propaganda among the masses inside and especially outside the Party. . . .

Communists parties must not neglect to make their influence felt in workers colleges, factory council schools, trade union educational institutions, which under the guise of "non-party institutions" engage in working class education, etc. They must combat the dangers which these schools present to proletarian class ideology and endeavour to get control over them in order to make them useful for communist education. . . .

The Central Committees of the Parties must also maintain direct contact with the propaganda institutions and Marxian-Leninist study circles in the most important working class districts in their respective countries. The Communist International must also be the medium for establishing connection between the communist universities, Party schools, Marxian-Leninist study circles of the Russian Communist Party, and the corresponding institutions abroad.

Party organs must take an active part in the establishment of similar educational institutions for the youth, in providing them with propagandists and by drawing the youth into the educational institutions of the Party.

Communist Parties must also concern themselves with the higher education of communist students and other intellectuals. Communist students must not be allowed to remain in a state of splendid isolation. The existing communist student fractions or nuclei which hitherto have been select self-education circles without any particular system, must be transformed, under the direct guidance of experienced Party workers well versed in Marxism and Leninism and familiar with the labour movement, into education bodies capable of turning out fully qualified propagandists. Moreover, members of these student groups must be induced to take part in practical group work.

— 13 —

THE COMMUNIST PARTY MEMBER ABOVE GROUND AND UNDERGROUND

Just as "cultural vigilantes" betray a tendency to see Communism in liberal or social-democratic movements of reform—movements which the Communists regard with envenomed bitterness as more dangerous to themselves than reactionary groups—so certain kinds of liberals, who may be called "ritualistic liberals," regard Communists as merely progressives, advanced liberals or agrarian reformers whose harmless heresies constitute no threat to the integrity of the democratic process. The following official directives concerning the necessity of combining legal and illegal activity by Communist Parties throughout the world, drawn up at the Second Congress of the Third Communist International, should disabuse those capable of learning from the official declarations of the Communists themselves, not to mention the actual history of Communist seizures of power in countries like the Soviet Union and Czechoslovakia. It is questionable whether any group organized along the lines described in the following directives can be considered "a political party" in the ordinary sense of political parties in a state, which accept the ground rules that regulate the political process, especially in a democratic community.

The Party must be so organized, that it shall always be in a position to adapt itself quickly to all the changes that may occur in the conditions of the struggle. The Communist Party must develop into a militant organization capable of avoiding a fight in the open against overwhelming forces of the enemy, concentrated upon a given point; but on the other hand, the very concentration of the enemy must be so utilized as to attack him in a spot where he least suspects it. It would be the greatest mistake for the Party organization to stake everything upon a rebellion and street fighting, or only upon condition of severe oppression. Communists must perfect their preliminary revolutionary work in every situation on a basis of preparedness, for it is frequently next to impossible to foresee the changeable wave of stormy and calm periods; and even in cases where it might be possible, this foresight cannot, in many cases, be made use of for reorganization, because the change as a rule comes quickly, and frequently quite suddenly.

The legal Communist Parties of the capitalist countries usually fail to grasp the importance of the task before the Party to be properly prepared for the armed struggle, or for the illegal fight in general. Communist organizations often commit the error of depending on a permanent legal basis for their existence, and of conducting their work according to the needs of the legal tasks.

On the other hand, illegal parties often fail to make use of all the possibilities of legal activity towards the building up of a party organization which would have constant intercourse with the revolutionary masses. Underground organizations which ignore these vital truths run the risk of becoming merely groups of conspirators, wasting their labors in futile Sysiphus tasks.

Both those tendencies are erroneous. Every legal communist organization must know how to insure for itself complete preparedness for an underground existence, and above all for revolutionary outbreaks. Every illegal communist organization must, on the other hand, make the fullest use of the possibilities offered by the legal labor movement, in order to become, by means of intensive party activity, the organizer and real leader of the great revolutionary masses.

Both among legal and underground Party circles there is a tendency for the illegal Communist organization activity to evolve into the establishment and maintenance of a purely military organization isolated from the rest of the Party organization and activity. This is absolutely erroneous. On the contrary, during the pre-revolutionary period the formation of our militant organizations must be mainly accomplished through the general work of the Communist Party. The entire Party must be developed into a militant organization for the Revolution.

Isolated revolutionary-military organizations, prematurely created in the pre-revolutionary periods, are apt to show tendencies towards dissolution, because of the lack of direct and useful party work.

It is of course imperative for an illegal party to protect its members and party organs from being found out by the authorities, and to avoid every possibility of facilitating such discovery by registration, careless collecting of contributions and injudicious distribution of revolutionary material. For these reasons, it cannot use frank organizational methods to the same extent as a legal party. It can, nevertheless, through practice, acquire more and more proficiency in this matter.

Therefore, our general party work must be apportioned in a manner which would ensure, even in the pre-revolutionary period, the foundation and consolidation of a fighting organization commensurate with the needs of the revolution. It is of the greatest importance that the directing body of the Communist Party should be guided in its entire activity by the revolutionary requirements, and that it should endeavor as far as possible, to gain a clear idea of what these are likely to be. This is, naturally, not an easy matter, but that should not be a reason for leaving out of consideration this very important point of communist organizational leadership.

Even the best organized party would be faced with very difficult and complicated tasks, if it had to undergo great functional changes in a period of open revolutionary uprising. It is quite possible that our Political Party will be called upon to mobilize in a few days its forces for the revolutionary struggle. Probably, it will have to mobilize, in addition to the party forces, their reserves, the sympathizing organizations, viz., the unorganized revolutionary masses. The formation of a regular red army is, as yet, out of the question. We must conquer without a previously organized army—through the party work, and not mere drilling which the practical worker of today rejects. One must also not forget that this kind of activity is for every Communist the best preparation for the exigencies of the final struggle.

* * *

On the other hand, a legal mass party must be fully prepared for illegal work and periods of struggle. It must never relax its preparations for any eventualities (viz., it must have safe hiding places for duplicates of members' files; must, in most cases, destroy correspondence, put important documents into safe keeping, . . .

— 14 —

WHY SHOULD COMMUNISTS PARTICIPATE IN ELECTIONS?

One of the most direct appeals the Communists make to the masses is an electoral appeal on every level. Few people vote for revolution, even when they are deeply dissatisfied with existing conditions. They vote for the promise of specific reforms or in protest. Very often, Communist parties capitalize on the desire of the masses for reforms by running candidates who make all sorts of promises to improve the immediate conditions and at the very least to alleviate distress. The following extract from the Theses of the Second Congress of the Third (Communist) International *spells out in bold detail the basic Communist attitude towards elections and social reforms. It establishes the futility of either allying oneself with them or supporting them if one is interested in improving the immediate conditions of the masses rather than in engineering a violent revolution. These directives indicate why Communist Parties, and other groups set up by the*

Communist Parties under other names, so often make a shambles of the parliamentary process instead of carrying out their promises to achieve the specific social reforms which they make when they solicit electoral support. As this document shows, the procedure to follow when Communists are elected to local or communal posts is carefully described. The responsibility and subordination of the elected candidate to "the Communist Party— whether lawful or unlawful" and "not to the wide mass of his constituents" is made with an explicitness that leaves no room for ambiguity. By and large, Communist Parties —whether in Italy or in Kerala, India—have faithfully carried out these instructions.

✓   ✓   ✓

Parliament at present can in no way serve as the arena of a struggle for reform, for improving the lot of the working people, as it has at certain periods of the preceding epoch. The centre of gravity of political life at present has been completely and finally transferred beyond the limits of parliament. On the other hand, owing not only to its relationship to the working masses, but also to the complicated mutual relations within the various groups of the bourgeois itself, the bourgeoisie, is forced to have some of its policies in one way or another passed through parliament, where the various cliques haggle for power, exhibit their strong sides and betray their weak ones, get themselves unmasked, etc., etc. Therefore it is the immediate historical task of the working class to tear this apparatus out of the hands of the ruling classes, to break and destroy it, and to create in its place a new proletarian apparatus. At the same time, however, the revolutionary general staff of the working class is vitally concerned in having its scouting parties in the parliamentary institutions of the bourgeoisie, in order to facilitate this task of destruction. . . .

Parliamentarism cannot be a form of proletarian government during the transition period between the dictatorship of the bourgeoisie and that of the proletariat. At the moment when the accentuated class struggle turns into civil war, the proletariat must inevitably form its State organization as a fighting organization, which cannot contain any of the representatives of the former ruling classes;

all fictions of a "national will" are harmful to the proletariat at that time, and a parliamentary division of
authority is needless and injurious to it; the only form of
proletarian dictatorship is a Republic of Soviets.

The bourgeois parliaments, which constitute one of the
most important instruments of the State machinery of the
bourgeoisie, cannot be won over by the proletariat any
more than can the bourgeois order in general. The task
of the proletariat consists in blowing up the whole
machinery of the bourgeoisie, in destroying it, and all the
parliamentary institutions with it, whether they be republican or constitutional-monarchial.

The same relates to the local government institutions of
the bourgeoisie, which theoretically it is not correct to
differentiate from State organizations. In reality they are
part of the same apparatus of the State machinery of the
bourgeoisie which must be destroyed by the revolutionary
proletariat and replaced by local Soviets of Workers'
Deputies.

Consequently, Communism repudiates parliamentarism
as the form of the future; it renounces the same as a
form of the class dictatorship of the proletariat; it
repudiates the possibility of winning over the parliaments;
its aim is to destroy parliamentarism. Therefore it is only
possible to speak of utilizing the bourgeois State organizations with the object of destroying them. The question can
be discussed only and exclusively on such a plane. . . .

When the elections are over, the organization of the
parliamentary factions must be wholly in the hands of the
Central Committee of the Communist Party—whether the
Party in general is a lawful or unlawful one at the given
moment. The chairman and the bureau of the parliamentary faction of Communists must be confirmed in their
functions by the Central Committee of the Party. The
Central Committee of the Party must have its permanent
representative in the parliamentary faction with the right
of veto. On all important political questions the parliamentary faction shall get preliminary instructions from
the Central Committee of the Party. . . .

A Communist delegate, by decision of the Central
Committee, is bound to combine lawful work with unlawful work. In countries where the Communist delegate
enjoys a certain inviolability, this must be utilized by way

of rendering assistance to illegal organizations and for the propaganda of the party. . . .

Each Communist member must remember that he is not a "legislator" who is bound to seek agreements with the other legislators, but an agitator of the Party, detailed into the enemy's camp in order to carry out the orders of the Party there. The Communist member is answerable not to the wide mass of his constituents, but to his own Communist Party—whether lawful or unlawful.

— 15 —

UNITED-FRONT TACTICS

When different political groups are struggling for what appear to be common or similar things, demanding what appear to be the same or similar measures in behalf of the oppressed or underprivileged, it is natural to hope for unity of action. In most situations, unity of action can be undertaken even where there is difference of opinion and differences about ultimate objectives. The Communist Party has always proclaimed its belief in "united-front tactics." Invariably, however, the united front has been nothing but a tactic by which the Communist Party seeks to reach the membership of other groups or parties in order to discredit their leadership and destroy their organization. The real operating maxim behind all united-front organizations into which Communists enter is: "Rule or ruin."

The following passages indicate quite clearly how the united front tactic is to be applied. Offer "united fronts," Communist organizations are instructed, to socialist or democratic organizations. If they refuse, denounce them as betrayers. If they accept, exploit the united-front action to turn their own members against them on the ground that they are selling the common program short. Whether it is in a trade union or a cultural group, or in forming a government, the Communist united–front tactic is the same. The first two excerpts are from the Theses of the Third Congress of the Communist International, *New York, 1921. The second set of excerpts are from* Resolutions and Speeches at the Seventh Congress of the Communist International, *New York, 1935.*

—A—

The tactics of the United Front imply the leadership of the Communist vanguard in the daily struggles of the large masses of the workers for their vital interests. In these struggles the Communists are even ready to parley with the treacherous leaders of the social-democrats and of Amsterdam. It is obviously our duty to make the most unequivocal denial of the allegations made by the Second International misrepresenting the United Front as the organisational amalgamation of all the "labour parties." The attempts of the Second International to win over the more advanced labour organisations under the cloak of the United Front (amalgamation of the social-democrats and independents in Germany), are in reality nothing but an opportunity for the social democratic leaders to deliver some other parts of the working masses into the hands of the bourgeoisie. . . .

The most important thing in the tactics of the United Front is and remains the agitational and organisational unification of the working masses. The real success of the United Front tactics is to come from "below," from the depth of the working masses themselves. At the same time, the Communists should not decline, under given circumstances, to negotiate with the leaders of the workers' parties in opposition to us. But the masses must be constantly and completely kept informed of the course of these negotiations. Even during such negotiations the Communist Party should not in any way circumscribe the independence of its agitation. . . .

—B—

In the struggle against the social democratic and other petty bourgeois trade union leaders, as well as against the leaders of various labor parties one cannot hope to achieve much by persuasion. The struggle against them should be conducted in the most energetic fashion, and the best way to do that is by depriving them of their following, showing up to the workers the true character of these treacherous socialist leaders who are only playing into the hands of capitalism. The Communists should endeavor to unmask these so-called leaders, and subsequently attack them in the most energetic fashion. . . .

Joint action with the Social-Democratic Parties and organizations not only does not preclude, but on the contrary, *renders still more necessary* the serious and well-founded criticism of reformism, of Social-Democracy as the ideology and practice of class collaboration with the bourgeoisie, and the patient exposition of the principles and program of Communism to the Social Democratic workers.

While revealing to the masses the meaning of the demagogic arguments advanced by the Right Social-Democratic leaders against the united front, *while intensifying the struggle against the reactionary section of Social-Democracy,* the Communists must establish *the closest cooperation with those Left Social-Democratic workers, functionaries and organizations, that fight against the reformist policy and advocate a united front with the Communist Party.* The more we intensify our fight against the reactionary camp of Social-Democracy, which is participating in a bloc with the bourgeoisie, the more effective will be the assistance we give to that part of Social-Democracy which is becoming revolutionized and the self-determination of the various elements within the Left camp will take place the sooner, the more resolutely the Communists fight for a united front with Social-Democratic Parties.

. . . we indicate the possibility of forming a government of the anti-fascist united front in the conditions of a political crisis. In so far as such a government will really prosecute the struggle against the enemies of the people, and give a free hand to the working class and the Communist Party, we Communists shall accord it our unstinted support, and as soldiers of the revolution shall take our place in the *first line of fire.* But we state frankly to the masses:

Final salvation this government *cannot bring.* It is not in a position to overthrow the class rule of the exploiters, and for this reason cannot finally eliminate the danger of fascist counter-revolution. Consequently it is necessary *to prepare for the socialist revolution!* Soviet Power and *only* Soviet power can bring such salvation!

— 16 —

AID TO REVOLUTIONARY MOVEMENTS

From the very outset the Soviet Union set about, both in its own interests and to further the Communist aim of world revolution, to organize subversive movements in other countries—including those with which it maintained friendly relations. Long before there was any foreign intervention in the Soviet Union, these activities were undertaken. The following document reveals that the distinction between the Soviet government (which pledged itself not to interfere in the internal affairs of other countries) and the Communist international movement was a pretence. The subsequent claim by Stalin and Khrushchev that Communist revolutions could not be exported concealed the fact that funds, literature, arms and Communist party organizers can and have been exported by the Soviet Union to almost every country in the world and that in accordance with Communist theory a Communist revolution cannot take place without a functioning Communist Party. The document first appeared in the Gazette *of the Temporary Workers and Peasants Government, December 13, 1917.*

✓   ✓   ✓

Taking into consideration how Soviet authority stands upon the principle of international solidarity of the proletariat and the brotherhood of toilers of all countries and that only a struggle against war and imperialism on an international scale can lead to complete victory, the Soviet of People's Commissars deems it necessary to render every possible assistance, including financial aid, to the left, internationalist wing of the workers movement of all countries, whether these countries are at war with Russia or are allied with her or whether they are remaining neutral.

With this in mind, the Soviet People's Commissars ordains the assigning of two million roubles for the needs of the revolutionary internationalist movement to be disbursed by foreign representatives of the Commissariat of Foreign Affairs.

> President of the Soviet of People's Commissars, V. ULYANOV (LENIN); People's Commissar for Foreign Affairs, L. TROTSKY; Administrator of the Soviet of People's Commissars, VLAD. BONCH-BRUEVITCH; Secretary of the Soviet, N. GORBOUNOV.

Part III

COMMUNISM IN
THE U.S.S.R.

THE MEANING OF
COEXISTENCE

*The following document will repay careful analysis. Its
study is mandatory in courses on Marxist-Leninism in the
Soviet Union. In February, 1920, Lenin gave an interview
to a reporter of the* New York Evening Journal *in which
he said: "Let American capitalists not touch us: we will
not touch them." This interview was not published in the
Soviet Union until April, 1950, when the formula about
coexistence came into play in Soviet propaganda. But on
November 20, 1920, Lenin made an address to the functionaries of the Communist Party in which he made clear
what coexistence means in the vocabulary of Communism.
He also showed how "concessions" must be used to further the Communist program. From Lenin's* Selected
Works, *Vol. 8, pp. 270ff.*

✓   ✓   ✓

The example of the Brest Peace has taught us a lot. We
are at present between two foes. If we are unable to defeat them both, we must know how to dispose our forces
in such a way that they fall out among themselves; because, as is always the case, when thieves fall out, honest
men come into their own. But as soon as we are strong
enough to defeat capitalism as a whole, we shall immediately take it by the scruff of the neck. Our strength is
growing, and very rapidly. . . .

Since the Second Congress of the Third International
we have secured a firm foothold in the imperialist countries, not only ideologically but also organisationally.
There are now nuclei in all countries which are carrying
on and will continue to carry on independent work. . . .

But, of course, it would be a great mistake to think that concessions imply peace. Nothing of the kind. Concessions are nothing but a new form of war. . . .

Economically, we have a vast deal to gain from concessions. Of course, when settlements are created they will bring capitalist customs with them, they will demoralise the peasantry. But watch must be kept, we must put up our Communist influence in opposition at every step. This also is a kind of war, the military rivalry of two methods, of two formations, two kinds of economy—communist and capitalist. We shall prove that we are the stronger. We are told: "Very good, you have held your own on the foreign front, you are beginning to build; well, build, and we shall see who will win. . . ." Of course, the task is a difficult one, but we said, and continue to say, that socialism has the power of example. Force is of avail in relation to those who want to restore their power. But that exhausts the value of force, and after that only influence and example are of avail. We must demonstrate the importance of communism practically, by example. We have no machines, the war has impoverished us, the war has deprived Russia of her economic resources; yet we do not fear this rivalry, because it will be useful to us in all respects.

This will also be a war in which not the slightest yielding is permissible. This war will be useful for us in all respects; and the transition from the old war to the new war will also be useful, not to mention the fact that there is a certain indirect guarantee of peace. At the meeting which was so badly reported in *Pravda,* I said that we have just passed from war to peace, but that we have not forgotten that war will again return. As long as capitalism and socialism exist, we cannot live in peace: in the end, one or the other will triumph—a funeral dirge will be sung either over the Soviet Republic or over world capitalism. This is a respite in war. The capitalists will seek pretexts for fighting. If they accept the proposal and agree to concessions, it will be harder for them. On the one hand, we shall have the best conditions in the event of war; on the other hand, those who want to go to war will not agree to concessions. The existence of concessions is an economic and political argument against war. The

states that might war on us will not war on us if they take
concessions. From the point of view of the danger of a
collision between capitalism and Bolshevism, it must be
said that concessions are a continuation of the war, but in
a different sphere. Every step of the enemy will have to be
watched. Every means of administration, surveillance,
influence and authority will be required. And this is war.
We have fought a much bigger war, yet in this war we
shall mobilise even larger numbers of the people than in
that war. In this war literally everybody who toils will be
mobilised; he will be told, and given to understand: "If
capitalism does this or that, you workers and peasants who
have overthrown the capitalists must do no less than they.
Learn."

— 18 —

CAN COMMUNISM SURVIVE WITHOUT WORLD REVOLUTION?

*Another light on the Communist view of coexistence is
thrown by the Communist theory that final safety for socialism in the U.S.S.R. cannot be guaranteed without victory for Communism throughout the world, or at least in
the major countries. Despite Stalin's differences with Trotsky, he insisted that, although socialism can be built in
one country, it cannot be preserved indefinitely in one
country without victory on an international scale. Consequently, in order to safeguard itself, the Soviet Communist
regime must work to overthrow the non-Communist regimes of the world in whatever way it can. Coexistence
endures until, as Lenin put it, the Communist world is
strong enough to take the non-Communist world "by the
scruff of its neck." This letter was first published in the
United States in the* Daily Worker *of February 17, 1938.*

To Comrade IVAN PHILIPOVICH IVANOV:

. . . Undoubtedly the question of the victory of Socialism in one country, in this case of our country, has two different sides.

The first side of the question of the victory of Socialism in our country embraces the problem of the mutual relations between the classes in our country. This concerns the sphere of internal relations. Can the working class of our country overcome the contradictions with our peasantry and establish an alliance, a collaboration with them? Can the working class of our country in alliance with our peasantry smash the bourgeoisie of our country, deprive it of the land, factories, mines, etc., and by its own efforts build a new, classless society, a complete Socialist society?

These are the problems connected with the first side of the question of the victory of Socialism in our country.

Leninism answers these problems in the affirmative. Lenin teaches that "we have all that is necessary for building a complete Socialist society." Hence we can and must by our own efforts overcome our bourgeoisie and build a Socialist society. Trotsky, Zinoviev, Kamenev and those other gentlemen who later became spies and agents of fascism, denied that it was possible to build Socialism in our country unless the victory of the Socialist revolution was first achieved in other countries, in the capitalist countries. As a matter of fact, these gentlemen wanted to turn our country back to the path of bourgeois development, and they concealed their apostasy by hypocritically talking about the "victory of the revolution" in other countries. This was precisely the point of controversy between our Party and these gentlemen. Our country's subsequent course of development proved that the Party was right and that Trotsky and Company were wrong. For during this period we succeeded in liquidating our bourgeoisie, in establishing fraternal collaboration with our peasantry, and in building, in the main, Socialist society, notwithstanding the fact that the Socialist revolution has not yet been victorious in other countries.

This is the position in regard to the first side of the question of the victory of Socialism in our country. . . .

The second side of the question of the victory of Socialism in our country embraces the problem of mutual relations between our country and the other countries, capitalist countries; the problem of the mutual relations between the working class of our country and the bourgeoisie of other countries. This concerns the sphere of external, international relations. Can the victorious Socialism of one country which is encircled by many strong capitalist countries, regard itself as being fully guaranteed against the danger of military invasion—intervention—and hence, against attempts to restore capitalism in our country? Can our working class and our peasantry, by their own efforts, without the serious assistance of the working class in capitalist countries, overcome the bourgeoisie of other countries in the same way as we overcame our own bourgeoisie? In other words: can we regard the victory of Socialism in our country as final, that is, as being free from the danger of military attack and of attempts to restore capitalism, assuming that Socialism is victorious only in one country and that the capitalist encirclement continues to exist?

These are the problems connected with the second side of the question of the victory of Socialism in our country.

Leninism answers these problems in the negative. Leninism teaches that "the final victory of Socialism, in the sense of the full guarantee against the restoration of bourgeois relations, is possible only on an international scale." (Resolution of the 14th convention of the Communist Party of the Soviet Union.) This means that the serious assistance of the international proletariat is a force without which the problem of the final victory of Socialism in one country cannot be solved. This, of course, does not mean that we must sit with folded arms and wait for assistance from outside. On the contrary, the assistance of the international proletariat must be combined with our work to strengthen the defense of our country, to strengthen the Red Army and the Red Navy, to mobilize the whole country for the purpose of resisting military attack and attempts to restore bourgeois relations.

This is what Lenin says on this score: "We are living not merely in a state, but in a system of states, and it is inconceivable that the Soviet Republic should continue to exist for a long period side by side with imperialist states. Ultimately, one or the other must conquer. Meanwhile, a number of terrible clashes between the Soviet Republic and the bourgeois states is inevitable. This means that if the proletariat, as the ruling class, wants to and will rule, it must prove this also by military organization." (*Collected Works,* Vol. 24, P. 122, Russian edition.) And further: "We are surrounded by people, classes and governments which openly express their hatred for us. We must remember that we are at all times but a hair's breadth from invasion." (*Collected Works,* Vol. 27, P. 117, Russian edition.)

This is said sharply and strongly, but honestly and truthfully, without embellishment, as Lenin was able to speak.

On the basis of these premises, Stalin stated in *Problems of Leninism* that "the final victory of Socialism is the full guarantee against attempts at intervention, and that means against restoration, for any serious attempt at restoration can take place only with serious support from outside, only with the support of international capital. Hence the support of our revolution by the workers of all countries, and still more, the victory of the workers in at least several countries, is a necessary condition for fully guaranteeing the first victorious country against attempts at intervention and restoration, a necessary condition for the final victory of Socialism." (*Problems of Leninism,* 1937 Russian edition, P. 134, *Leninism,* Vol. I, by Joseph Stalin, P. 299.)

— 19 —

DEFENSE OF THE SOVIET UNION AT ALL COSTS

The coördination of the struggle of Communist Parties everywhere with the needs and interests of the Soviet Union has been emphasized from the very beginning. Since the Soviet Union is proclaimed to be the citadel of world revolution, this in effect has always meant the subordination of Communist struggle everywhere to the state interests of the Soviet Union. The justification is that any-thing which strengthens the Soviet Union weakens the non-Communist world and ultimately contributes to the triumph of world Communism. Communist movements in other countries, therefore, receive not only their general strategic directives from the Kremlin, but also the tactical signals when to attack, whom to attack, when to unite and with whom, when to retreat and where. Sometimes they are ruthlessly sacrificed, together with the interests of the workers of those countries, to the policies of the Soviet Union. In Germany, for example, during the years pre-ceding Hitler's seizure of power, the Soviet Union de-clared that the German Socialists were the chief enemy of the Communist movement; the German Communist Party was instructed to make common cause, and sometimes to take common action, with the German National Socialists, as the Nazis called themselves. The first of the three se-lections here reprinted is from the Resolutions and Theses of the Fourth Congress of the Communist International, London, 1923, p. 21; *the second is from the* Resolutions of the Sixth Congress of the Communist International (1928) *New York, 1934; the third is from the* Seventh World Congress of the Communist International: Resolu-tions, *New York, 1935, pp. 45*ff.

↗   ↗   ↗

—A—

The Fourth World Congress reminds the proletarians of all countries that the proletarian revolution can never be completely victorious within one single country, but that it must win the victory internationally, as the world revo-lution. The work and struggle of Soviet Russia for its existence and for the achievement of the revolution, is the struggle for the emancipation of the proletarians, the op-pressed and exploited of the whole world from slavery and servitude. The Russian proletarians have done more than their duty as the revolutionary pioneers of the world proletariat. The world proletariat must at last do its share. In all countries, the workers, the disinherited and the en-slaved, must show morally, economically and politically the most active solidarity with Soviet Russia. Their own interest, and not only international solidarity, demand that they should engage for this purpose in the most energetic struggle against the bourgeoisie and the capitalist State. In all countries their watchword must be "Hands off Soviet Russia!" "De jure" recognition of Soviet Russia!

—B—

The proletariat in the Soviet Union harbors no illusions as to the possibility of a durable peace with the imperialists. The proletariat knows that the imperialist attack against the Soviet Union is inevitable; that in the process of proletarian world revolution, wars between proletarian and bourgeois States, wars for the emancipation of the world from capitalism, will *necessarily* and *inevitably arise*. Therefore, the primary duty of the proletariat, as the fighter for Socialism, is to make all the necessary political, economic and military preparations for these wars, to strengthen its Red Army—that mighty weapon of the proletariat—and to train the masses of the toilers in the art of war. There is a glaring contradiction between the imperialists' policy of piling up armaments and their hypocritical talk about peace. There is no such contradiction, however, between the Soviet Government's preparations for defense and for revolutionary war and a consistent peace policy. Revolutionary war of the proletarian dictatorship is but a continuation of revolutionary peace policy "by other means."

The Red Army is not an "enemy" army, but the army of the international proletariat. In the event of a war against the Soviet Union, the workers in capitalist countries must not allow themselves to be scared from supporting the Red Army and from expressing this support by fighting against their own bourgeoisie, by the charges of treason that the bourgeoisie may hurl against them.

—C—

From the historic balance of achievements secured since the Sixth Congress of the Communist International, with which the world proletarian movement is approaching the second round of wars and revolutions and which *determines the basic tasks of the world proletarian revolution,* follows the primary duty of the working class and the toilers of the world and of all Sections of the C. I.:

To help with all their might and by all means to

strengthen the U.S.S.R. and to fight against the enemies of the U.S.S.R., both under peace conditions and in the circumstances of war directed against the U.S.S.R. the interests of strengthening the U.S.S.R., of increasing its power, of ensuring its victory in all spheres and in every sector of the struggle, coincide fully and inseparably with the interests of the toilers of the whole world in their struggle against the exploiters with the interests of the colonial and oppressed peoples fighting against imperialism; they are the conditions for, and they contribute to, the triumph of the world proletarian revolution, the victory of socialism throughout the world.

— 20 —

THE POPULATION BOMB
AND MOTHER HEROINES

In the early days of the Russian Revolution comparatively progressive measures were adopted which permitted planned parenthood through birth control. During the mid-thirties all these progressive measures were abandoned despite the strong evidence of their popularity. From that time on the Soviet state has systematically fostered a policy of encouraging large families despite the chronic shortage in housing and consumer goods which makes family life extremely onerous in most centers of the Soviet Union. The system of prizes and awards for large families introduced by Mussolini and Hitler was adopted by the U.S.S.R. Any theory or doctrine that saw some good in the movement of birth control, whether in relation to social or economic planning or in relation to intelligent organization of personal family life, was denounced as "Malthusian cannibalism." The following paragraphs are extracts from the Edict of the Supreme Soviet of the U.S.S.R. on the Increase of State Aid for Mothers and Children, printed in

Information Bulletin of the Embassy *of the U.S.S.R., July 25, 1944.*

✓   ✓   ✓

. . . Thirdly, on the institution of a Motherhood Medal and the Order of Glory of Motherhood, and on the establishment of the honorary title Mother Heroine.

To institute a Motherhood Medal, First and Second Class, for award to mothers who have given birth to and reared six and five children respectively.

To institute the Order of Glory of Motherhood, First, Second and Third Class, for award to mothers who have given birth to and reared nine, eight, and seven children respectively.

To establish that the title of Mother Heroine is to be conferred upon mothers who have given birth to and reared 10 children, this award being accompanied by the presentation of the Order of Mother Heroine and a scroll from the Presidium of the Supreme Soviet of the USSR.

The award of the Order of Glory of Motherhood and the Motherhood Medal, as well as the Mother Heroine title, comes into effect when the last child born reaches the age of one year, if the remaining children from the same mother are living.

Children killed or reported missing on fronts of the Patriotic War are to be included when these awards are made to mothers.

Fourthly, on the tax on single men and women and citizens with small families.

In modification of the Edict of the Presidium of the Supreme Soviet of the USSR of November 21, 1941 "On the tax on single men and women and childless citizens of the USSR," the tax will henceforth be levied upon citizens who have no children and on citizens who have one or two children: for men over 20 and up to 50 years of age and for women over 20 and up to 45.

LENIN'S TESTAMENT

The following "testament" was dictated by Lenin a year before his death in the form of a communication to the Central Committee of the Communist Party. It was first made public in The New York Times, *October 18, 1926, by Max Eastman, who had secured a copy from Leon Trotsky, For many years its authenticity was denied, although Stalin quoted from it on occasion in his polemics with Bukharin. Those critics of Soviet terror who referred to the testament at the time of the Moscow Trials and later, were denounced as guilty of malicious fabrication by Communists outside the Soviet Union. Khrushchev distributed it as a background document to the delegates of the 20th Party Congress in connection with his speech.*

↗   ↗   ↗

By the stability of the Central Committee, of which I spoke before, I mean measures to prevent a split, so far as such measures can be taken. For, of course, the White Guard in *Russkaya Mysl* (I think it was S. E. Oldenburg) was right when, in the first place, in his play against Soviet Russia he banked on the hope of a split in our party, and when, in the second place, he banked for that split on serious disagreements in our party.

Our party rests upon two classes, and for that reason its instability is possible, and if there cannot exist an agreement between those classes its fall is inevitable. In such an event it would be useless to take any measures or in general to discuss the stability of our Central Committee. In such an event no measures would prove capable of preventing a split. But I trust that is too remote a future, and too improbable an event, to talk about.

I have in mind stability as a guarantee against a split in the near future, and I intended to examine here a series of considerations of a purely personal character.

I think that the fundamental factor in the matter of stability—from this point of view—is such members of the Central Committee as Stalin and Trotsky. The relation between them constitutes, in my opinion, a big half of the danger of that split, which might be avoided, and the avoidance of which might be promoted, in my opinion, by raising the number of members of the Central Committee to fifty or one hundred.

Comrade Stalin, having become General Secretary, has concentrated an enormous power in his hands; and I am not sure that he always knows how to use that power with sufficient caution. On the other hand, Comrade Trotsky, as was proved by his struggle against the Central Committee in connection with the question of the People's Commissariat of Ways and Communications, is distinguished not only by his exceptional abilities—personally he is, to be sure, the most able man in the present Central Committee—but also by his too far-reaching self-confidence and a disposition to be too much attracted by the purely administrative side of affairs.

These two qualities of the two most able leaders of the present Central Committee might, quite innocently, lead to a split; if our party does not take measures to prevent it, a split might arise unexpectedly.

I will not further characterize the other members of the Central Committee as to their personal qualities. I will only remind you that the October episode of Zinoviev and Kamenev was not, of course, accidental, but that it ought as little to be used against them personally as the non-Bolshevism of Trotsky.

Of the younger members of the Central Committee, I want to say a few words about Bukharin and Pyatakov. They are in my opinion, the most able forces (among the youngest) and in regard to them it is necessary to bear in mind the following: Bukharin is not only the most valuable and biggest theoretician of the party, but also may legitimately be considered the favorite of the whole party; but his theoretical views can only with the very greatest doubt be regarded as fully Marxist, for there is something scholastic in him (he never has learned, and I think never has fully understood, the dialectic).

And then Pyatakov—a man undoubtedly distinguished in will and ability, but too much given over to administration and the administrative side of things to be relied on in a serious political question.

Of course, both these remarks are made by me merely with a view to the present time, or supposing that these two able and loyal workers may not find an occasion to supplement their knowledge and correct their one-sidedness.
December 25, 1922

Postscript: Stalin is too rude, and this fault, entirely supportable in relations among us Communists, becomes insupportable in the office of General Secretary. Therefore, I propose to the comrades to find a way to remove Stalin from that position and appoint to it another man who in all respects differs from Stalin only in superiority—namely, more patient, more loyal, more polite and more attentive to comrades, less capricious, etc. This circumstance may seem an insignificant trifle, but I think that from the point of view of preventing a split and from the point of view of the relation between Stalin and Trotsky which I discussed above, it is not a trifle, or it is such a trifle as may acquire a decisive significance.
January 4, 1923   LENIN

— 22 —

THE NAZI-SOVIET PACT, AUGUST 23, 1939

The following documents bear on one of the great turning points in the relations of the Soviet regime with the Western powers. From January 30, 1933, to August 23, 1939, the Soviet Union claimed to be in the forefront of the world opposition to Nazism. It joined the League of Nations and signed non-aggression pacts with France, Poland and the Baltic countries. It entered into direct military negotiations with England and France for mutual assistance in the event of German attack. Suddenly, with-

out warning, even while the negotiators of the democratic powers were still hopeful of signing an agreement, Hitler's lieutenant Ribbentrop flew to Moscow and the Nazi-Soviet Pact was signed, while Stalin looked on with beaming countenance. Shortly thereafter, Nazi and Soviet troops moved against Poland, and the Baltic states were overrun. Stalin telegraphed Hitler at the 1940 Nazi Parteitag that "the agreement between the U.S.S.R. and the German Republic was sealed in blood" and pledged loyal support.

For two years the Soviet Union, as Molotov claimed, "most faithfully abided by all the provisions of the treaty." During this period the U.S.S.R. supplied oil and other essential materials to Hitler's war machine. Stalin dismissed warnings from the Western democratic powers that Hitler would turn East as provocations designed to embroil him with his Nazi ally. When Hitler struck, the most surprised of all parties was the Soviet regime. The first extract contains some relevant sections from Stalin's Report to the 18th Congress of the Communist Party of the Soviet Union, March 10, 1939; the second is the text of the Nazi-Soviet Pact plus the "secret additional agreement"; the third is part of the text of Molotov's statement after the Pact was signed; the fourth again from Molotov after Hitler launched his attack.

✓   ✓   ✓

—A—

Extracts from Stalin's Report to the 18th Congress of the Communist Party of the Soviet Union

In order to strengthen its international position, the Soviet Union decided to take certain other steps. At the end of 1934 our country joined the League of Nations, considering that despite its weakness the League might nevertheless serve as a place where aggressors can be exposed, and as a certain instrument of peace, however feeble, that might hinder the outbreak of war. The Soviet Union considers that in alarming times like these even so weak an international organization as the League of Nations should not be ignored. In May 1935 a treaty of mutual assistance against possible attack by aggressors was signed between France and the Soviet Union. A similar treaty was simultaneously concluded with Czechoslovakia. In March 1936 the Soviet Union concluded a treaty of mutual assistance with the Mongolian People's Republic. In August 1937 the Soviet Union concluded a pact of nonaggression with the Chinese Republic.

It was in such difficult international conditions that the Soviet Union pursued its foreign policy of upholding the cause of peace.

The foreign policy of the Soviet Union is clear and explicit.

1. We stand for peace and the strengthening of business relations with all countries. That is our position; and we shall adhere to this position as long as these countries maintain like relations with the Soviet Union, and as long as they make no attempt to trespass on the interests of our country.

2. We stand for peaceful, close and friendly relations with all the neighbouring countries which have common frontiers with the U.S.S.R. That is our position; and we shall adhere to this position as long as these countries maintain like relations with the Soviet Union, and as long as they make no attempt to trespass, directly or indirectly, on the integrity and inviolability of the frontiers of the Soviet state.

3. We stand for the support of nations which are the victims of aggression and are fighting for the independence of their country.

4. We are not afraid of the threats of aggressors, and are ready to deal two blows for every blow delivered by instigators of war who attempt to violate the Soviet borders.

—B—

Text of the Nazi-Soviet Pact, August 23, 1939 [1]

Guided by the desire to strengthen the cause of peace between Germany and the Union of Socialist Soviet Republics, and basing themselves on the fundamental stipulations of the Neutrality Agreement concluded between

[1] From: German Library of Information, *Documents on the Events Preceding the Outbreak of the War* (compiled and published by the German Foreign Office, Berlin, 1939; New York, 1940), No. 348, pp. 370-371.

Germany and the Union of Socialist Soviet Republics in April, 1926, the German Government and the Government of the Union of Socialist Soviet Republics have come to the following agreement:

ARTICLE 1. The two contracting parties undertake to refrain from any act of force, any aggressive act, and any attacks against each other undertaken either singly or in conjunction with any other Powers.

ARTICLE 2. If one of the contracting parties should become the object of war-like action on the part of a third Power, the other contracting party will in no way support the third Power.

ARTICLE 3. The Governments of the two contracting parties will in future remain in consultation with one another in order to inform each other about questions which touch their common interests.

ARTICLE 4. Neither of the two contracting parties will join any group of Powers which is directed, mediately or immediately, against the other party.

ARTICLE 5. In case disputes or conflicts on questions of any kind should arise between the two contracting parties, the two partners will solve these disputes or conflicts exclusively by friendly exchange of views or if necessary by arbitration agreements.

ARTICLE 6. The present agreement is concluded for the duration of ten years with the stipulation that unless one of the contracting parties denounces it one year before its expiration, it will automatically be prolonged by five years.

ARTICLE 7. The present agreement shall be ratified in the shortest possible time. The instruments of ratification are to be exchanged in Berlin. The treaty comes into force immediately it has been signed.

Done in two original documents in the German and Russian languages, respectively.

Moscow, August 23, 1939

    For the German Government
        V. RIBBENTROP
    As plenipotentiary of the Government of the Union of Socialist Soviet Republics
        V. MOLOTOV

Secret Additional Protocol to the Nazi-Soviet Pact, August 23, 1939 [2]

On the occasion of the signature of the Nonaggression Pact between the German Reich and the Union of Socialist Soviet Republics the undersigned plenipotentiaries of each of the two parties discussed in strictly confidential conversations the question of the boundary of their respective spheres of influence in Eastern Europe. These conversations led to the following conclusions:

1. In the event of a territorial and political rearrangement in the areas belonging to the Baltic States (Finland, Estonia, Latvia, Lithuania), the northern boundary of Lithuania shall represent the boundaries of the spheres of influence of Germany and the U.S.S.R. In this connection the interest of Lithuania in the Vilna area is recognized by each party.

2. In the event of a territorial and political rearrangement of the areas belonging to the Polish state the spheres of influence of Germany and the U.S.S.R. shall be bounded approximately by the line of the rivers Narew, Vistula, and San.

The question of whether the interests of both parties make desirable the maintenance of an independent Polish state and how such a state should be bounded can only be definitely determined in the course of further political developments.

In any event both Governments will resolve this question by means of a friendly agreement.

3. With regard to Southeastern Europe attention is called by the Soviet side to its interest in Bessarabia. The German side declares its complete political disinterestedness in these areas.

4. This protocol shall be treated by both parties as strictly secret.

Moscow, August 23, 1939.

For the government of the German Reich	Plenipotentiary of the Government of the U.S.S.R.:
V. RIBBENTROP	V. MOLOTOV

[2] From: Raymond James Sontag and James Stuart Beddie, eds., *Nazi-Soviet Relations, 1939-1941* (Documents from the Archives of the German Foreign Office as Released by the Department of State) (Didier, New York, 1948), p. 78.

—C—

Part of Text of Molotov's Statement after Signing of Nazi-Soviet Pact[3]

The decision to conclude a nonaggression pact between the U.S.S.R. and Germany was adopted after military negotiations with France and Great Britain had reached an impasse owing to the insuperable differences I have mentioned. As the negotiations had shown that the conclusion of a pact of mutual assistance could not be expected, we could not but explore other possibilities of ensuring peace and eliminating the danger of war between Germany and the U.S.S.R. If the British and French governments refused to reckon with this, that is their affair. It is our duty to think of the interests of the Soviet people, the interests of the Union of Soviet Socialist Republics. All the more since we are firmly convinced that the interests of the U.S.S.R. coincide with the fundamental interests of the peoples of other countries. But that is only one side of the matter.

Another circumstance was required before the Soviet-German Non-Aggression Pact could come into existence. It was necessary that in her foreign policy Germany should make a turn towards good neighborly relations with the Soviet Union. . . .

*   *   *

The Soviet-German Pact has been the object of numerous attacks in the English, French, and American press. Conspicuous in these efforts are certain "Socialist" newspapers, diligent servitors of "their" national capitalism, servitors of gentlemen who pay them decently. It is clear that the real truth cannot be expected from gentry of this caliber. Attempts are being made to spread the fiction that the signing of the Soviet-German Pact disrupted the negotiations with England and France on a mutual assistance pact. This lie has already been nailed in the interview given by Voroshilov.

In reality, as you know, the very reverse is true. The

[3] From: V. M. Molotov's "The Meaning of the Soviet-German Non-Aggression Pact," *The Communist International*, Sept., 1939, pp. 951*ff*.

Soviet Union signed the Non-Aggression Pact with Germany, for one thing, in view of the fact that the negotiations with France and England had run into insuperable differences and ended in failure through the fault of the ruling classes of England and France.

—D—

Molotov's Statement after Hitler Launched His Attack[4]

MOSCOW, June 22.—The following is the text of V. M. Molotov's statement:

"Citizens of the Soviet Union!

"The Soviet Government and its head, Comrade Stalin, have authorized me to make the following statement:

"Today at four o'clock in the morning, without presenting any claims to the Soviet Government and without any declaration of war, German troops attacked our country, attacked our borders at many points and bombed from their airplanes our cities—Zhitomir, Kiev, Sevastopol, Kaunas, and some others, killing and wounding over 200 persons.

"There were also enemy air-raids and artillery shelling from Rumanian and Finnish territory.

"This unheard of attack upon our country is perfidy unparalleled in the history of civilized nations. The attack on our country was perpetrated despite the fact that a treaty of non-aggression had been signed by the Union of Soviet Socialist Republics and Germany and that the Soviet Government had most faithfully abided by all the provisions of this treaty. The attack upon our country was perpetrated despite the fact that during the entire period of operation of this treaty the German government could not find grounds for a single complaint against the U.S.S.R. as regards observance of the treaty.

"The entire responsibility for this predatory attack upon the Soviet Union falls fully and completely upon the German fascist rulers.

"At 5:30 A.M., that is, after the attack had already been perpetrated (Count Friedrich W. Von der) Schulenburg, the German Ambassador in Moscow, made a state-

[4] From: *Daily Worker,* June 23, 1941.

ment on behalf of his government to me as People's Commissar of Foreign Affairs to the effect that the German Government had decided to launch a war against the U.S.S.R. in connection with the concentration of Red Army units near the eastern German frontier.

"In reply to this I stated on behalf of the Soviet Government that up to the very last moment the German government had not presented any claims to the Soviet government, that Germany had attacked the U.S.S.R. despite the peaceable position of the Soviet Union, and that for this reason Fascist Germany is the aggressor.

"On instruction of the Government of the Soviet Union, I must also state that at no point had our troops or our airforce committed any violation of the frontier and that therefore the statement made this morning by the Rumanian radio to the effect that Soviet aircraft had allegedly fired on Rumanian airdromes is a sheer lie and provocation. Likewise, lie and provocation is the entire declaration made today by Hitler, who is trying belatedly to concoct accusations charging the Soviet Union with failure to observe the Soviet-German pact.

— 23 —

BEFORE AND AFTER HITLER STRUCK AGAINST HIS ALLY

The following two documents, representative of many, show how faithfully the line of the American Communist Party veered and tacked and reversed course in accordance with signals transmitted by the Kremlin. The first is a call by the American Peace Mobilization, a front organization set up by the Communist Party when the Nazi-Soviet Pact made it necessary to bury the American League for Peace and Democracy, the most successful of all Communist front organizations during the period of

the Popular Front. It appeared in the Communist World
News and Views, *February 15, 1941. On June 22, 1941,
Hitler turned against his ally and invaded the Soviet
Union. The second document appeared in the same
periodical on October 4, 1941, hardly more than three
months later.*

*These documents tell a story that sometimes was more
graphically illustrated. On June 22, 1941, the Young
Communist League paraded on the campus of universities
in New York City with banners reading "The Yanks Are
Not Coming" (a take-off on the popular World War I
song "The Yanks Are Coming"). A few days later they
appeared with the same banners bearing an altered device.
"The Yanks Are Not Coming—Too Late."*

↗   ↗   ↗

—A—

America—Call For a People's Peace

NEW YORK (By Cable).—The "American Peace
Mobilisation" has called on the people of the American
nation to rally to a great "American People's Meeting" in
New York on April 5 and 6 to halt the drive to war.

The text of the call reads:

*"To all friends of peace and liberty! Fellow Americans
—We are endangered. The tragic days of 1917 and of the
American Expeditionary Force are almost here again.
Our trade unions are under attack. The right to strike is
being taken away. Our farmers are being driven from
their land, their products are selling below cost. We are
paying more for food. Our rents are being increased. Our
wages are being held down. Unemployment continues
and our relief is being cut.*

*"Discrimination against our Negro people is increasing.
Attacks against the Jewish people are being intensified.
Our 'non-citizens' have been fingerprinted.*

*"There are virtually no jobs for the youth. Four million
people are being placed under military law.*

*"Congress continues to deny the vote to ten million
American citizens. The minority parties are being rapidly
suppressed. We are being intimidated and spied upon.
Persons and papers are being seized without warrant. Our
constitutional rights are being taken from us.*

"This is how democracy was blacked out in Germany and France, how it is being blacked out in England, and how it will be blacked out here unless labour and the people unite and act.

"These things have happened to us because our statesmen and the economic royalists are violating the will of the people. Men in high places are dragging us into a war 3,000 miles away. It is not a war to defend democracy—it is a war to line the pockets of the corporate interests at the expense of the peoples of the world.

"All-out aid to the British Empire or any other such warring empire means total war for the American people.

"There is a way out. The drive toward fascist rule in America and to total war CAN be stopped. Sovereignty belongs to the people. A united people's anti-war movement can save America from the horrors of war and from the barbarity of fascism.

"In order to get out and stay out of World War No. 2; to fight every step of the war; to regain and strengthen our democracy; to secure the rights of Labour: WORK FOR A PEOPLE'S PEACE.

"We call on the workers of mill and mine and factory and office and railroad and ships, upon the farmers, the unemployed, the Churches, upon the Negro people, the youth and aged; to meet in their unions and organisations and shops and mass meetings and Churches, to elect representatives to the American People's Meeting, to take steps to mobilise the people for Peace, Liberty and the Common Welfare."

—B—

Appeasers Don't Represent America

BY A CORRESPONDENT

For many months before June 22 reactionary groups had been playing up the Communist and Bolshevist bogies and had achieved some success, such as the banning of the Communist Party from elections in certain states and the imprisonment of Earl Browder. Many newspapers were plugging the "Communist-Nazi-no-difference" line. To such as these the attack on the Soviet Union came as a shock.

At first the change in attitude was slow, even in trade

union circles. But the march of events, the resistance of the Soviet forces; and the realisation that the Nazis are really out for world domination, including domination of the United States and Latin America, has steadily brought about a change which is now becoming clear.

Summing up the situation at the end of August, the *Daily Worker* wrote: "The tide is turning. The arrogance of the Vichymen and Fifth Columnists have revealed the danger. Within the past few days there have been such developments against Hitlerism as the New York State A. F. of L. position for all out struggle; the support of the New York C.I.O. Council for the Madison Square Garden anti-Hitler rally addressed by Admiral Bird and Supreme Court Justice Robert; the anti-Hitler speeches at the Knights of Columbus Convention . . . and similar action. These are belated beginnings, but they show the trend. . . . The working people of the country now need to speed the movement for national unity of all anti-Hitler forces, with a definite programme of action based on crushing Hitlerism."

This list must be supplemented by similar calls for support for Britain, the U.S.S.R. and China from the Vermont State Federation of Labour, the Wisconsin Federation of Labour, the powerful Wayne County (Detroit) C.I.O., representing 325,000 workers, the Iowa (Nebraska) C.I.O. and hundreds of smaller union branches and councils. The United Maritime Workers was the first of the great national unions to call for support to the Soviet Union, and though Lewis, of the mineworkers, ex-head of the C.I.O., some weeks ago put his name to an isolationist letter, also signed by Hoover and Landon, it is doubtful whether this represents a considered stand, or whether it has any support in his union. . . .

Much, however, still remains to be done to consolidate U.S. opinion behind the world front of peoples against Hitler. It is good news that the C.I.O. may soon make an official pro-Ally statement. It is good news that the progressive anti-Hitler *P.M.*, whose publisher, Ralph Ingersoll, has just been on a visit to Moscow, is to fight the isolationists of Chicago in their own territory. And especially is it good news that the Roosevelt administration is taking a steadily stronger line against the dark forces of Nazi-Fascism.

— 24 —

THE MOSCOW TRIALS

In the course of the Moscow Trials, conducted from 1936 through 1938, the Soviet regime, under the leadership of Stalin, sought to prove to the entire world that most of the general staff of the Bolshevik October Revolution were spies, traitors and saboteurs, that some—like Trotsky, who was the chief defendant—had been in the pay of enemies of the Soviet Union from the very beginning, and had made a compact with Fascist Germany and Japan to divide up the Soviet Union. Most of those arrested confessed. A great mystery was made of the Confessions, although subsequently Khrushchev explained the simple means by which they were obtained. An intense campaign to popularize the Moscow Trials was made by the Communist Parties throughout the world. In many countries and by many individuals in all countries, the official Kremlin version was swallowed whole. Joseph Davies, the American Ambassador to the Soviet Union, was convinced of the justice of the Moscow Trials. A long list of American writers, professors and intellectuals also endorsed them.

Because of the importance of ascertaining the truth, an International Commission of Inquiry, headed by John Dewey, the dean of American philosophers at the time, was established to investigate the charges, the evidence and the conduct of the trial. It brought in a verdict of "Not Guilty" for the defendants and charged that the Trials had been staged, that the defendants were victims of one of the most elaborately staged frame-ups in history. Dewey and the Commission he headed were themselves defamed as Fascists by the Communists throughout the world, including the United States. After Stalin's death, Khrushchev, who had abetted Stalin in the purges, revealed in his secret report before the 20th Congress of the Communist Party, some of the truth about the Moscow Trials.

The Moscow Trials constituted one of the turning points in the history of American liberalism. It drew a sharp line between those who were prepared to take the propaganda handouts of the Kremlin on faith and those who insisted on applying the same standards of inquiry and truth which all liberals had adopted in appraising the Reichstag Fire Trials and other injustices in democratic as well as totalitarian countries.

The first excerpt consists of the official Soviet account of the Trials; the second, an examination of the evidence by the author written at the time of the trials; and the third, the judgment of the Dewey Commission of Inquiry. Some excerpts from Khrushchev's secret speech to the 20th Congress of the Communist Party being on the Moscow Trials will be found in Readings No. 24, 25 and 26.

✓   ✓   ✓

—A—

The Enemies of the People

In 1937, new facts came to light regarding the fiendish crimes of the Bukharin-Trotsky gang. The trial of Pyatakov, Radek and others, the trial of Tukhachevsky, Yakir and others, and, lastly, the trial of Bukharin, Rykov, Krestinsky, Rosengoltz and others, all showed that the Bukharinites and Trotskyites had long ago joined to form a common band of enemies of the people, operating as the "Bloc of Rights and Trotskyites."

The trials showed that these dregs of humanity, in conjunction with the enemies of the people, Trotsky, Zinoviev and Kamenev, had been in conspiracy against Lenin, the Party and the Soviet state ever since the early days of the October Socialist Revolution. The insidious attempts to thwart the Peace of Brest-Litovsk at the beginning of 1918, the plot against Lenin and the conspiracy with the "Left" Socialist-Revolutionaries for the arrest and murder of Lenin, Stalin and Sverdlov in the spring of 1918, the villainous shot that wounded Lenin in the summer of 1918, the revolt of the "Left" Socialist-Revolutionaries in the summer of 1918, the deliberate aggravation of differences in the Party in 1921 with the object of undermining and overthrowing Lenin's leadership from within, the attempts to overthrow the Party leadership during Lenin's illness and after his death, the betrayal of state secrets and the supply of information of an espionage character to foreign espionage services, the vile assassination of Kirov, the acts of wrecking diversion and explosions, the dastardly murder of Menzhinsky, Kuibyshev and Gorky—all these and similar villainies over a period of twenty years were committed, it transpired, with the participation or under the direction of Trotsky, Zinoviev, Kamenev, Bukharin, Rykov and their henchmen, at the behest of espionage services of bourgeois states.

The trials brought to light the fact that the Trotsky-Bukharin fiends, in obedience to the wishes of their masters—the espionage services of foreign states—had set out to destroy the Party and the Soviet state, to undermine the defensive power of the country, to assist foreign military intervention, to prepare the way for the defeat of the Red Army, to bring about the dismemberment of the U.S.S.R., to hand over the Soviet Maritime Region to the Japanese, Soviet Byelorussia to the Poles, and the Soviet Ukraine to the Germans, to destroy the gains of the workers and collective farmers, and to restore capitalist slavery in the U.S.S.R.

These Whiteguard pigmies, whose strength was no more than that of a gnat, apparently flattered themselves that they were the masters of the country, and imagined that it was really in their power to sell or give away the Ukraine, Byelorussia and the Maritime Region.

These Whiteguard insects forgot that the real masters of the Soviet country were the Soviet people, and that the Rykovs, Bukharins, Zinovievs and Kamenevs were only temporary employees of the state, which could at any moment sweep them out from its offices as so much useless rubbish.

These contemptible lackeys of the fascists forgot that the Soviet people had only to move a finger, and not a trace of them would be left.

The Soviet court sentenced the Bukharin-Trotsky fiends to be shot.

The People's Commissariat of Internal Affairs carried out the sentence.

The Soviet people approved the annihilation of the Bukharin-Trotsky gang and passed on to next business.

—B—

The Mystery of the Moscow Trials

—A LOGICAL ANALYSIS—

BY SIDNEY HOOK

No political trial in modern times has had consequences more far flung than those of the Moscow trials. The Dreyfus case threw France into turmoil. The fate of Carl von Ossietsky stirred a wave of international protest. But the repercussions of the Moscow trials have been much more profound. Not only have they shattered the unity of all forces left of center in every major country of the world, they have had a direct influence upon the foreign policy of at least half a dozen European chancelleries. All informed observers are agreed that the decline in Russian prestige which began after August, 1936, the date of the first trial, contributed to forcing a realignment of the European powers. The vital cause of this loss of prestige has been the Moscow trials and the continuous purges resulting therefrom.

Many have been the speculations hatched to account for the psychology of the defendants or the psychology of Stalin. A tangled web of motives has been spun around every dramatic event in the bizarre spectacle of the "fathers of the Russian Revolution" confessing to crimes of which even their bitterest political enemies never dared to accuse them. Comparatively little concern, however, has been manifested in the nature and weight of the evidence itself. Yet, fascinating as psychological speculations are, especially when the *dramatis personae* are regarded as characters out of Dostoyevsky, in the last analysis all questions, except the immediate political consequences of the trials, turn upon the issue of the guilt or innocence of the defendants. This is the primary question, and although it may be difficult to answer, a certain hunger for justice makes men ask it.

The Sources. The basic source materials of the Moscow trials with which the student of the subject must familiarize himself consist of five volumes. They read like detective stories and light up many an obscure corner in the history of the Russian Revolution. Presenting the case for the Prosecution are three volumes reporting the court proceedings: *The Trotskyite-Zinovievite Terrorist Center,* (Moscow 1936); *The Anti-Soviet Trotskyite Center,* (Moscow 1937); *The Anti-Soviet Bloc of Rights and Trotskyites,* (Moscow 1938). Presenting the case of the chief defendant is *The Case of Leon Trotsky,* Report of Hearings on the Charges Made Against Him in the Moscow Trials, (New York, 1937). This is a verbatim account of the hearings held at Mexico City before the Preliminary Commission of Inquiry headed by John Dewey. The fifth volume is *The Final Report of the Commission of Inquiry into Charges Made Against Leon Trotsky and Leon Sedov* (Trotsky's son) *in the Moscow Trials.* (New York, 1938, in press).

The Evidence. A careful reading of all the evidence presented at the trials shows that it consists almost exclusively of the confessions of the defendants and of self-incriminated witnesses. The confessions themselves constitute evidence of a sort. But their logical and legal weight depends entirely upon the extent to which they can be substantiated. The question of substantiation in this case is all the more important for a number of special reasons. First, the character of the charges made and historical rôle of the persons involved are such as to provoke a legitimate bewilderment and incredulity. Second, the publicly formulated principles of Russian criminal procedure demand that confessions be confirmed by material evidence. For example, in a well-known textbook on criminal trials, edited by the State Prosecutor Vyshinsky, we read:

> In no measure whatsoever does it correspond to the principles of the Soviet criminal trial to depend on it [*the testimony of the accused*] as the fundamental and most important proof. Such significance the testimony of the accused in a Soviet trial does not and cannot possess; the testimony of the accused, in particular his admission of guilt, like every other piece of evidence, is subject to verification and

careful evaluation as a result of juxtaposing it with all the other evidence gathered in the case.

Thirdly, since the State Prosecutor himself explained the confessions on the ground that the defendants were confronted by incontrovertible evidence of their guilt, it is natural to expect him to produce that evidence, or at least part of it, in open court.

The most surprising feature of the Moscow trials in the eyes of the Western World was the failure of the Prosecution to produce a scrap of material evidence bearing in any relevant way on the specific charges against the defendants. Even when the Prosecutor cites from the record of the Preliminary Investigation, only confessions are introduced. That is to say, later confessions are sometimes checked by earlier confessions but no material evidence is given to show which ones, if any, are true. When we bear in mind that the defendants were accused of almost all crimes on the calendar from high treason to putting nails in butter, in a conspiracy which lasted a dozen years or more and involved tens of thousands in all fields of Russian life—the glaring absence of material evidence throws a huge question mark on all the trials. With the best will and friendliest feelings in the world towards the Russian government, no individual who holds that justice and truth are above geographical and political boundaries, can accept the Moscow trials on their face value. Nor, as far as *this* aspect of the evidence goes, can he yet declare all the charges to be false.

The Logical Key. But there is another aspect of the evidence. This aspect concerns not what is alleged to have transpired in Russia but outside of it. It introduces into the picture people in other countries of the world who, by the confession of the defendants, are integrally involved in the plot. Indeed, as will be seen in a moment, the entire logical structure of the evidence rests upon this aspect of the evidence.

The defendants all confessed that they were members of a political organization. They are unanimous that the policy and directives for the organization were transmitted from abroad by Leon Trotsky. He is alleged to have given personal instructions to certain emissaries from among the defendants and self-implicated witnesses who passed them on to the rest of the group. The official indictment, the verdict, the speeches of the Prosecution and defendants reiterate these charges against Trotsky. The basic testimony of *all* the defendants rests upon the testimony of the eight men who asserted that they were the intermediaries between Trotsky and the other defendants. They testified to having met Trotsky, as well as his confederates, at certain times, in certain places, and under certain conditions. Here we have the key to everything else deposed in the Moscow court. For fortunately this is evidence which can be checked publicly under the very eyes of the world. It does not require clairvoyant guesswork about what occurred in the cellars of the Lubianka Prison.

The alleged intermediaries between Trotsky and the other defendants were Berman-Yurin, David, Olberg, Holtzmann, Pyatakov and Romm in the first two trials, Bessonov and Krestinsky in the third. From the first day that these intermediaries told their story, down to the present, a mountain of evidence has accumulated which proves their testimony to have been completely false. Accounts of this evidence appeared in the N. Y. *Times* as it came to light. Even while the trials were in progress, witnesses in Norway, Denmark and France came forward with affidavits and documents impugning the testimony of the intermediaries and requesting the Russian government to postpone execution of the verdict until it could check on the counter-evidence. The investigation of the Dewey Commission of Inquiry has resulted in the discovery of unimpeachable documentary evidence and witnesses which completely invalidates the confessions of every one of the intermediaries. And on these confessions, the confessions of all the other defendants hang.

No less damaging to the prosecution were revelations concerning individuals, other than Trotsky, residing outside of Russia, who were mentioned in the Moscow trials. Those defendants who claimed to be espionage agents of foreign powers told of having been recruited by prominent figures in Western Europe. Every living person named offered proof that these allegations were false from start to finish. Among them were Theodore Dan, close friend of Léon Blum, and supposedly acting for the leaders of the Labor and Socialist International, Madelaine Paz,

Alfred Rosmer, Paul Sheffer, I. Maslow, Lady Paget and Max Eastman.

Positions Reversed. The situation then is as follows. At all points where empirical confirmation is possible, the testimony of the Moscow defendants is demonstrably untrue. Everything else turns out to be "conversations about conversations." For the confessions no material proof of any kind is offered. But from outside of Russia material proof is available that the key confessions are false. Further, the evidence is overwhelming that the Prosecutor Vyshinsky was aware of the existence of essential portions of the counter-evidence. For example, no sooner had Pyatakov testified that he flew from Berlin to Oslo in December, 1935, to visit Trotsky, than officials of the Oslo airport certified that not a single foreign airplane landed in Oslo during the entire month. The next day, Vyshinsky brought the matter up again and this time Pyatakov testified that he landed in an airport *near* Oslo which Vyshinsky identified as the Kjeller Airdrome. The very same day Director Gulliksen of the Kjeller Airdrome produced his records which showed that no foreign plane had landed from September, 1935, to May, 1936. The information was wired to Vyshinsky by Konrad Knudsen, Storting deputy, with the request that Pyatakov be questioned further on this central point. Instead Pyatakov was shot. During the last trial Chernov testified that Paul Sheffer, correspondent of the *Berliner Tageblatt* had visited him in Moscow in 1930, to give him instructions from the espionage department of the Weimar Republic. Sheffer immediately offered proof that Chernov could not be telling the truth because Sheffer had quit Russia early in 1929. The next day Vyshinsky recalled Chernov who corrected the date to bring it in line with Sheffer's denial.

In the light of all this, the positions of the Prosecution and the chief defendants are reversed. Keeping the evidence in mind, and only the evidence, it is no longer incumbent upon Leon Trotsky to prove that he is not guilty as charged. It is the Prosecution which must now disprove the evidence that it has been guilty of a gigantic frame-up. Political partisans on one side or another may come to any conclusion which their faith dictates. But this is the only logical conclusion which the available evidence supports.

—C—

Summary of Findings

CONDUCT OF TRIALS

Independent of extrinsic evidence, the Commission finds:

1. That the conduct of the Moscow trials was such as to convince any unprejudiced person that no effort was made to ascertain the truth.

2. While confessions are necessarily entitled to the most serious consideration, these confessions themselves contain such inherent improbabilities as to convince the Commission that they do not represent the truth, irrespective of any means used to obtain them.

THE CHARGES

3. On the basis of all the evidence, we find that Trotsky never gave Smirnov any terrorist instructions through Sedov or anybody else.

4. On the basis of all the evidence, we find that Trotsky never gave Dreitzer terrorist instructions either through Sedov or anybody else.

5. On the basis of all the evidence, we find that Holtzman never acted as go-between for Smirnov on the one hand and Sedov on the other for the purposes of any terrorist conspiracy.

6. We find that Holtzman never met Sedov in Copenhagen; that he never went with Sedov to see Trotsky; that Sedov was not in Copenhagen during Trotsky's sojourn in that city; that Holtzman never saw Trotsky in Copenhagen.

7. We find that Olberg never went to Russia with terrorist instructions from Trotsky or Sedov.

8. We find that Berman-Yurin never received terrorist instructions from Trotsky in Copenhagen, and that Berman-Yurin never saw Trotsky in Copenhagen.

9. We find that David never received terrorist instructions from Trotsky in Copenhagen and that David never saw Trotsky in Copenhagen.

10. We find no basis whatever for the attempt to link Moissei Lurye and Nathan Lurye with an alleged Trotskyist conspiracy.

11. We find that Trotsky never met Vladimir Romm in the Bois de Boulogne; that he transmitted no messages through Romm to Radek. We find that Trotsky and Sedov never had any connection with Vladimir Romm.

12. We find that Pyatakov did not fly to Oslo in December, 1935; he did not, as charged, see Trotsky; he did not receive from Trotsky any instructions of any kind. We find that the disproof of Pyatakov's testimony on this crucial point renders his whole confession worthless.

13. We find that the disproof of the testimony of the defendant Pyatakov invalidates the testimony of the witness Bukhartsev.

14. We find that the disproof of Vladimir Romm's testimony and that of Pyatakov completely invalidates the testimony of the defendant Radek.

15. We find that the disproof of the confessions of Smirnov, Pyatakov and Radek completely invalidates the confessions of Shestov and Muralov.

16. We are convinced that the alleged letters in which Trotsky conveyed alleged conspiratorial instructions to the various defendants in the Moscow trials never existed; and that the testimony concerning them is sheer fabrication.

17. We find that Trotsky throughout his whole career has always been a consistent opponent of individual terror. The Commission further finds that Trotsky never instructed any of the defendants or witnesses in the Moscow trials to assassinate any political opponent.

18. We find that Trotsky never instructed the defendants or witnesses in the Moscow trials to engage in sabotage, wrecking, and diversion. On the contrary, he has always been a consistent advocate of the building up of socialist industry and agriculture in the Soviet Union and has criticized the present régime on the basis that its activities were harmful to the building up of socialist economy in Russia. He is not in favor of sabotage as a method of opposition to any political régime.

19. We find that Trotsky never instructed any of the accused or witnesses in the Moscow trials to enter into agreements with foreign powers against the Soviet Union. On the contrary, he has always uncompromisingly advocated the defense of the U.S.S.R. He has also been a most forthright ideological opponent of the fascism rep-

resented by the foreign powers with which he is accused of having conspired.

20. On the basis of all the evidence we find that Trotsky never recommended, plotted, or attempted the restoration of capitalism in the U.S.S.R. On the contrary, he has always uncompromisingly opposed the restoration of capitalism in the Soviet Union and its existence anywhere else.

21. We find that the Prosecutor fantastically falsified Trotsky's role before, during and after the October Revolution.

CONCLUSIONS

22. We therefore find the Moscow trials to be frame-ups.

23. We therefore find Trotsky and Sedov not guilty.

Signed: JOHN DEWEY, *Chairman*
BENJAMIN STOLBERG
WENDELIN THOMAS
ALFRED ROSMER
JOHN R. CHAMBERLAIN
CARLO TRESCA
E. A. ROSS
OTTO RUEHLE
F. ZAMORA
SUZANNE LA FOLLETTE, *Secretary*

Session of the Commission on
Monday, September 20, 1937,
held at 231 East 14th St.,
New York City

— 25 —

WHY DID THEY CONFESS?

Ever since the Moscow Trials there has been intense speculation as to why the obviously innocent defendants confessed to the most fantastic improbabilities. Many apologists for these trials, confronted by the glaring discrepancies in the testimony, fell back upon the fact of the confessions, although it was known that some people in the past had confessed to being witches or in league with the Devil. In this excerpt from his secret speech, Khrushchev explains why innocent people confessed. What should be added is that those who withstood "the pressures" to confess were never brought to trial, but were either shot or shipped off to concentration camp by administrative decree of the Secret Police.

　　　✓　　　　　✓　　　　　✓

When Stalin said that one or another should be arrested, it was necessary to accept on faith that he was an "enemy of the people." Meanwhile, Beria's gang, which ran the organs of state security, outdid itself in proving the guilt of the arrested and the truth of materials which it falsified. And what proofs were offered? The confessions of the arrested, and the investigative judges accepted these "confessions." And how is it possible that a person confesses to crimes which he has not committed? Only in one way—because of application of physical methods of pressuring him, tortures, bringing him to a state of unconsciousness, deprivation of his judgment, taking away of his human dignity. In this manner were "confessions" acquired.

When the wave of mass arrests began to recede in 1939, and the leaders of territorial party organizations began to accuse the NKVD workers of using methods of physical pressure on the arrested, Stalin dispatched a coded telegram on January 20, 1939 to the committee secretaries of *oblasts* and *krais,* to the central committees of republic Communist parties, to the People's Commissars of Internal Affairs and to the heads of NKVD organizations. This telegram stated:

"The Central Committee of the All-Union Communist Party (Bolsheviks) explains that the application of methods of physical pressure in NKVD practice is permissible from 1937 on in accordance with permission of the Central Committee of the All-Union Communist Party (Bolsheviks) . . . It is known that all bourgeois intelligence services use methods of physical influence against the representatives of the socialist proletariat and that they use them in their most scandalous forms.

"The question arises as to why the socialist intelligence service should be more humanitarian against the mad agents of the bourgeoisie, against the deadly enemies of the working class and of the *kolkhoz* workers. The Central Committee of the All-Union Communist Party (Bolsheviks) considers that physical pressure should still be used obligatorily, as an exception applicable to known and obstinate enemies of the people, as a method both justifiable and appropriate." . . .

Let us also recall the "affair of the doctor-plotters." (Animation in the hall.) Actually there was no "affair" outside of the declaration of the woman doctor Timashuk, who was probably influenced or ordered by someone (after all, she was an unofficial collaborator of the organs of state security) to write Stalin a letter in which she declared that doctors were applying supposedly improper methods of medical treatment.

Such a letter was sufficient for Stalin to reach an immediate conclusion that there are doctor-plotters in the Soviet Union. He issued orders to arrest a group of eminent Soviet medical specialists. He personally issued advice on the conduct of the investigation and the method of interrogation of the arrested persons. He said that the academician Vinogradov should be put in chains, another one should be beaten. Present at this Congress as a delegate is the former Minister of State Security, Comrade Ignatiev. Stalin told him curtly, "If you do not obtain confessions from the doctors we will shorten you by a head." (Tumult in the hall.)

Stalin personally called the investigative judge, gave him instructions, advised him on which investigative methods should be used; these methods were simple—beat, beat and, once again, beat.

KHRUSHCHEV ON STALIN'S CRIMES

After Stalin's death, there ensued a struggle for the succession. Khrushchev and Malenkov eliminated Beria, then Khrushchev triumphed over Malenkov and his supporters. In order to strengthen his position in this struggle, Khrushchev made his secret report to the 20th Congress of the Communist Party of the Soviet Union on February 24, 1956, in which he revealed some of the crimes committed under Stalin's rule (crimes which he had loyally supported as one of Stalin's chief lieutenants). The Report has not been published in the Soviet Union to this day, but some copies sent to Communists abroad fell into the hands of the U.S. State Department, which published the Report without comment. The repercussions were felt throughout the world, especially among Communist Parties abroad which had canonized Stalin. Khrushchev criticizes mainly the "cult of the individual" which Stalin had encouraged, but indicates clearly that Stalin had suffered in his later years from megalomania. But the differences between the actions of Stalin sane and Stalin insane were hardly distinguishable.

The impact of Khrushchev's speech was so shattering that for a brief moment the Communists in other countries were shocked. Howard Fast, for example, the American Communist novelist and winner of the Stalin Prize, proclaimed: "It is a strange and awful document perhaps without a parallel in history . . . it itemizes a record of barbarism and paranoic blood lust that will be a lasting and shameful memory to civilized man." Similar sentiments were expressed in other countries by some of Stalin's faithful followers. None of them noted the fact that almost every revelation made by Khrushchev confirmed charges and criticisms uttered years before by critics of the Communist regime who had been slandered as "Trotskyite Fascists" and "running dogs of imperialism" by Communists throughout the world, including those who cried quits as well as those who substituted Khrushchev for Stalin in their political orthodoxy.

Soon, however, the Communist Parties of the world lost their embarrassment. Khrushchev's speech gave them an opportunity to explain away every act of Soviet brutality and repression—previously denied as canards or inventions—as the fault of Stalin and to hail Khrushchev as the harbinger and executor of a new dispensation in the Communist world. None explained how it was possible for Stalin to have succeeded in his criminal career for more than a score of years except through means and institutions integral to the Communist totalitarian system itself. None sought to explain along Marxist lines how one man could be guilty of so much harm and evil without the support of the Communist organization and bureaucracy. None observed that Khrushchev's action in giving the signal for the massacre of the Hungarian revolutionists—a few months after the Report was made—equalled, if it did not surpass, the scale of Stalin's terrorism.

All quotations are from the text of the State Department's release, June 4, 1956.

✓   ✓   ✓

Stalin acted not through persuasion, explanation and patient cooperation with people, but by imposing his concepts and demanding absolute submission to his opinion. Whoever opposed this concept or tried to prove his viewpoint and the correctness of his position was doomed to removal from the leading collective and to subsequent moral and physical annihilation. This was especially true during the period following the 17th Party Congress, when many prominent party leaders and rank-and-file party workers, honest and dedicated to the cause of Communism, fell victim to Stalin's despotism. . . .

Stalin originated the concept "enemy of the people." This term automatically rendered it unnecessary that the ideological errors of a man or men engaged in a controversy be proven; this term made possible the usage of the most cruel repression, violating all norms of revolutionary legality, against anyone who in any way disagreed with

Stalin, against those who were only suspected of hostile intent, against those who had bad reputations. This concept "enemy of the people" actually eliminated the possibility of any kind of ideological fight or the making of one's views known on this or that issue, even those of a practical character. In the main, and in actuality, the only proof of guilt used, against all norms of current legal science, was the "confession" of the accused himself; and, as subsequent probing proved, "confessions" were acquired through physical pressures against the accused. This led to glaring violations of revolutionary legality and to the fact that many entirely innocent persons, who in the past had defended the party line, became victims.

We must assert that, in regard to those persons who in their time had opposed the party line, there were often no sufficiently serious reasons for their physical annihilation. The formula "enemy of the people" was specifically introduced for the purpose of physically annihilating such individuals. . . .

Arbitrary behavior by one person encouraged and permitted arbitrariness in others. Mass arrests and deportations of many thousands of people, execution without trial and without normal investigation created conditions of insecurity, fear and even desperation. . . .

It was determined that of the 139 members and candidates of the party's Central Committee who were elected at the 17th Congress, 98 persons, *i.e.*, 70 per cent, were arrested and shot (mostly in 1937-1938). (Indignation in the hall.) What was the composition of the delegates to the 17th Congress? It is known that 80 per cent of the voting participants of the 17th Congress joined the Party during the years of conspiracy before the Revolution and during the civil war; this means before 1921. By social origin the basic mass of the delegates to the Congress were workers (60 per cent of the voting members).

For this reason, it was inconceivable that a congress so composed would have elected a Central Committee a majority of whom would prove to be enemies of the party. The only reason why 70 per cent of Central Committee members and candidates elected at the 17th Congress were branded as enemies of the party and of the people was because honest Communists were slandered, accusations against them were fabricated, and revolutionary legality was gravely undermined.

The same fate met not only the Central Committee members but also the majority of the delegates to the 17th Party Congress. Of 1,966 delegates with either voting or advisory rights, 1,108 persons were arrested on charges of anti-revolutionary crimes, *i.e.*, decidedly more than a majority. This very fact shows how absurd, wild and contrary to common sense were the charges of counterrevolutionary crimes made out, as we now see, against a majority of participants at the 17th Party Congress. (Indignation in the hall.). . .

It must be asserted that to this day the circumstances surrounding Kirov's murder hide many things which are inexplicable and mysterious and demand a most careful examination. There are reasons for the suspicion that the killer of Kirov, Nikolayev, was assisted by someone from among the people whose duty it was to protect the person of Kirov.

Mass repressions grew tremendously from the end of 1936 after a telegram from Stalin and [Andrei] Zhdanov, dated from Sochi on September 25, 1936, was addressed to Kaganovich, Molotov and other members of the Political Bureau. The content of the telegram was as follows:

"We deem it absolutely necessary and urgent that Comrade Yezhov be nominated to the post of People's Commissar for Internal Affairs. Yagoda has definitely proved himself to be incapable of unmasking the Trotskyite-Zinovievite bloc. The OGPU is four years behind in this matter. This is noted by all party workers and by the majority of the representatives of the NKVD."

Strictly speaking, we should stress that Stalin did not meet with and, therefore, could not know the opinion of party workers.

This Stalinist formulation that the "NKVD is four years behind" in applying mass repression and that there is a necessity for "catching up" with the neglected work directly pushed the NKVD workers on the path of mass arrests and executions.

We should state that this formulation was also forced on the February-March plenary session of the Central Committee of the All-Union Communist Party (Bolsheviks) in 1937. The plenary resolution approved it on the basis of Yezhov's report, "Lessons flowing from the harmful activity, diversion and espionage of the Japanese-German-Trotskyite agents," stating:

"The plenum of the Central Committee of the All-Union Communist Party (Bolsheviks) considers that all facts revealed during the investigation into the matter of an anti-Soviet Trotskyite center and of its followers in the provinces show that the People's Commissariat of Internal Affairs has fallen behind at least four years in the attempt to unmask these most inexorable enemies of the people."

The mass repressions at this time were made under the slogan of a fight against the Trotskyites. Did the Trotskyites at this time actually constitute such a danger to our party and to the Soviet state? We should recall that in 1927, on the eve of the 15th Party Congress, only some 4,000 votes were cast for the Trotskyite-Zinovievite opposition while there were 724,000 for the party line. During the 10 years which passed between the 15th Party Congress and the February-March Central Committee plenum, Trotskyism was completely disarmed; many former Trotskyites had changed their former views and worked in the various sectors building socialism. It is clear that in the situation of socialist victory there was no basis for mass terror in the country.

— 27 —

THE CASE OF COMRADE EIKHE

In his secret report Khrushchev quotes the case of "Comrade Eikhe" as a typical illustration of Comrade Stalin's outrages. What Khrushchev does not report is that the same treatment which was meted out to members of the Communist Party who ran afoul of Stalin's terror was applied to all elements in the population which for any reason ran afoul of the Communist Party dictatorship— except that, instead of executions, long sentences were imposed at killing labor in concentration camps. Khrushchev mentions, in addition to atrocities against Communist Party members, the deportation of the entire popula-

tion of Kalmuck, Chechen-Inguish, and the Kabardino-Balkan Republics (there were others, too). But he does not mention the genocide of more than two million so-called kulaks during the enforced collectivization program from 1929 to 1932, an operation which he himself directed in the Ukraine.

✓   ✓   ✓

An example of vile provocation, of odious falsification and of criminal violation of revolutionary legality is the case of the former candidate for the Central Committee Political Bureau, one of the most eminent workers of the party and of the Soviet Government, Comrade Eikhe, who was a party member since 1905. (Commotion in the hall.)

Comrade Eikhe was arrested on April 29, 1938 on the basis of slanderous materials, without the sanction of the Prosecutor of the USSR, which was finally received 15 months after the arrest.

Investigation of Eikhe's case was made in a manner which most brutally violated Soviet legality and was accompanied by willfulness and falsification.

Eikhe was forced under torture to sign ahead of time a protocol of his confession prepared by the investigative judges, in which he and several other eminent party workers were accused of anti-Soviet activity.

On October 1, 1939 Eikhe sent his declaration to Stalin in which he categorically denied his guilt and asked for an examination of his case. In the declaration he wrote: "There is no more bitter misery than to sit in the jail of a government for which I have always fought."

A second declaration of Eikhe has been preserved which he sent to Stalin on October 27, 1939; in it he cited facts very convincingly and countered the slanderous accusations made against him, arguing that this provocatory accusation was on the one hand the work of real Trotskyites whose arrests he had sanctioned as First Secretary of the West Siberian Krai [Territory] Party Committee and who conspired in order to take revenge on him, and, on the other hand, the result of the base falsification of materials by the investigative judges.

Eikhe wrote in his declaration:

". . . On October 25 of this year I was informed that the investigation in my case has been concluded and I was given access to the materials of this investigation. Had I been guilty of only one hundredth of the crimes with which I am charged, I would not have dared to send you this pre-execution declaration; however, I have not been guilty of even one of the things with which I am charged and my heart is clean of even the shadow of baseness. I have never in my life told you a word of falsehood, and now, finding my two feet in the grave, I am also not lying. My whole case is a typical example of provocation, slander and violation of the elementary basis of revolutionary legality. . . .

". . . The confessions which were made part of my file are not only absurd but contain some slander toward the Central Committee of the All-Union Communist Party (Bolsheviks) and toward the Council of People's Commissars, because correct resolutions of the Central Committee of the All-Union Communist Party (Bolsheviks) and of the Council of People's Commissars which were not made on my initiative and without my participation are presented as hostile acts of counterrevolutionary organizations made at my suggestion. . . .

"I am now alluding to the most disgraceful part of my life and to my really grave guilt against the party and against you. This is my confession of counterrevolutionary activity. . . . The case is as follows: Not being able to suffer the tortures to which I was submitted by Ushakov and Nikolayev—and especially by the first one—who utilized the knowledge that my broken ribs have not properly mended and have caused me great pain, I have been forced to accuse myself and others.

"The majority of my confession has been suggested or dictated by Ushakov, and the remainder is my reconstruction of NKVD materials from Western Siberia for which I assumed all responsibility. If some part of the story which Ushakov fabricated and which I signed did not properly hang together, I was forced to sign another variation. The same thing was done to Rukhimovich, who was at first designated as a member of the reserve net and whose name later was removed without telling me anything about it; the same was also done with the leader of the reserve net, supposedly created by Bukharin in 1935. At first I wrote my name in, and then I was instructed to insert Mezhlauk. There were other similar incidents.

". . . I am asking and begging you that you again examine my case, and this not for the purpose of sparing me but in order to unmask the vile provocation which, like a snake, wound itself around many persons in a great degree due to my meanness and criminal slander. I have never betrayed you or the party. I know that I perish because of vile and mean work of the enemies of the party and of the people, who fabricated the provocation against me."

It would appear that such an important declaration was worth an examination by the Central Committee. This, however, was not done, and the declaration was transmitted to Beria while the terrible maltreatment of the Political Bureau candidate, Comrade Eikhe, continued.

On February 2, 1940 Eikhe was brought before the court. Here he did not confess any guilt and said as follows:

"In all the so-called confessions of mine there is not one letter written by me with the exception of my signatures under the protocols, which were forced from me. I have made my confession under pressure from the investigative judge, who from the time of my arrest tormented me. After that I began to write all this nonsense. . . . The most important thing for me is to tell the court, the party and Stalin that I am not guilty. I have never been guilty of any conspiracy. I will die believing in the truth of party policy as I have believed in it during my whole life."

On February 4 Eikhe was shot. (Indignation in the hall.)

— 28 —

KHRUSHCHEV'S "REVISION" OF LENINISM

As we have seen, it is a firmly held axiom of Bolshevik-Leninism that war between the Western democratic world and the Communist world is inevitable. War is inevitable primarily because the nature of a capitalist economy compels it to expand. Sooner or later this expansion will touch on the territory of the Soviet Union. Consequently, although the Soviet Union seeks to avoid war, it must be prepared for it. In the meantime it must seek to aid Communist Parties to come to power in other countries by all possible means, including military, unless such action threatened to provoke a world war for which it was not yet prepared.

The development of nuclear weapons, especially the hydrogen bomb, makes total war a risk for all nations, Communist and non-Communist alike. Khrushchev therefore argues that war is not inevitable if it threatens the destruction of both sides. The Chinese Communist Party holds to the old Leninist view that war is inevitable and denies that it will lead to the destruction of all mankind. It will lead only to the destruction of the West.

The issue has been widely misunderstood. Khrushchev is as committed today as in the past to the goal of world communism. "We will bury you," he has told the West. When Prime Minister Macmillan complained to Khrushchev after the latter torpedoed the Summit Conference at Paris in June, 1960, and wrote "I simply do not understand your purpose today," Khrushchev replied: "You may remember my speech in America when I said that our grandchildren will live under Communism." Shortly after he visited Austria and proclaimed in another speech: "Life is short, and I want to see the Red Flag fly over the whole world in my lifetime."

Khrushchev, therefore, has not renounced the goal of world communism. Nor has he renounced the policy of military aggression and expansion if this does not risk a world war with nuclear weapons. He counts upon the decline of the Western powers, which is to be facilitated by economic war and internal subversion. He also counts upon the threat of war. He threatened to hurl rockets against England, Turkey, Norway and Pakistan and Japan if they continued to provide bases for American reconnaissance planes. He threatened to hurl rockets against the United States if it intervened in Cuba or the Congo. He has declared that his rockets make "England, France and Italy hostages" in his hands.

Khrushchev thus is prepared to use war and the threat of war and all other weapons to aid Communist expansion provided these policies do not precipitate an atomic war in which the Soviet Union could gain only a Pyrrhic victory. This is a clue to the Soviet Union's disarmament policy.

The following speech was delivered by Khrushchev to the Roumanian Communist Party in Bucharest on June 21, 1960. From text in Soviet News *#4229, released by Soviet Embassy, June 22, 1960.*

Comrades, questions of international relations, questions of war and peace, have always deeply concerned the mass of the people. That is natural. More than once in history the anti-national policy of the imperialists, their desire for a redivision of the world, for the seizure of new colonies, have subjected mankind to the horrors of devastating wars. But no matter how terrible wars have been in the past, if the imperialist circles should succeed in unleashing another world war, its calamities would be incomparably more terrible. For millions of people might burn in the conflagration of hydrogen explosions, and for some states a nuclear war would be literally a catastrophe. That is why the Marxist-Leninist parties, in all their activity, have always been consistent champions of a reasonable peaceloving policy, of the prevention of another world war. . . .

We do not intend to yield to provocations and to deviate from the general line of our foreign policy, which was laid down by the 20th C.P.S.U. Congress and approved in the Declaration of the Communist and Workers' Parties, adopted in 1957, during the celebrations of the 40th anniversary of the Great October Socialist Revolution.

This is a policy of coexistence, a policy of consolidating peace, easing international tension and doing away with the cold war.

The thesis that in our time war is not inevitable has a direct bearing on the policy of peaceful coexistence proclaimed at the 20th and 21st Congresses of our party. Lenin's propositions about imperialism remain in force and are still a lodestar for us in our theory and practice. But it should not be forgotten that Lenin's propositions on imperialism were advanced and developed tens of years ago, when the world did not know many things that are now decisive for historical development, for the entire international situation.

Some of Lenin's propositions on imperialism date back to the period when there was no Soviet Union, when the other socialist countries did not exist.

The powerful Soviet Union, with its enormous economic and military potential, is now growing and gaining in strength; the great socialist camp, which now numbers over 1,000 million people, is growing and gaining in strength; the organisation and political consciousness of the working class have grown, and even in the capitalist countries it is actively fighting for peace. Such factors are in operation now as, for instance, the broad movement of peace champions; the number of countries coming out for peace among nations is increasing. It should also be pointed out that imperialism no longer has such a rear to fall back upon as the colonial system which it had formerly.

Besides, comrades, one cannot mechanically repeat now on this question what Vladimir Ilyich Lenin said many decades ago on imperialism, and go on asserting that imperialist wars are inevitable until socialism triumphs throughout the world. We are now living in such a period when the forces of socialism are increasingly growing and becoming stronger, where ever-broader masses of the working people are rallying behind the banner of Marxism-Leninism.

History will possibly witness such a time when capitalism is preserved only in a small number of states, maybe states for instance, as small as a button on a coat. Well? And even in such conditions would one have to look up in a book what Vladimir Ilyich Lenin quite correctly said for his time, would one just have to repeat that wars are inevitable since capitalist countries exist?

Of course, the essence of capitalism, of imperialism, does not change even if it is represented by small countries. It is common knowledge that a wolf is just as bloodthirsty a beast of prey as a lion or a tiger, although he is much weaker. That is why man fears less to meet a wolf than a tiger or a lion. Of course, small beasts of prey can also bite, essentially they are the same but they have different possibilities, they are not so strong and it is easier to render them harmless.

Therefore one cannot ignore the specific situation, the changes in the correlation of forces in the world and repeat what the great Lenin said in quite different historical conditions. If Lenin could rise from his grave he would take such people, as one says, to task and would teach them how one must understand the essence of the matter.

We live in a time when we have neither Marx, nor Engels, nor Lenin with us. If we act like children who, studying the alphabet, compile words from letters, we shall not go very far. Marx, Engels and Lenin created their immortal works which will not fade away in centuries. They indicated to mankind the road to communism. And we confidently follow this road. On the basis of the teaching of Marxism-Leninism we must think ourselves, profoundly study life, analyse the present situation and draw the conclusions which benefit the common cause of communism.

One must not only be able to read but also correctly understand what one has read and apply it in the specific conditions of the time in which we live, taking into consideration the existing situation, and the real balance of forces. A political leader acting in this manner shows that he not only can read but can also creatively apply the revolutionary teaching. If he does not do this, he resembles a man about whom people say: "He looks into a book, but sees nothing!"

All this gives grounds for saying with confidence that under present conditions war is not inevitable.

He who fails to understand this does not believe in the strength and creative abilities of the working class, underestimates the power of the socialist camp, does not believe in the great force of attraction of socialism, which has demonstrated its superiority over capitalism with the utmost clarity.

Is the possibility of the imperialists unleashing war under present conditions ruled out? We have said several times and we repeat once again: No, it is not. But the imperialist countries cannot fail to take into account the [strength of the Soviet Union]. . . . Naturally, the imperialists do not want to trigger off war in order to perish in it. They would like to destroy the socialist countries. Therefore today even the stupid, frenzied representatives of the imperialist circles will think twice about our power before they start a military gamble. . . .

The U.S.S.R. pursued a policy of peace even when it stood alone, facing the powerful camp of imperialist states. We are also pursuing this policy now when the forces of peace are undoubtedly superior to the forces of war and aggression.

This position of ours stems from our firm belief in the stability of the socialist system, in our system, and therefore don't worry about the future of socialism.

No world war is needed for the triumph of socialist ideas throughout the world. These ideas will get the upper hand in the peaceful competition between the countries of socialism and capitalism. . . .

— 29 —

SOVIET ANTI-SEMITISM

In mid-March 1962, four Republican U.S. Senators (Jacob K. Javits and Kenneth B. Keating of New York, Leverett B. Saltonstall of Massachusetts, and Prescott Bush of Connecticut) expressed fear that a new round of anti-Semitism was being unleashed behind the Iron Curtain. Two weeks later, on March 29, 1962, a provincial Soviet newspaper in the Georgian city of Tbilisi reported the execution of two Jews for alleged economic offenses. For years Russian authorities had been attacking synagogues as havens for spies and denouncing Jews for supposed economic offenses such as currency speculation and black-marketing. No matter what it was called in the Soviet Union, it was in practice planned anti-Semitism, sponsored by the regime.

The official Soviet position on Jews in the U.S.S.R. was stated by Khrushchev in August 1956 when he denied the "slanderous accusations of anti-Semitism" directed against him and his party. He repeated the view that the majority of Soviet Jews have become integrated into the country's general life. This integration, he insisted, was "historically progressive."

In October 1956 the British Communist party dispatched an eight-man delegation to the Soviet Union. Its three-part report on all facets of Soviet life appeared in consecutive issues of the London Communist weekly, World News. Here is the second part, devoted exclusively to Soviet Jewry. It was signed by the entire delegation, including party Secretary J. R. Campbell. In effect, this constituted a Communist reply to the official Soviet position on Jews in the U.S.S.R.

✓   ✓   ✓

A Communist Reply[1]

For some years prior to the death of Stalin, rumors began to spread that all was not well in [the Jewish] field, and that well-known Jewish writers and intellectuals had disappeared. Then came the revelations of the 20th Congress [of the Soviet Communist Party] and later (April 4, 1956) specific charges in the *Folkshtimme,* a Polish Jewish workers' paper, that could not be ignored, for these charges were consistent with the kind of accusations which Khrushchev had leveled against Stalin, Beria and the security police.

The charges specifically named a number of Jewish writers, artists and intellectuals as having been tortured and physically destroyed, particularly during the period 1948-52, and this included the whole of the Jewish Anti-Fascist Committee, which had done such yeoman service in helping mobilize Jewish support and sympathy for the struggle of the Soviet Union during the darkest days of the war. The charges implied also that deliberate efforts had been made to repress all expressions of Jewish culture; that the Moscow Jewish State Theater had been shut down; that Jewish papers had ceased publication and the Yiddish Publishing House had been closed.

Naturally all these charges created consternation and

[1] From: *World News,* London, January 12, 1957. As quoted in *The New Leader,* September 14, 1959, pp. 9-11.

bewilderment in the ranks of Jewish Communists in all countries, so that it became a matter of urgency and of importance to expose their truth or falsehood. Moreover, these again in their minds became an acid test of the extent, if any, to which the Soviet Union had moved away from the path of socialism. Accordingly, one of the members of the delegation, Comrade [Hyman] Levy, was given the specific task to examine this problem and to report on it.

". . . The first piece of concrete information came from a visit to the Lenin State Library. . . . Here there exist a Yiddish and a Hebrew section. . . . It turned out that there is nothing in Yiddish later than 1948, when publication of Yiddish papers and journals must therefore have ceased.

"The Soviet Encyclopedia, which in its 1932 edition devoted about 160 columns to the Jews, reduces this in the 1952 edition to four columns. The biographies of many eminent Jews had been removed. Marx was no longer referred to as a Jew.

"While the changes in content of the Encyclopedia could have been the individual decision of the editor himself, interpreting what he conceived to be the official mood, the cessation of publication of Yiddish books and papers could hardly be anything else than official policy. For example, *Heimland*, a Yiddish journal, was in the library up to the volumes of 1948 and no later. The collected works of [Samuel] Halkin and [Aron] Vergelis, Yiddish poets still alive, were there up to 1948. That year seemed to be marked out as a significant date.

"The first task, therefore, was to meet a few Jewish writers and to examine their reactions to this. Official requests to this end were made, but we were informed this was not possible as they were all on holiday, while Halkin, who was at home, was too ill to receive anyone. . . .

"Then came the discovery from private conversations by Comrade Levy with Jews that the years 1948-52 were known among them as 'The Black Years,' the period during which many Jews were dismissed from their posts, Jewish poets and writers were arrested and charged with treason and executed; Yiddish disappeared from the street and the market place, the population closed up together, becoming tense and nervy, and young Jews who might otherwise have merged with the general population and have forgotten that they were Jews awoke to a new sense of unity in distress. . . . But let it be said that this fear did not emanate from any general feeling of antagonism from among the Russian population, but from official or quasi-official sources; from the security police, in fact.

"Conversations with the relatives of cultural workers who had been liquidated seemed to suggest that the procedure was invariable. Those arrested and charged in secret were prominent political or cultural workers. Shortly after his arrest, the immediate relatives of the arrested man would be deported to some distant place and there set to work, and often at low wages. Finally, the husband would be shot, perhaps after torture to try to force him to confess or to incriminate others. In this way, practically the whole of the Jewish Anti-Fascist Committee was liquidated. . . . It was not until after the 20th Congress revelations that steps were taken to bring back the families of the murdered men, to reinstate them in their homes, and to recompense them in some measure for the suffering through which they had passed. . . .

"What is the present policy of the Soviet Union toward the Jews? What perspectives can be said to exist for Jews —as a people—in the cultural sphere? For it might be supposed obvious, from what has been said, that the printing of books in Yiddish, the publication of Yiddish papers, and the re-institution of the Yiddish theater would follow as a matter of course. Not at all. . . .

"Jews in official positions both in Moscow and Leningrad explained that it was easier to close an institution than to reopen it. . . . Among ordinary Jews of the older generation—of the type of the 2,000 who gathered in the Leningrad Synagogue this summer to celebrate the festival of the Rejoicing of the Law (*Simchas Torah*)—the non-existence of a Yiddish paper was regarded as a deprivation and an injustice. Just before the delegation departed, however, it had a long interview with Comrade [Mikhail] Suslov, the chairman of the Central Committee, and this question of the re-institution of the theater and the Yiddish press was raised clearly and specifically. The answer came back equally clearly and unequivocally: Unless there is a specific demand for them from Soviet Jewry, *no, these things will not be re-instituted*. . . .

"If there actually existed a demand for it, if a large enough group of Soviet Jews put forward a request for it, they could have their theater and their press. Novels and poems written in Yiddish would indeed be published —we were also assured of this by the Secretary of the Union of Soviet Writers—and would be immediately translated into Russian and other languages, so that others could understand and share in these contributions. The Jewish Almanac would shortly be produced. (Translations of Yiddish poems by Peretz Markish and others who were shot have appeared recently in Soviet literary journals. Madame Markish is at present engaged in translating her husband's play, written before he was shot, on the uprising in the ghetto, and it is to be performed publicly in 1957.) Where Jewish cultural life spontaneously expressed itself, facilities would be given; but no artificial encouragement would be forthcoming.

"This attitude was in no way shaken by the argument that it did not reflect the usual approach to cultural work to expect that it should pay for itself; that it was usually held that such things have to be nurtured and encouraged. Nor was there any response to the point that there seemed to be little recognition of the importance attached to such matters in influential Jewish circles in the capitalist world; and yet Jewish intellectuals in the USSR had just published an appeal to precisely such Jews asking them to use their influence to restrain Israel in its attack on Egypt.

"The Soviet authorities appeared to be oblivious to, or at least unimpressed by, the effect produced in the outside world by the criminal treatment of Jewish intellectuals during the Beria period.

"It seems quite clear, then, that accepting Comrade Suslov's statement as official policy, that policy expects that the Jewish people in the Soviet Union will become completely absorbed . . . that there is no need, therefore, for special encouragement of Yiddish culture, and that it is undesirable to take such steps. . . .

"It remains now to attempt to give a rational explanation of how it happened that this particular kind of drive against certain elements in Jewry developed. Its importance lies in the fact that although it is concerned particularly with the Jewish problem, it nevertheless appears to throw considerable light on the general situation. That many Soviet intellectuals must themselves be puzzled and confused and indeed ashamed of it seems clear from a uniform attitude adopted everywhere when this question was raised. . . .

"Crimes and distortions of this type cannot be the work of one man. It must have been the case that sectors of the administrative personnel must have been aware of what was taking place and must have taken the steps necessary to implement it. This argues a certain level of degeneration in this sector; a certain measure of indifference to human values which does violence to those of us, brought up in bourgeois capitalist society, who have given our support to the Socialist cause. Rightly or wrongly, we have expected something vastly different from this. . . ."

— 30 —

THE SOVIET UNION
AND THE UNITED NATIONS

The following passage indicates Communist thinking about the United Nations before the end of the Second World War. It should be appraised in the light of the hundred Soviet vetoes in the U.N. Security Council, the Soviet defiance of the U.N. on the occasions of the invasion of South Korea and the brutal repression of the Hungarian Revolution, and the campaign against NATO, which was organized to defend Western Europe against Soviet aggression. These paragraphs are taken from Stalin's speech on the 27th Anniversary of the Russian October Revolution, November 6, 1944, as reprinted in the Daily Worker, *November 8, 1944.*

What means are there to preclude fresh aggression on Germany's part, and if war should start nevertheless, to nip it in the bud and give it no opportunity to develop into a big war?

This question is the more appropriate since history shows that aggressive nations, the nations which attack, are usually better prepared for a new war than peace-loving nations which, having no interest in a new war, are usually behindhand with their preparations for it. It is a fact that in the present war the aggressive nations had an invasion army all ready even before the war broke out, while the peace-loving nations did not have even a fully adequate army to cover their mobilisation.

One cannot regard as an accident such distasteful facts as the Pearl Harbour incident, the loss of the Philippines and other Pacific Islands, the loss of Hong-Kong and Singapore, when Japan, as the aggressive nation, proved to be better prepared for war than Great Britain and the United States of America, which pursued a policy of peace. Nor can one regard as an accident such a distasteful fact as the loss of the Ukraine, Byelorussia and the Baltic area in the very first year of the war, when Germany, as the aggressive nation, proved better prepared for war than the peace-loving Soviet Union.

It would be naive to explain these facts by the personal qualities of the Japanese and the Germans, their superiority over the British, the Americans and the Russians, their foresight, etc. The reason here is not personal qualities but the fact that aggressive nations, interested in a new war, being nations that prepare for war over a long time and accumulate forces for it, usually are, and are bound to be, better prepared for war than peace-loving nations which have no interest in a new war.

This is natural and understandable. It is, if you like, a law of history, which it would be dangerous to ignore.

Accordingly it is not to be denied that in the future the peace-loving nations may once more find themselves caught off their guard by aggression unless, of course, they work out special measures right now which can avert it.

Well, what means are there to preclude fresh aggression on Germany's part and, if war should start nevertheless, to stifle it at its very beginning and give it no opportunity to develop into a big war?

There is only one means to this end, apart from the complete disarmament of the aggressive nations: This is to establish a special organisation made up of representatives of the peace-loving nations for the defence of peace and safeguarding of security; to put at the disposal of the directing body of this organisation the necessary minimum of armed forces required to avert aggression, and to oblige this organisation to employ these armed forces without delay if it becomes necessary, to avert or stop aggression, and to punish those guilty of aggression.

This must not be a repetition of the dismal memory of the League of Nations, which had neither the rights nor the means for averting aggression. It will be a new, special, fully authorised international organisation having at its command everything necessary to defend peace and avert new aggression.

Part IV

COMMUNISM IN THE UNITED STATES

— 31 —

RECOGNITION OF THE SOVIET UNION BY THE UNITED STATES

The Soviet regime set great store on diplomatic recognition by the United States, which had been refused because of public evidence that the Communists had established a "fifth column" in the United States to overthrow the government. In the following official letter, the Communist regime solemnly pledges not to intervene in the internal affairs of the United States. Before two years were out, at the Seventh Congress of the Communist International in Moscow, Earl Browder, then Secretary of the American Communist Party (appointed by Stalin after the purge of the American Party in 1929), described in detail how the American Communists were carrying out the Communist program for the conquest of power. A protest of the American government at the violation of the agreement of November 16, 1933, went unheeded.

✓   ✓   ✓

WASHINGTON, *November 16, 1933.*

MY DEAR MR. PRESIDENT: I have the honor to inform you that coincident with the establishment of diplomatic relations between our two Governments it will be the fixed policy of the Government of the Union of Soviet Socialist Republics:

1. To respect scrupulously the indisputable right of the United States to order its own life within its own jurisdiction in its own way and to refrain from interfering in any manner in the internal affairs of the United States, its territories or possessions.

2. To refrain, and to restrain all persons in government service and all organizations of the Government or under its direct or indirect control, including organizations in

receipt of any financial assistance from it, from any act overt or covert liable in any way whatsoever to injure the tranquility, prosperity, order, or security of the whole or any part of the United States, its territories or possessions, and, in particular, from any act tending to incite or encourage armed intervention, or any agitation or propaganda having as an aim, the violation of the territorial integrity of the United States, its territories or possessions, or the bringing about by force of a change in the political or social order of the whole or any part of the United States, its territories or possessions.

3. Not to permit the formation or residence on its territory of any organization or group—and to prevent the activity on its territory of any organization or group, or of representatives or officials of any organization or group—which makes claim to be the Government of, or makes attempt upon the territorial integrity of, the United States, its territories or possessions; not to form, subsidize, support or permit on its territory military organizations or groups having the aim of armed struggle against the United States, its territories or possessions, and to prevent any recruiting on behalf of such organizations and groups.

4. Not to permit the formation or residence on its territory of any organization or group—and to prevent the activity on its territory of any organization or group, or of representatives or officials of any organization or group—which has as an aim the overthrow or the preparation for the overthrow of, or the bringing about by force of a change in, the political or social order of the whole or any part of the United States, its territories or possessions.

I am, my dear Mr. President,

Very sincerely yours,

MAXIM LITVINOFF,
People's Commissar for Foreign Affairs,
Union of Soviet Socialist Republics.

Mr. FRANKLIN D. ROOSEVELT,
President of the United States of America,
The White House.

— 32 —

THE MECHANICS OF CONTROL OF AMERICAN COMMUNISTS BY THE SOVIET UNION

The following document was found on the person of a Soviet secret courier captured by the Latvian government in 1919 and made available to the American government. Since then, specific directives to American Communists have been transmitted in more skillful ways through special delegates sent by the Communist International under the cloak of anonymity and through leading American Communists who travelled to the Soviet Union. The extremist character of these early instructions, calling for the establishment of Soviets and armed insurrection as soon as possible, can only be explained in terms of the euphoric revolutionary mood in Communist Petrograd at the time. Lenin and his followers expected Soviet revolutions in Western Europe, England and America. At that time they believed this was the only way the October Russian Revolution could be saved.

These fantastic expectations soon evaporated, and there developed a more sober sense of the realities of American political life, bringing with it newer sets of specific directives to achieve the underlying strategic revolutionary purposes. The authors of the communication, Bukharin and Berzin, together with Zinoviev, President of the Communist International, were liquidated by Stalin in the 1930's on charges of having been in the pay of capitalist powers from the very beginning.

This document was published by Special Committee to Investigate Communist Activities in the United States, 71st Congress, in session June 17, 1930. Investigation of Communist Propaganda, *Part 3, Vol. 2, p. 79.*

✦   ✦   ✦

Copy of Document Taken From a Soviet Courier En Route to the United States

DEAR COMRADES: Allow us to express ourselves as to your work in America.

1. We consider that, after the expulsion of certain national sections of the American Socialist Party, the time is ripe to form a Communist Party of America, officially affiliated with the Communist International. In our opinion, such a party should be organized out of (*a*) the former Socialist Propaganda League, (*b*) the left expelled elements of the A.S.P., (*c*) left elements of the S.L.P., which must at all costs be split, (*d*) the I.W.W., whose nonpolitical attitude will vanish on its recognition of the Soviet Government and the workers' dictatorship.

Upon the formation of the Communist Party, measures should be taken to have a representative at Moscow.

2. We consider that one of the most important tasks before you is the organization of communist groups in the Army and Navy, which should carry on energetic propaganda in favor of soldiers' and sailors' soviets and denunciatory agitation against officers and generals.

3. Workers' soviets should on no account be allowed to develop into bodies for philanthropic or educative ends. We fear that in America a danger of this kind exists. We therefore insist that the soviets shall be fighting organizations for seizing control of the state, for the overthrow of government, and the establishment of the workers' dictatorship. This is their sole task. The leading of strikes, of unemployment agitation, and of insurrection—such must be their activity. Secondly, care must be taken to forestall the division of the workers into national groups. Strive, therefore, to create soviets consisting of various nationalities. The backbone of the revolution will always be American.

4. Your chief slogans must be: Down with the Senate and Congress; long live the government of workers' councils; away with capitalists from the factories; long live the workers' control of the factories and mills; down with speculators; all food organizations in the hands of workmen; and so on. Everywhere the strongest agitation must be conducted for the seizure by the workers of all organs of economic administration. Make a clear distinction

between nationalization of industry under capital and our socialization. It will be useful also to practice calumniation of Wilson as the most hypocritical robber, and also of the League of Nations. Besides denouncing the hangman's rôle of the "great democracies," point out also how we have been crushed in Hungary.

5. Especial attention must be given to the American Federation of Labor. It must be broken, agitating with the energetic aid of the International Workers of the World for the creation of revolutionary trade-unions.

6. Propagate with all possible force the idea of the arming of the workers. Let not demobilized revolutionary soldiers give up their rifles. The general motto should be: An international soviet republic. Scare the workers with the new wars that capital is preparing. Prevent by every means, not hesitating to resort to the most extreme measures, the formation of a white guard.

7. Act centrally. Do not fall asunder. Organize conspirative revolutionary headquarters.

With communist greeting of the bureau of the executive committee of the Communist International.

N. BUKHARIN.
I. BERZIN.

— 33 —

STALIN AND THE AMERICAN COMMUNIST PARTY

The American Communist Party has always been of special concern to the Soviet Union. Since the fortunes of world communism depend upon developments in the United States, the activities of the American Communist Party are of the first importance. Actually, except for a few years in the thirties, the American Communist Party has been a negligible force in the life of the country.

Potentially, however, it has always appeared to the Soviet Union as capable of leading the American working class and of contributing, by both legal activities and underground activities, to the victory of communism.

The measure of the interest which the Soviet regime has taken in the American Communist is indicated not only by Lenin's *Letter to the American Working Class*, but by the fact that Stalin, at the height of his struggle against the so-called right-wing faction of the Russian Communist Party which was headed by Bukharin, took time out to make three extended speeches on the American Communist Party—one before the American Commission of the Presidium of the Executive Committee of the Communist International (*May 6, 1929*) and two before the Presidium of that organization when the Report of the American Commission was considered. In these speeches Stalin condemns the American leadership (which had been raised to power by the Comintern) for its theory of exceptionalism, according to which the special historical condition of the United States required a special approach. Stalin argued that the revolutionary activity of the American Communist Party "must base itself on the general features of capitalism, which are the same for all countries, and not its specific features in any given country." He did more than argue. He commanded that the American leadership be transferred from the Lovestone faction to the Foster faction, and that the Lovestone faction liquidate itself and its chief members retire from commanding posts. He scoffed at the idea that because Lovestone claimed to have the support of 99% of the American Communist Party behind him, which was true, that he could still keep that support after the Comintern had decided against him. Stalin's prediction also turned out to be true.

These speeches were published under the title of Stalin's *Speeches on the American Communist Party*, New York, 1930. This was the last disagreement any group or individual had with Stalin which did not prove fatal to them if they happened to be on the soil of the Soviet Union.

I. Speech Delivered in the American Commission of the Presidium of the E. C. C. I.

(May 6, 1929)

Comrades, since quite a few speeches have been delivered here and the political position of both groups in the Communist Party of the United States of America has been sufficiently clarified, I do not intend to speak at great length. I shall not deal with the political position of the leaders of the majority and the minority. I shall not do so since it has become evident during the course of the discussion that both groups are guilty of the fundamental error of exaggerating the specific features of American capitalism. You know that this exaggeration lies at the root of every opportunist error committed both by the majority and the minority group. It would be wrong to ignore the specific peculiarities of American capitalism. The Communist Party in its work must take them into account. But it would be still more wrong to base the activities of the Communist Party on these specific features, since the foundation of the activities of every Communist Party, including the American Communist Party, on which it must base itself, must be the general features of capitalism, which are the same for all countries, and not its specific features in any given country. It is on this that the internationalism of the Communist Party is founded. Specific features are only supplementary to the general features. The error of both groups is that they exaggerate the significance of the specific features of American capitalism and thereby overlook the basic features of American capitalism which are characteristic of world capitalism as a whole. Therefore, when the leaders of the majority and the minority accuse each other of elements of a Right deviation, it is obviously not without some measure of truth. It cannot be denied that American conditions form a medium in which it is easy for the American Communist Party to be led astray and to exaggerate the strength and stability of American capitalism. These conditions lead our comrades from America, both the majority and the minority, into errors of the type of the Right deviation. Owing to these conditions, at times one section, at others, the other section, fails to realize the full extent of reformism in America, underestimates the leftward swing of the working class and, in general, is inclined to regard American capitalism as something apart from the above world capitalism. That is the basis for the unsteadiness of both sections of the American Communist Party in matters of principle.

Having made these general observations, let us now pass to practical political questions.

What are the main defects in the practice of the leaders of the majority and the minority?

Firstly, that in their day-to-day work they, and particularly the leaders of the majority, are guided by motives of unprincipled factionalism and place the interests of their faction higher than the interests of the Party.

Secondly, that both groups, and particularly the majority, are so infected with the disease of factionalism that they base their relations with the Comintern, not on the principle of confidence, but on a policy of rotten diplomacy, a policy of diplomatic intrigue. . . .

A word or two regarding the tasks and the mission of the American Communist Party. I think, comrades, that the American Communist Party is one of those few Communist Parties in the world upon which history has laid tasks of a decisive character from the point of view of the world revolutionary movement. You all know very well the strength and power of American capitalism. Many now think that the general crisis of world capitalism will not affect America. That, of course, is not true. It is entirely untrue, comrades. The crisis of world capitalism is developing with increasing rapidity and cannot but affect American capitalism. The three million now unemployed in America are the first swallows indicating the ripening of the economic crisis in America. The sharpening antagonism between America and England, the struggle for markets and raw materials and, finally, the colossal growth of armaments—that is the second portent of the approaching crisis. I think the moment is not far off when a revolutionary crisis will develop in America. And when a revolutionary crisis develops in America, that will be the beginning of the end of world capitalism as a whole. It is essential that the American Communist Party should be capable of meeting that historical moment fully prepared and of assuming the leadership of the impending class struggle in America. Every effort and every means must be employed in preparing for that, comrades. For that end the American Communist Party must be improved and bolshevized. . . .

A few words regarding the vaunting manner in which the group of Comrade Lovestone speaks and represents itself here in the name of the whole Party, in the name of 99 percent of the Communist Party of America. They never represent themselves otherwise than in the name of 99 percent of the Party. One would think they have that 99 percent in their pockets. That is a bad manner, comrades of the American delegation. Let me remind you that Zinoviev and Trotzky also at one time played trumps with percentages, and assured everybody that they had secured, or at any rate, would secure, a 99 percent majority in the ranks of the C.P.S.U. You know, comrades, in what a farce the vain glory of Trotzky and Zinoviev ended. I would therefore advise you not to play trumps with percentages. You declare you have a certain majority in the American Communist Party and that you will retain that majority under all circumstances. That is untrue, comrades of the American delegation, absolutely untrue. You had a majority because the American Communist Party until now regarded you as the determined supporters of the Communist International. And it was only because the Party regarded you as the friends of the Comintern that you had a majority in the ranks of the American Communist Party. But what will happen if the American workers learn that you intend to break the unity of the ranks of the Comintern and are thinking of conducting a fight against its executive bodies—that is the question, dear comrades? Do you think that the American workers will follow your lead against the Comintern, that they will prefer the interests of your factional group to the interests of the Comintern? There have been numerous cases in the history of the Comintern when its most popular leaders, who had greater authority than you, found themselves isolated as soon as they raised the banner against the Comintern. Do you think you will fare better than these leaders? A poor hope, comrades! At present you still have a formal majority. But tomorrow you will have no majority and you will find yourselves completely isolated if you attempt to start a fight against the decisions of the Presidium of the Executive Committee of the Comintern. You may be certain of that dear comrades.

THE COMRADES SQUABBLE—FATHER DECIDES

The following document is instructive, but should also provide some comic relief. It reveals the presence of factional strife in the Communist Party—which was to last until 1929—and at the same time makes clear who it is who makes all the chief decisions. Whether a particular group in a particular country had a majority of the party membership in support of its position, was completely immaterial. The decisions of the Comintern made and unmade programs, plans, and leaders. It even decided where the party headquarters would be. Since the Bolsheviks were the more experienced revolutionists, they overrode what they regarded as sectarianism on the part of American Communists and their isolation from the American masses. The question whether the American Communist Party should support and work within a reformed Labor Party agitated the American Communists for years. A majority opposed such action. They were constantly overruled by the Comintern. When the Party finally came to heel and accepted the directive, with the minority transformed by fiat into a majority, it discovered that the genuine labor movement would have none of it. The following is extracted from an article by Max Bedacht in The Inprecorr *of September 24, 1925.*

✓   ✓   ✓

A few days after the conclusion of the presidential elections in November, the majority of the Central Committee passed, over the protests of the then minority, a declaration that the Labour Party movement is dead.

Finally, later in November 1924, the then majority adopted a thesis declaring against the Labour Party policy and campaign and denouncing the pro-Labour Party group in the Committee as opportunists, liquidators, and reformists.

The differences in the Party were finally submitted to the Communist International. But not after some struggle. The combined experience of our World Party was to help our American Section out of its entanglement.

The Comintern decided for a Labour Party. But that did not settle the controversy. The "trades unionist" anti-Labour Party group of the Central Committee realised that the decision of the Comintern was a political defeat, which in any ripe communist Party would lead to the defeat of the Executive Committee in a convention. To avoid such a defeat our right wing therefore decided to raise false issues and to claim a victory at the Comintern. The CI. in its decision declared that it had detected errors on both sides. This sentence was ridden to death. The anti-Labour Party group completely forgot its political duty toward the Party. It had submitted to the Comintern a general orientation for judgment; so had the left wing of the party. The Comintern accepted the general line of the left wing and rejected that of the right. While the general line of the left was found correct, the Comintern rightly criticised tactical errors made by that group in applying a correct line. The right wing seized upon these criticisms as the main issue and thus prevented a thorough discussion of its major error. Thus it prevented the Party from really learning to understand not only that the old CEC majority had made a mistake, but the nature and basis of the mistake. Only a clear understanding of the nature and the basic causes of a mistake is a guarantee against the repetition of it. The right wing prevented this Leninist self-criticism in order to be able to further exploit the prejudices which it had created against the left wing on the basis of its former demagogic accusations of reformism, opportunism, and pink flagism.

But the comrades of the then majority of the Central Committee were not satisfied with a politically dishonest fight against the left wing. They were determined to retain the leadership of the Party at all costs. With this aim in mind, they initiated a campaign of suspensions and expulsions. In Cleveland this campaign found its classic climax. Branches which supported the left wing of the CEC were changed into supporters of the anti-Labour

Party group by suspending from membership as many as thirty left wing adherents in one single branch. When these suspended comrades were reinstated by a decision of a Party commission established by action of the CI., the District Organiser found new ground for suspension. The District Organiser in this district, to assure his domination took upon himself even the right of two votes in committees.

With such actions as a preliminary the Fourth Convention of the Workers Communist Party began under dangerous auspices. Dual delegations presented themselves from the most important districts, like Boston, New York, Philadelphia, and Cleveland.

The political theses and resolutions submitted to the convention were adopted unanimously in the Party Commission. The struggle in the Convention therefore centred on the credentials and on the past actions of the Executive Committee.

The report of the minority of the credentials committee disclosed such utterly uncommunist manoeuvres that it seemed impossible to appease the outraged delegation of the left wing and prevent a split.

But the fever heat of resentment was overcome by the loyalty to, and the confidence of the comrades in the Comintern. The left wing delegation returned from its caucus to the convention and declared that under no conditions will it permit itself to be provoked into a split.

All throughout the debates of the convention, the fundamental differences between the groups manifested themselves. The lack of a political concept which could unify all the activities and all the analyses of the Party manifested itself on the one hand,—and an effort to give such a unifying concept was apparent on the other hand.

The debates were bitter but contributed to the clarity of the Party. The role of the Party in the class struggle was discussed, on the concrete basis of American conditions. A clear understanding of the resolution of the Second World Congress of the Comintern on that matter was thus created.

The real object of the Party's work in the trades unions, —not as industrial, but as political work—was made clear. This will contribute to a more conscientious application of the Party's forces to this task. It will help to eliminate the dangerous ideological division of the Party into trades unionists, and politicals. It will establish as the most important prerequisite and fundamentally necessary qualification for a Party member, that of being a Communist.

The Convention took up the problem of a serious reformist crystalization in the Party. This social democratic wing centred around Ludwig Lore, the editor of the New York Volkszeitung. Lore was an ally of the "trades unionists" in their revolt against the "politicals" in the Third Convention of the Party. As a true opportunist he supported the criticism of the "trades unionists," by the "politicals," but voted with the former to oust the latter from leadership. From the convention in January 1924 Lore wired to his paper that "the Trotskyites have won the Party." This was never repudiated by the majority. Lore and his adherents became an integral part of the majority caucus.

With the bolshevization of the Party, which manifested itself in an ever-accelerating tendency away from abstractions and toward concretization and action, the social-democratic remnants in the Party came into an ever sharper conflict with the Party's policies. Opposition to these policies became fundamental opposition to action. In the period when this reformist crystallization took definite form, it was imperatively necessary that the Party should join issue with it and thus preserve the unity and the purity of the Party. But the fact that the Lore group was an integral part of the leading group in the Central Committee favoured this opportunist crystallization.

The then minority took up the question of Loreism with the Comintern at the Fifth World Congress in April 1924. The CI. supported the left wing and condemned Lore and Loreism. But the alliance of the "trades unionist" majority with Lore continued. Only a new decision of the Comintern made at the last Enlarged Session of the Executive Committee in April 1925 at the urgent request of the left wing severed the ties between Lore and the majority. But the division is by no means definite. The bulk of the rank and file which is under the ideological influence of Lore and Loreism, together with the least active sections of our Party, supported the anti-Labour Party right wing in its struggle for further leadership before the convention. But the decision of the Comintern succeeded in driving home to the Party as a whole the seriousness of the Loreistic disease of our Party. As a result of this it was possible to unite the majority and minority fractions for a unanimously accepted proposal to expel Lore from the Party. On the initiative of the left wing the removal of Askeli, another Loreite, from the position of editor on the Finnish Daily, "Tyomies," was also decided unanimously.

The pro-Labour Party left wing did everything in its power to keep the discussion on the level of a political debate. This was very hard because of the right wing's persistent efforts to lead the discussion away from political fundamentals into the field of petty details. But in spite of all that, the Convention proceeded under the slogan of bolshevization. The very debates of the convention were a contribution to bolshevization. Whatever efforts might have been made to divert this main aim were finally frustrated by the Comintern when it made and transmitted to the convention an eleventh hour decision in which among other things it stated categorically that:

> "It has finally become clear that the Ruthenberg group (pro-Labour Party left wing group) is more loyal to the decisions of the Comintern and stands closer to its view."

This CI. decision had the effect of a bombshell in the convention. The majority, which, by its questionable methods characterized by the CI. as "excessive mechanical and ultra fractional," had succeeded in having a majority of the delegates, after a long struggle in its caucus submitted to this decision. A Central Executive Committee was elected, with equal representation from both groups and a representative of our World Party as chairman.

Under the leadership of this Committee, the decisions of the Fourth Convention will be put into effect. The reorganisation of the Party as a necessary pre-requisite to its bolshevization will be the immediate task. Out of a union of numerous language federations, each one in itself a political party, this Executive Committee will weld a unified centralised Communist Party, worthy of membership in the Comintern and adapted to the tremendous tasks awaiting it in the American class struggle.

35

THE COMMUNIST PLEDGE OF ALLEGIANCE

The Communist movement has sometimes functioned as a religion in the lives of its members and participants. All sorts of rituals have been developed to commemorate the major experiences of life in such a way as to reinforce the individual Communist Party member's sense of identification with a transcendent cause, the movement of history, and specifically the triumph of the Soviet Union, and ultimately of world communism. Organizations for the children, youth, college students, married women; coöperatives, burial and benevolent associations; sports, clubs and committees for relief, art, cinema, soccer, music, literature, have proliferated over the years. Every avenue of experience has been organized in order to reinforce the stimulus as well as the symbols of Communist identification. One of the most effective of Communist rituals is the mass meeting, which is organized with the voluntary assistance of members and fellow-travellers skilled in the theatrical arts. The Communists have outdone their totalitarian rivals in staging and dramatic effect.

The following passages are from The Communist Party: A Manual on Organization, *New York, July 1935, pp. 104-5. Peters subsequently went underground and headed one of the most notorious Soviet espionage rings in the United States; its members included Whittaker Chambers and Alger Hiss. The pledge given by Browder to the fledgling members of the Communist Party conveys something of the quality of meetings of this sort as well as indicating the conditions of membership.*

✦   ✦   ✦

Who Is Eligible For Membership in the Communist Party?

Any person from the age of eighteen up, who accepts the program and statutes of the C.I., and the Communist Party of the U.S.A.

If a worker who is less than 18 years of age wants to join the Party, and there is no Young Communist League in the town or factory, the Party Unit has the right to accept him into the Unit, get him a book and permit him to remain of the Party Unit until, with the help of the Party Unit, he is able to build up a Unit of the Y.C.L.

What Are the Conditions For Membership in the Communist Party?

The conditions for membership in our Party are contained in the following pledge read by Comrade Browder to 2,000 workers who were initiated into the Party in the New York District in 1935.

"I now take my place in the ranks of the Communist Party, the Party of the working class. I take this solemn oath to give the best that is in me to the service of my class. I pledge myself to spare no effort in uniting the workers in militant struggle against fascism and war. I pledge myself to work unsparingly in the unions, in the shops, among the unemployed, to lead the struggles for the daily needs of the masses. I solemnly pledge to take my place in the forefront of the struggle for Negro rights; against Jim-Crowism and lynching, against the chauvinist lies of the ruling class. I pledge myself to rally the masses to defend the Soviet Union, the land of victorious Socialism. I pledge myself to remain at all times a vigilant and firm defender of the Leninist line of the Party, the only line that insures the triumph of Soviet Power in the United States."

Our Party application carries this declaration:

"The undersigned declares his adherence to the program and statutes of the C.I. and the Communist Party of the U.S.A. and agrees to submit to the discipline of the Party and to engage actively in its work."

On the basis of this declaration we could enumerate the conditions for membership in the Party in the following way:

1. Activity in a unit;
2. Regular payment of membership dues;
3. Adherence to all decisions of the Comintern and of the Party;
4. Adherence to the discipline of the Party.

36

HOW TO ACHIEVE
A SOVIET AMERICA

Two questions are often confused: whether Communists have a legal right to advocate overthrow of democratic government by force and violence, and whether they do advocate it. According to present law, as interpreted by the United States Supreme Court, they have such a right except when advocacy becomes an incitement or when it creates a clear and present danger that certain substantive evils will result which Congress has a right to prevent. With respect to the second question, the following passage from William Z. Foster's Towards Soviet America *together with other documents in this book should be decisive. Foster was Chairman of the American Communist Party for many years and left the United States to die in the odor of sanctity in the Soviet Union.*

Despite these passages, some apologists for the Communist Party and the Soviet Union have argued that the Communist theory and practice of seizure of power express in modern idiom the philosophy of the American Declaration of Independence. They overlook the essential difference between a revolution against a tyrannical undemocratic government and the use of revolutionary violence against a democratic government whose processes permit reforms and the abolition of abuses by peaceful means. Sometimes by arbitrary semantic fiat, they declare that governments which they seek to overthrow are not "true" democracies because their policies differ from those of the Communist Party which, by definition, represents the "true" interests of the people or working masses. This Communist conception of "democracy" implies that the will of the people gives a democratic mandate only when other "capitalistic" political parties have been liqui-

dated. A "capitalistic" party is any party, even if consti-
tuted of workers, declared such by the leaders of the
Communist Party.

The following passage is from p. 275 of Foster's book,
published by Coward, McCann, Publishers, New York,
1932.

✓   ✓   ✓

Even before the seizure of power, the workers will
organize the Red Guard. Later on this loosely constructed
body becomes developed into a firmly-knit, well-disci-
plined Red Army.

The leader of the revolution in all its stages is the
Communist party. With its main base among the industrial workers, the Party makes a bloc with the revolutionary farmers and impoverished city petty bourgeoisie,
drawing under its general leadership such revolutionary
groups and organizations as these classes may have.
Under the dictatorship all the capitalist parties—Republican, Democratic, Progressive, Socialist, etc.—will be
liquidated, the Communist party functioning alone as the
Party of the toiling masses. Likewise, will be dissolved
all other organizations that are political props of the
bourgeois rule, including chambers of commerce, employers' associations, rotary clubs, American Legion,
Y.M.C.A., and such fraternal orders as the Masons, Odd
Fellows, Elks, Knights of Columbus, etc.

37

ROOSEVELT'S MARCH TO FASCISM

Roosevelt's New Deal was a turning point in the development of the United States as a welfare state. The Roosevelt Administration, through the Wagner Labor Relations Act, helped to organize more workers into trade unions than had ever been enrolled by the labor unions themselves. Roosevelt thereby won a mass support for his regime, leaving the Communist Party isolated and ignored. The Communists thereupon resolved on a two-pronged tactic. They denounced the New Deal as a movement towards Fascism and at the same time infiltrated into the trade union movement, particularly the C.I.O., in order to win strategic posts so that they could call strikes for political reasons whenever it served the purpose of the Soviet Union by exploiting industrial grievances. Subsequently, as the line of the Soviet Union changed, they appealed to the spirit of the New Deal in their attacks on American legislative policies. The unions which they captured by their techniques of infiltration were expelled by both the A.F. of L. and C.I.O.

The following excerpts are from a speech made by Earl Browder, Secretary of the American Communist Party, before the Thirteenth Plenum of the Executive Committee of the Communist International and printed in The Communist International, *January 15, 1934.*

✓   ✓   ✓

Characteristic for the whole system of policies known as the New Deal is their nature as preparations for war. The economic contents of these measures are those of war economy. The famous three-billion-dollar building program turns out in reality to be a program of Navy building, mechanization of the Army, building of military roads, and the putting into operation of the Muscle Shoals explosive plant abandoned at the close of the World War. The "unemployment relief" program turns out to be first of all the setting up of a network of military training camps, under the direction of the War Department, where 300,000 young men are being prepared for the Army. The *National Recovery Administration* follows the pattern laid down by the War Industries Board of the World War. Never before has there been such gigantic war preparations at a time when the "enemy" is as yet unnamed. . . .

International social-fascism has hailed the Roosevelt policies as "steps in the direction of socialism." The British Labor Party and Trade Union Congress have adopted the Roosevelt program as their own, demanding that it be imitated in Britain. In this way they are but continuing, in the period of crisis, that complete ideological subordination to the bourgeoisie which, during the period of American prosperity created out of the figure of Henry Ford the reformist "Saviour." The American Socialist Party has not lagged behind in this respect; Norman Thomas and Morris Hillquit hastened to pay a public visit to Roosevelt, upon his assumption of office, to congratulate him upon his policies, which they hailed as nothing less than a "revolution" in the interests of the masses.

But the fascist direction in which the Roosevelt policies are carrying the U.S. is becoming clear to the whole world. Nowhere is this more manifest than in the efforts to merge the reformist American Federation of Labor into the machinery of government, under the avowed banner of the fascist conception of the "corporate state," prohibition of strikes, compulsory arbitration, governmental fixing of wages, and even control of the inner life of the trade unions. For the edification of the masses this was spoken of as a "partnership of capital and labor, together with the government." Under this program the A.F. of L. is given governmental support and even financial assistance, and a determined effort is made to control and eventually choke off the strike movement, by driving the workers into the A.F. of L. where it is hoped the official leadership will be able to bring the masses under control. . . .

Our Party and the Red unions came out openly and boldly against the N.R.A., and exposed it as a general attack against the workers' standards, and as a movement toward fascism. In this we had to go sharply against the stream of mass illusions that had been aroused by the Roosevelt demagogy.

— 38 —

SELF-DETERMINATION FOR THE BLACK BELT

Wherever there is a grievance, the Communist Party strategy is to inflate it and make political capital out of the distress of the oppressed and unfortunate. The Negroes in the United States were early regarded by the Kremlin as inflammable material that could be used to help light the fires of class and civil war. Judging by the European experience, and applying categories that were appropriate to oppressed national minorities with a distinctive cultural history and language, the Kremlin concluded that the Negroes in the United States, although not a colony, nonetheless suffered from national oppression. The area in which most Negroes lived was regarded not as an integral part of the United States, but as a zone or belt which should have the right to liberate itself from "the yoke of American imperialism" and to set itself up, if it wished, as an independent nation. The Negroes in the United States were not considered part and parcel of American culture, but carriers of another, distinctive culture whose development was presumably being thwarted by the foreign pattern imposed upon them by their white masters. Some Russian Communists assumed, until they were disabused, that the Negroes of America spoke a language of their own.

These conclusions were imposed on the American Communist Party by the Kremlin at the behest of Stalin and his agent in the Comintern, Otto Kuusinen. For some years after the Sixth World Congress in 1928, the

*slogan "self-determination for the black belt" was de rigeur
in the agitation and propaganda of the American Communist Party. At best this program called for the establishment of a Jim Crow state for Negroes: at the worst, it
was an invitation to civil war and secession. There was
absolutely no sentiment for the program even among the
few radical American Negroes in the Communist Party.
But the discipline of the Communist International over
the American Communist Party was so tight that no
leading member, black or white, dared to oppose the
slogan of "self determination for the black belt" publicly,
even though any attempt to implement the insurrectionary
program behind it, would have been drowned in rivers
of blood.*

*Although never formally withdrawn or rescinded, the
program and slogan of "self-determination" was permitted
to fall into desuetude during the period of the Popular
Front. It illustrated the mechanical way in which the
Bolshevik theses on the problem of national minorities,
formulated by Stalin, was imposed from abroad, and the
ruthlessness with which the Communists were prepared
to exploit politically the sufferings of an oppressed group.*

*The following excerpts are from the "Resolution on the
Negro Question in the United States" issued by the
Political Commission of the Executive Committee of the
Communist International and published in its American
organ,* The Communist, *February, 1931. The reader will
note that the final paragraph of the excerpt stresses the
fact that the right of self-determination must include the
right of separation or secession from the United States.*

✓   ✓   ✓

The slogan of the right of self-determination occupies
the central place in the liberation struggle of the Negro
population in the Black Belt against the yoke of American
imperialism. But this slogan, as we see it, must be carried
out only in connection with two other basic demands.
Thus, there are three basic demands to be kept in mind in
the Black Belt, namely, the following:

(a) *Confiscation of the landed property of the white
landowners and capitalists for the benefit of the Negro
farmers.* The landed property in the hands of the white

American exploiters constitutes the most important material basis of the entire system of national oppression and serfdom of the Negroes in the Black Belt. More than three-quarters of all Negro farmers here are bound in actual serfdom to the farms and plantations of the white exploiters by the feudal system of "share cropping." Only on paper and not in practice are they freed from the yoke of their former slavery. The same holds completely true for the great mass of black contract laborers. Here the contract is only the capitalist expression of the chains of the old slavery, which even today are not infrequently applied in their natural iron form on the roads of the Black Belt (chain gang work). These are the main forms of present Negro slavery in the Black Belt, and no breaking of the chains of this slavery is possible without confiscating all the landed property of the white masters . . .

(b) *Establishment of the state unity of the Black Belt*. At the present time this Negro zone—precisely for the purpose of facilitating national oppression—is artificially split up and divided into a number of various states which include distant localities having a majority of white population. If the right of self-determination of the Negroes is to be put into force, it is necessary wherever possible to bring together into one governmental unit all districts of the South where the majority of the settled population consists of Negroes. Within the limits of this state there will of course remain a fairly significant white minority which must submit to the right of self-determination of the Negro majority. There is no other possible way of carrying out in a democratic manner the right of self-determination of the Negroes. Every plan regarding the establishment of the Negro state with an exclusively Negro population in America (and of course, still more exporting it to Africa) is nothing but an unreal and reactionary caricature of the fulfillment of the right of self-determination of the Negroes, and every attempt to isolate and transport the Negroes would have the most damaging effect upon their interests. Above all, it would violate the right of the Negro farmers in the Black Belt not only to their present residences and their land, but also to the land owned by the white landlords and cultivated by Negro labor.

(c) *Right of self-determination.* This means complete and unlimited right of the Negro majority to exercise governmental authority in the entire territory of the Black Belt, as well as to decide upon the relations between their territory and other nations, particularly the United States. It would not be right of self-determination in our sense of the word if the Negroes in the Black Belt had the right of determination only in cases which concerned *exclusively* the Negroes and did not affect the whites, because the most important cases arising here are bound to affect the whites as well as Negroes. First of all, true right to self-determination means that the Negro majority and not the white minority in the entire territory of the administratively united Black Belt exercises the right of administering governmental, legislative, and judicial authority. At the present time all this power is concentrated in the hands of the white bourgeoisie and landlords. It is they who appoint all officials, it is they who dispose of public property, it is they who determine the taxes, it is they who govern and make the laws. Therefore, *the overthrow of this class rule* in the Black Belt is unconditionally necessary in the struggle for the Negroes' right to self-determination. This, however, means at the same time the overthrow of the yoke of American imperialism in the Black Belt on which the forces of the local white bourgeoisie depend. Only in this way, only if the Negro population of the Black Belt wins its freedom from American imperialism even to the point of deciding *itself* the relations between its country and other governments, especially the United States, will it win real and complete self-determination. One should demand from the beginning that no armed forces of American imperialism should remain on the territory of the Black Belt.

As stated in the letter of the Political Secretariat of the E.C.C.I. of March 16, 1930, the Communists must *"unreservedly* carry on a struggle" for the self-determination of the Negro population in the Black Belt in accordance with what has been set forth above. It is incorrect and harmful to interpret the Communist standpoint to mean that the Communists stand for the right of self-determination of the Negroes only up to a certain point but not beyond this, to, for example, the right of separation. It is also incorrect to say that the Communists are only to carry on propaganda or agitation for the right of self-determination, but not to develop any activity to bring this about. No, it is of the utmost importance for the Communist Party to reject any such limitation of its struggle for this slogan. Even if the situation does not yet warrant the raising of the question of uprising, one should not limit oneself at present to propaganda for the demand, "Right to Self-Determination," but should organize mass actions, such as demonstrations, strikes, tax boycott movements, etc.

— 39 —

THE STUDENT MOVEMENT

It would be hard to keep track of the multiplicity of Communist youth movements organized among the students of the United States. Beginning with sectarian organizations which were regarded as weird irrelevancies during the 1920's the Communist organizers sent to the campuses by the Communist Party soon learned how to sell their wares under more attractive labels. Aided by the uncertainties and hardships of the depression, in the thirties the Communists succeeded in dominating the politically articulate section of American youth. During this decade, the high point was the student strike against war in 1936 in which thousands of students publicly took the Oxford pledge never to bear arms in defense of their country. In the forties, after Hitler invaded the Soviet Union, the Communist student movement proved to be more patriotic than the Daughters of the American Revolution. The Young Communist League formally dissolved and reconstituted itself as American Youth for Democracy. After 1945 it reversed course once more. The AYD strongly advocated the foreign policy of the Soviet Union against the United States and the UN. It supported the Progressive Party campaign in 1948. In the fifties, the Communist youth movement went underground and oper-

ated through the guise of Marxist study groups. The following account of the Student Strike appeared in Inprecorr, May 30, 1936.

✓   ✓   ✓

United States—The Student Strike

BY ADAM LAPIN (NEW YORK)

The student anti-war strike in the United States on April 22, under the leadership of the American Student Union, fulfilled in actual numbers even the wildest expectations of its sponsors. Some 500,000 students participated, according to letters and telegrams received in the office of the Student Union. This figure was also accepted by the Associated Press, largest and most conservative of American news agencies.

Colleges and universities provided 350,000 of the strikers. The remaining 150,000 were in High Schools. The largest number to strike in any single city was about 90,000 in New York. The greatest gains over previous strikes were in the South, which in former years had been almost untouched by such movements. Not only were many important white universities involved, but thousands of Negro students in Negro colleges in the South took part in the strike.

Important schools in every section of the country were out on strike, even the supposedly highly conservative schools with aristocratic traditions in New England and other Eastern sections. High schools in the squalid slums of New York took part in the strike at the same time as students on the secluded and cultured campuses of Princeton and Harvard Universities. While 3,500 City College students in New York were attending a strike meeting, 5,000 on the beautiful campus of the University of California at Berkeley were on strike.

On April 13, 1934, the first strike took place under the joint auspices of the National Student League, led largely by Communists, and the Student League for Industrial Democracy, a Socialist organisation. A few months before the strike these two organisations had concluded a united front pact, and the strike was their first ambitious demonstration on a nation-wide scale. Although the total membership of the two groups was no more than 7,000, the number of students to answer their strike call totaled 25,000. The first student strike indicated the possibilities of united front action on a national scale, and it introduced into the arena of the anti-war movement in America a new weapon.

In the second student strike, on April 12, 1935, the number participating was 185,000. This time the united front had been extended to include several new organisations, among which were the National Council of Methodist Youth, the Inter-seminary Council, and the American Youth Congress, that federation of student and youth organisations. The second student strike was the greatest success, up to that time, of the student anti-war movement.

The third student strike, this year, showed an even more startling growth of anti-war sentiment among students. Within one year the number of participants was almost tripled. The leadership of the American Student Union was undoubtedly one of the chief factors making the success of the strike possible. . . .

During the year between the second and third student strikes this new organisation had entered the field as a result of the merger of the two previous organisations which claimed the allegiance of the militant students. The National Student League and the Student League for Industrial Democracy merged with other groups in December, 1935, and formed a new united body which represented a coalition of Communists, Socialists and Liberals. For the first time, with the formation of the American Student Union, all students had a common focal point for their adherence and loyalty. . . .

On the whole the programme of the strike was excellent. It emphasised the need for fighting against the war preparations of the Roosevelt administration. One of its chief demands was a slogan calling for the abolition of the Reserve Officers' Training Corps, the prevalent form of military training in the schools. As a step toward the total abolition of the R.O.T.C., the strike call urged the passage by Congress of the Nye-Kvale bill, which revokes the compulsory features of military training in schools.

The strike call took cognisance of the danger of war against the Soviet Union, by attack from either Germany or Japan. One of its main slogans stated, "War anywhere means war everywhere," stressing the indivisibility of peace.

It is hardly a coincidence that the leaders of the American Student Union were informed the day after the strike that there would probably be no hearings on the Nye-Kvale bill, and that the day after the strike the news appeared that a bill had unanimously passed the lower house of the federal congress setting up a Reserve Air Training Corps, and establishing an air division for the training of students.

Why is it that the government was able, during the very course of the strike action, during the sweep of its preparations and at the high point of its actual execution, to defy the admittedly powerful student movement?

The fact is, and this goes for the entire student anti-war movement, that there is an inability to translate the sentiment, and even the action, of the students for peace into terms of concrete proposals and specific achievements in the United States.

In the case of the present strike, it is true that one of the major slogans was the abolition of military training in the schools, but this slogan did not become the focal point of the preparations for the strike in most schools.

There was stressed the idea that the strike was a dress rehearsal for the future, that it was an indication of what students would do when war would break out, that it expressed the determination of the students to disrupt the entire school system when it again becomes incorporated in the war machine.

Together with this idea, there was also stressed, especially by members of the Young People's Socialist Society, the idea that the most important present action of the student anti-war movement was adhesion to the Oxford Pledge, which states, in this country, that "we will support no war undertaken by the United States government."

But it seems hardly necessary to point out that a pledge of that sort is hardly sufficient in times of actual crisis. It is hardly necessary to say that a dress rehearsal is all the more effective if it is capable of scoring immediate results.

THE COMMUNIST PARTY "DISAFFILIATES" FROM THE COMMUNIST INTERNATIONAL

After the passage of the Voorhis Act in 1940, it was expected that the Communist Party would be compelled to register as an agent of a foreign power. Instead the Communist Party resorted to a ruse. It went through the motions of formally disaffiliating itself from the Communist International. In every other respect it carried on as usual, as subsequent documents will show. The following is extracted from an article in the Communist publication World News and Views (*a successor to* International Press Correspondence), *October 30, 1940, pp. 691-692.*

✓   ✓   ✓

The American Communists and the Communist International

The Voorhis Act forces the Communist Party in the U.S.A. to disaffiliate from the Communist International. Earl Browder puts the issues to a special convention of the Party's National Committee which reaffirms loyalty to working class internationalism.

A Special Convention of the National Committee of the Communist Party in the U.S.A. has voted to cancel its organisational affiliation to the Communist International to meet the requirements of the Voorhis "Blacklist" Act so that it can continue to struggle against the involvement of the U.S.A. in the imperialist war.

In taking this decision the Convention reaffirmed the Party's loyalty to working-class internationalism.

Earl Browder, General Secretary of the Party, reported on the issues involved and submitted in the name of the

National Committee the proposal that the Party cancel its organisational link with the International.

The following resolution, proposed by Browder, was then unanimously adopted by the Convention:

That the Communist Party of the United States in Convention assembled does hereby cancel and dissolve its organisational affiliation to the Communist International as well as any and all other bodies of any kind outside the boundaries of the United States of America, for the specific purpose of removing itself from the terms of the so-called Voorhis Act which has been enacted and goes into effect on January 19, 1941, which law would otherwise tend to destroy and would destroy the position of the Communist party as the legal and open party of the American working class;

that the Convention denounces the Voorhis Act as harmful and destructive of the democratic rights of the people, as designed to coerce the people into submission to the entry of the United States into the imperialist war, and as part of the sweep of fascisation over the capitalist world;

that the Convention pledges the Party to work untiringly to secure the repeal of this law to the end that Labour and our Party shall be secure and unmolested in its sacred rights of international affiliation of all workers which, in the words of Lincoln, express 'the strongest bond of human sympathy outside the family relationship';

that the Convention reaffirms the unshakable adherence of our Party to the principles of proletarian internationalism in the spirit of its greatest leaders and teachers Marx, Engels, Lenin and Stalin, which offers the only road to the future for suffering humanity;

that the Convention formally and officially declares that the Communist Party of the United States is responsible for no political document, policy, book, article or other expression of political opinion except such as are issued by itself through its regularly constituted leadership on the basis of the Eleventh National Convention deliberations and decisions, etc., of this present special Convention;

that the Convention does now elect a sub-committee to consider the constitution and bylaws of the Communist Party of the United States as adopted at the Tenth National Convention and bring back to this Convention recommendations for such amendments, changes or relations which shall most effectively express these basic decisions in such constitution and bylaws.

— 41 —

THE DISSOLUTION OF THE COMMUNIST INTERNATIONAL

During the Second World War the existence of the Communist International became a liability to the Soviet Union, especially since the Communist Parties in allied countries professed to be interested only in saving the world from Fascism and not in revolution. Representations by Roosevelt to Stalin at the Yalta and Teheran Conferences resulted in the decision of the Kremlin to liquidate the organizational form of the Communist International. Nonetheless, the structure and files of the Comintern were retained, and evidence introduced in the Canadian espionage trials (see Document No. 43.) showed that operatives working for the Soviet Embassy in Canada were checked against information relayed from the offices of the Comintern in Moscow. After the war, the controls over the international Communist movement by the Kremlin were routed through spokesmen of various national parties, e.g., Jacques Duclos' letter to the American Communist Party signaled it to resume its revolutionary line. (See Document No. 40.) Although the reason given for the dissolution of the Communist International was that differences in historical conditions required different approaches to the conquest of power—which, if true, had always been true, although dissident Communists had sometimes been expelled for maintaining this view—in fact, the Kremlin continued to lay down the law to Communist Parties on what strategy to follow. The original text of the Resolution on the dissolution of the Comintern appeared in Pravda, May 22, 1943, and was reprinted in World News and Views *on May 29, 1943.*

✐   ✐   ✐

. . . long before the war it became more and more clear that, with the increasing complications in the internal and international relations of the various countries, any sort of international centre would encounter insuperable obstacles in solving the problems facing the movement in each separate country. The deep differences of the historic paths of development of various countries, the differences in their character and even contradictions in their social orders, the differences in the level and tempo of their economic and political development, the differences, finally, in the degree of consciousness and organisation of the workers, conditioned the different problems facing the working class of the various countries.

The whole development of events in the last quarter of a century, and the experience accumulated by the Communist International convincingly showed that the organisational form of uniting the workers chosen by the first congress of the Communist International answered the conditions of the first stages of the working-class movement but has been outgrown by the growth of this movement and by the complications of its problems in separate countries, and has even become a drag on the further strengthening of the national working-class parties.

The World War that the Hitlerites have let loose has still further sharpened the differences in the situation of the separate countries, and has placed a deep dividing line between those countries which fell under the Hitlerite tyranny and those freedom-loving peoples who have united in a powerful anti-Hitlerite coalition.

In the countries of the Hitlerite *bloc* the fundamental task of the working class, the toilers and all honest people consists in giving all help for the defeat of this *bloc,* by sabotage of the Hitlerite military machine from within, and by helping to overthrow the Governments who are guilty of the war. In the countries of the anti-Hitlerite coalition, the sacred duty of the widest masses of the people, and in the first place of the foremost workers, consists in aiding by every means the military efforts of the Governments of these countries aimed at the speediest defeat of the Hitlerite *bloc* and the assurance of the friendship of nations based on their equality.

Already the Seventh Congress of the Communist International, meeting in 1935, taking into account the change that had taken place both in the international situation and in the working-class movements that demand great flexibility and independence of its sections in deciding the problems confronting them, emphasised the necessity for the Executive Committee of the Communist International, in deciding all questions of the working-class movement arising from the concrete conditions and peculiarities of each country, to make a rule of avoiding interference in the internal organisational affairs of the Communist Parties. These same considerations guided the Communist International in considering the resolution of the Communist Party of the U.S.A. of November, 1940, on its withdrawal from the ranks of the Communist International. . . .

In consideration of the above, and taking into account the growth and political maturity of the Communist Parties and their leading cadres in the separate countries, and also having in view the fact that during the present war some sections have raised the question of the dissolution of the Communist International as the directing centre of the International Working-Class Movement.

The Presidium of the Executive Committee of the Communist International, in the circumstances of the World War not being able to convene a Congress of the Communist International, puts forward the following proposal for ratification by the sections of the Communist International:

The Communist International, as the directing centre of the International Working-Class Movement, is to be dissolved, thus freeing the section of the Communist International from their obligations arising from the statutes and resolutions of the Congresses of the Communist International.

The Presidium of the Executive Committee of the Communist International calls on all supporters of the Communist International to concentrate their energies on whole-hearted support of and active participation in the war of liberation of the peoples and States of the anti-

Hitlerite coalition for the speediest defeat of the deadly enemy of the working class and toilers—German-Fascism and its associates and vassals.

— 42 —

THE DUCLOS LETTER REVISING THE POLITICAL STRUCTURE OF THE COMMUNIST PARTY

In 1943, in order to allay Roosevelt's objections to the existence of the Communist International and in exchange for concessions which solidified Soviet expansionist aims in Eastern Europe, Stalin adopted the stratagem on the international scene which paralleled the action of the Communist Party in 1940 in formally disaffiliating from the Communist International. Stalin formally dissolved the Comintern. Using the Teheran agreements between Roosevelt, Churchill and Stalin in 1943 as his foundation, Earl Browder, the then Secretary of the American Communist Party, with the full approval of the Kremlin, proposed the transformation of the American Communist Party into the Communist Political Association. This proposal was adopted with practical unanimity.

In 1945, after the Second World War had been safely won, Stalin resumed the full Communist offensive against his erstwhile allies, especially the United States. The American Communist Political Association was ordered to resume political life. Since the Communist International formally did not exist, instructions were issued through Jacques Duclos, Secretary of the French Communist Party, in the form of a letter to the readers of the French Cahiers du Communisme, *whose readers allegedly had shown a sudden interest in the action taken almost two years before by the American Communist Party. This was the first time in the history of the Communist movement that a statement by an officer of a Communist Party in another country was used as a medium for communicating the command of the Kremlin. The American Communist Political Association became a Party once more with hardly any dissenting voices. Browder himself approved the changes, but was sacrificed in order to signify that the turn was considered to be significant. The dissolution of the Communist Party in 1943 was a contribution to the war effort, an expression of willingness to insure domestic peace so long as the United States was an ally of the Soviet Union and prepared to do its bidding. Once the war was over the Communists were to return to their main revolutionary task. The Duclos letter appeared in* the Daily Worker *of May 24, 1945, with a warm introduction by Browder. The following is from the closing section.*

✓   ✓   ✓

Without analyzing in detail Browder's full position on the dissolution of the CPUSA and creation of the Communist Political Association, and without making a developed critique of this position, one can nevertheless deduce from it the following conclusions:

1. The course applied under Browder's leadership ended in practice in liquidation of the independent political party of the working class in the U.S.

2. Despite declarations regarding recognition of the principles of Marxism, one is witnessing a notorious revision of Marxism on the part of Browder and his supporters, a revision which is expressed in the concept of a long-term class peace in the United States, of the possibility of the suppression of the class struggle in the postwar period and of establishment of harmony between labor and capital.

3. By transforming the Teheran declaration of the Allied governments, which is a document of a diplomatic character, into a political platform of class peace in the United States in the postwar period, the American Communists are deforming in a radical way the meaning of the Teheran declaration and are sowing dangerous opportunist illusions which will exercise a negative influence on the American labor movement if they are not met with the necessary reply.

4. According to what is known up to now, the Communist Parties of most countries have not approved Browder's position and several Communist Parties (for example that of the Union of South Africa and that of Australia) have come out openly against this position, while the Communist Parties of several South American countries (Cuba, Colombia) regarded the position of the American Communists as correct and in general followed the same path.

Such are the facts. Such are the elements of understanding which permit passing judgement on the dissolution of the American Communist Party. French Communists will not fail to examine in the light of Marxist-Leninist critique the arguments developed to justify the dissolution of the American Communist Party. One can be sure that, like the Communists of the Union of South Africa and of Australia, the French Communists will not approve the policy followed by Browder for it has swerved dangerously from the victorious Marxist-Leninist doctrine whose rigorously scientific application could lead to but one conclusion, not to dissolve the American Communist Party but to work to strengthen it under the banner of stubborn struggle to defeat Hitler Germany and destroy everywhere the extensions of fascism.

In the United States the omnipotent trusts have been the object of violent criticism. It is known, for instance, that the former Vice-President of the United States, Henry Wallace, has denounced their evil doings and their antinational policy.

We too, in France, are resolute partisans of national unity, and we show that in our daily activity, but our anxiety for unity does not make us lose sight for a single moment of the necessity of arraying ourselves against the men of the trusts.

Furthermore one can observe a certain confusion in Browder's declarations regarding the problem of nationalization of monopolies and what he calls the transition from capitalism to socialism.

Nationalization of monopolies actually in no sense constitutes a socialist achievement, contrary to what certain people would be inclined to believe. No, in nationalization it is simply a matter of reforms of a democratic character, achievement of socialism being impossible to imagine without preliminary conquest of power.

Everyone understands that the Communists of the United States want to work to achieve unity in their country. But it is less understandable that they envisage the solution of the problem of national unity with the good will of the men of the trusts, and under quasi-idyllic conditions as if the capitalist regime had been able to change its nature by some unknown miracle.

In truth, nothing justifies the dissolution of the American Communist Party, in our opinion. Browder's analysis of capitalism in the United States is not distinguished by a judicious application of Marxism-Leninism. The predictions regarding a sort of disappearance of class contradictions in the United States correspond in no wise to a Marxist-Leninist understanding of the situation.

As to the argument consisting of a justification of the Party's dissolution by the necessity of not taking direct part in the presidential elections, this does not withstand a serious examination. Nothing prevents a Communist Party from adapting its electoral tactics to the requirements of a given political situation. It is clear that American Communists were right in supporting the candidacy of President Roosevelt in the last elections, but it was not at all necessary for this to dissolve the Communist Party.

It is beyond doubt that if, instead of dissolving the Communist Party of the United States all had been done to intensify its activity in the sense of developing an ardent national and anti-fascist policy, it could very greatly have consolidated its position and considerably extended its political influence. On the contrary, formation of the Communist Political Association could not but trouble the minds and obscure the perspectives in the eyes of the working masses.

In France, under cover of Resistance unity, certain suggestions for the liquidation of the parties have been circulated, with more or less discretion, during the last months, but none among us has ever thought of taking such suggestions seriously. It is not by liquidating the Party that we would have served national unity. On the contrary we are serving it by strengthening our Party. And as far as the American Communists are concerned, it is clear that their desire to serve the unity of their country and the cause of human progress places before them tasks which pre-suppose the existence of a powerful Communist Party.

After the Teheran decisions came the Yalta decisions which expressed the will of the Big Three to liquidate fascism in Germany and to help the liberated peoples to liquidate the remnants of fascism in the different countries.

It is scarcely necessary to recall that the material bases for fascism reside in the trusts, and the great objective of this war, the annihilation of fascism, can only be obtained to the extent in which the forces of democracy and progress do not shut their eyes to the economic and political circumstances which engendered fascism.

The American Communists have an especially important role to play in the struggle taking place between the progressive forces of the earth and the fascist barbarism.

Without any doubt they would have been in a better position to play this role in the interests of their country and human progress if, instead of proceeding to dissolve their Party, they had done everything to strengthen it and make of it one of the elements of the assembling of the broad democratic masses of the United States for the final crushing of fascism, that shame of the 20th Century. It would be useless to hide the fact that fascism has more or less concealed sympathizers in the United States, as it has in France and other countries.

The former Vice-President of the U.S., Henry Wallace, present Secretary of Commerce, said rightly that one cannot fight fascism abroad and tolerate at home the activity of powerful groups which intend to make peace "with a simple breathing spell between the death of an old tyranny and the birth of a new."

The Yalta decisions thwart these plans, but the enemies of liberty will not disarm of their free will. They will only retreat before the acting coalition of all the forces of democracy and progress.

And it is clear that if Comrade Earl Browder had seen, as a Marxist-Leninist, this important aspect of the problems facing liberty-loving peoples in this moment in their history, he would have arrived at a conclusion quite other than the dissolution of the Communist Party of the United States.

43

COMMUNISTS, LOYALTY
AND WAR

The standing injunction to Communists throughout the world in case their country is embroiled in an imperialist war is "Turn the Imperialist War into a Civil War." What is an imperialist war? It is any war which the Communist International or the Soviet Union declares to be one. Even a nation which is defending itself against aggression, unless it is a co-belligerent and ally of the Soviet Union, is conducting an imperialist war. Since the true fatherland of every Communist is the Soviet Union, if his country finds itself at war with the Soviet Union, his duty is clear. He must fight against his country with whatever means are at his disposal. To avow this openly, of course, is impolitic. It not only outrages the natural sentiments of patriotism and local piety, it invites administrative measures on the part of the government to establish security programs and see to it that members of the Communist Party and individuals who, although not formally members, are under its discipline, do not worm themselves into positions of trust and responsibility.

Consequently, whenever American Communists are asked where their allegiance would lie in the event of a war between the Soviet Union and the United States, they refuse to answer clearly and resort to all sorts of evasions. The usual gambit is to maintain that "if" or "hypothetical questions concerning such eventualities are illegitimate." This is all the more surprising since the stock-in-propaganda of the American Communist Party, as well as other Communist Parties, has always been that the Soviet Union is in danger of being invaded by its encircling enemies or by a coalition of imperialist powers, chief among whom is the United States. If any question can be considered as not hypothetical, but actual and relevant in the political outlook of Communists, this is it.

The following colloquy took place between William Z. Foster, National Chairman of the American Communist Party, and the Chairman of the Special Committee on Un-American Activities, House of Representatives, 76th Congress, 1st Session, Investigation of Un-American Propaganda Activities in the U.S., *Vol. 7, September 5, 1939, p. 4347. At the time the Soviet Union had just signed a pact with Nazi Germany and was soon to invade Poland and overrun the Baltic States. In subsequent statements, following the Second World War and the resumption of the cold war of the Soviet Union against the democratic West, Foster was more outspoken in declaring his position.*

The CHAIRMAN. If there was war between Russia and the United States, where would your allegiance lie? Do you decline to answer that question?

Mr. FOSTER. I refuse to accept "if" questions as a determining factor. I will say this. I am for the defense of the United States.

The CHAIRMAN. I did not ask you that.

Mr. FOSTER. I am answering your question. I cannot be put on a "yes" or "no" answer to such a question.

I am for the defense of the United States and the maintenance of its national independence within a democratic system, and the development of democratic systems in the world, the establishment of socialism in the United States, and so, insofar as it goes, in a war against any country, I will not blindly walk into that war, but will examine what is involved in the war and decide my personal conduct accordingly.

If it is an imperialist war against some other country, I will not support it.

The CHAIRMAN. In other words, if the United States entered the present war, you would not support the United States?

Mr. FOSTER. Not an imperialist war.

The CHAIRMAN. I say, in the present war that is existing —you know there is a war?

Mr. FOSTER. I have heard about it.

The CHAIRMAN. If the United States entered the war, would you support the United States?

Mr. FOSTER. If the United States entered this war on an imperialist basis, I would not support it.

The CHAIRMAN. In other words, if the United States entered this war as an ally of France and England, you would not support the United States?

Mr. FOSTER. Under the present set-up I would say that is an imperialist war, and the workers have no interest in it, and I would speak against it.

The CHAIRMAN. You would not support the United States?

Mr. FOSTER. Not in such a war.

The CHAIRMAN. Do you regard it as a paramount duty of a Communist to defend the Soviet Union?

Mr. FOSTER. It depends on what you mean by defend.

The CHAIRMAN. Is not that the slogan of the party?

Mr. FOSTER. There are many ways to defend.

The CHAIRMAN. You have heard that stated, that the paramount duty is to defend the fatherland, the Soviet Union, have you not?

Mr. FOSTER. Yes.

The CHAIRMAN. Is that correct?

Mr. FOSTER. That is correct, but it depends on what you mean by defend.

The CHAIRMAN. What did you mean by that when you used it?

Mr. FOSTER. We use the term "defend" for many explanations, explanations of policy.

The CHAIRMAN. As chairman of the Communist Party of the United States, if the United States entered this present war—which you say is an imperialistic war—on the side of France and England, would the Communist Party support the United States Government?

Mr. FOSTER. First of all, the Communist Party would take up the question and discuss it and would take a stand accordingly.

The CHAIRMAN. What is your opinion as chairman of the Communist Party; would it support the United States Government?

Mr. FOSTER. I stated——

The CHAIRMAN. You stated your personal opinion.

Mr. FOSTER. I stated my personal opinion, and I would certainly advocate that in the party.

The CHAIRMAN. And you think that would prevail, don't you?

Mr. FOSTER. Well, we would see.

The CHAIRMAN. Well, if it did not prevail it would be the first time in which the Communist Party did not follow the party line?

Mr. FOSTER. It would not be the first time it did not follow my line.

The CHAIRMAN. I am not asking you about "your line"; I am talking about the party line.

Mr. FOSTER. It would not be the party line until they adopted it; just because I advocated it would not make it the party line.

The CHAIRMAN. I understand that; but I say if they did not follow the party line, it would be the first time they did not do so?

Mr. FOSTER. After they work out the party line, they would follow it, of course.

The CHAIRMAN. That party line has to be worked out by the Comintern, as well as the Communist Party of the United States, don't it?

Mr. FOSTER. No; the American party would settle that question.

The CHAIRMAN. Independent of the Comintern?

Mr. FOSTER. Yes; independent of the Comintern.

The CHAIRMAN. Have you ever settled any question regarding the party line independent of the Comintern?

Mr. FOSTER. Tens of thousands.

The CHAIRMAN. Independent of the Comintern?

Mr. FOSTER. Independent, of course; every day; every day, on every question that comes along, we make settlements.

The CHAIRMAN. Every day—can you cite a single instance where any decision of the Communist Party finally taken has conflicted with the decision of the Comintern?

Mr. FOSTER. Well, no; I cannot—no major decision.

44

HENRY A. WALLACE TO
HERBERT A. PHILBRICK

*The most successful episode in the many political mas-
querades of the Communist Party of the United States was
its organization of the Progressive Party, which ran Henry
A. Wallace for President in 1948. Herbert A. Philbrick,
an undercover operative of the government for many
years, revealed in his book* I Led Three Lives, *and in other
writings, the way in which the Communist Party maneu-
vered and stage-managed the affairs of the Progressive
Party behind the scenes. The following letter was addressed to Mr. Philbrick by Mr. Wallace and printed in*
The New York Herald Tribune *of February 14, 1952. In
the interests of historical accuracy it must be stated that
long before Philbrick's revelations, Mr. Wallace waved
aside evidence that the Communist Party had taken over
the strategic, organizational controls of the Progressive
Party, and the prediction that acceptance of support from
Communists would compromise the liberal cause.*

✓   ✓   ✓

DEAR MR. PHILBRICK:

When I wrote you yesterday in care of McGraw-Hill I
had had opportunity to read only page 245 of your book
entitled "I Led Three Lives." Since then I have read the
other references to me as they are indicated in your index
and I must say that in the main they seem to me to be
both factual and fair. Undoubtedly the Communists had
no use whatever for my faith in God and in "Progressive
Capitalism." You are correct, it seems to me, in saying
that the Communists used their influence against me in
the Progressive party. At Center Sandwich, N.H., in the
fall of 1948 I recognized the damage which the Communists were doing the Progressive party when I said, "If the
Communists would only run a ticket of their own, the

Progressive party would gain 3,000,000 votes." Your analysis of the relationship of the Communists to the Progressive party seems to me in retrospect to be essentially correct. They did make a shambles out of a party which could have served a very useful function. They also broke the hearts of liberal, well meaning people who desperately wanted peace but who hated the force, deceit and intrigue for which Communism stands.

HENRY A. WALLACE

— 45 —

THE FINDINGS OF THE SUBVERSIVE ACTIVITIES CONTROL BOARD

In 1950 Congress adopted the Internal Security Act, which set up a Board to determine, after public hearings, which organizations were Communist action organizations and therefore required to register as such with the Attorney General of the United States. Hearings were conducted for a period of two years. Thousands of pages of testimony were taken and hundreds of exhibits introduced into evidence which covered the entire history of the Communist Party in its various embodiments as listed herewith:

Communist Party of America: September 1919 to April 1923

Communist Labor Party of America: September 1919 to May 1920

United Communist Party of America: May 1920 to May 1921

Workers Party of America: December 1921 to August 1925

Workers (Communist) Party of America: August 1925 to March 1929

Communist Party of the USA (CPUSA): March 1929 to May 1944

Communist Political Association: May 1944 to July 1945

Communist Party of the USA: July 1945 to date

For reasons of space, only the conclusions of the Subversive Activities Control Board are given. The reader should be in a position on the basis of the documents included in this volume to check for himself the justice of the findings of the Board.

✔   ✔   ✔

Conclusion

The evidence in this proceeding discloses the history and activities of the Communist Party of the United States (Respondent herein) over the period of its entire existence. From its inception in 1919, it has been a subsidiary and puppet of the Soviet Union.

Since the late 1930's, when it was faced with adverse legislation, Respondent has become increasingly diligent and resourceful in its efforts to appear as a domestic political party while continuing its subservience to the Soviet Union. Many of its practices were contrived to conceal its revolutionary objectives. Thus, it continues as an avowed Marxist-Leninist organization but, except to initiates, disclaims so much of Marxism-Leninism as would endanger its continued legal existence to espouse. As in the present proceeding, this frequently entails disavowing the core of Marxism-Leninism.

Consequently, Respondent is met with the dilemma of appearing to reject but yet maintain its reason for being. As our findings in this report reveal, this dual role is so fundamentally incongruous as to be incapable of fulfillment under scrutiny. It is so innate in Respondent's nature that it seek and accept Soviet Union direction and control that, in actuality, it does not function as the purely domestic political party whose role it would, de jure, assume. Rather, nurtured by the Soviet Union, it labors unstintingly to advance the world Communist movement.

With consummate patience, the Party strives for the establishment of a dictatorship of the proletariat in the

United States; a goal which would rob the American people of the freedoms they have forged. While using the cloak of the United States Constitution, it struggles unremittingly to synthesize from the complexities of our time a condition in this country which would enable it to shackle our institutions and preside over a Soviet America, under the hegemony of the Soviet Union.

Upon the overwhelming weight of the evidence in this proceeding, we find that Respondent is substantially directed, dominated, and controlled by the Soviet Union, which controls the world Communist movement referred to in Section 2 of the Act; and that Respondent operates primarily to advance the objectives of such world Communist movement.

Accordingly, we find that the Communist Party of the United States is a Communist-action organization and required to register as such with the Attorney General of the United States under Section 7 of the Act.

An appropriate order will be entered.

By the Board:

(Signed)   PETER CAMPBELL BROWN,
Chairman.

(Signed)   KATHRYN MCHALE,
Member.

(Signed)   WATSON B. MILLER,
Member.

Dated: April 20, 1953, at Washington, D.C.

Part V

THE COMMUNIST MOVEMENT IN OTHER COUNTRIES

THE COMMUNIST MOVEMENT IN MEXICO, FRANCE AND INDIA

The detailed story of the relations between the Kremlin and countries other than the United States would require many volumes. The pattern, however, is the same—with a few exceptions in which attempts were made to resist complete domination. As a rule, the decisions on the program, leaders, main directives—all emanated from Moscow. The cases of Jugoslavia, Hungary, Poland and China will be treated elsewhere. Here we very briefly cite representative *documents indicating the extent to which the keys of control and power were held by the Kremlin.*

A. Mexico

The citation is from the beginning and conclusion of A Letter from the Communist International to the Mexican Communist Party *of August 21, 1923, an English translation of which was issued in Chicago under the imprint of the Workers Party of America.*

✓   ✓   ✓

The resolutions adopted at your Congress indicate that the process of securing ideological clarity within the Party is progressing favorably. But we deem it our duty to go into some detail with reference to certain concrete problems on which we do not find that a clear attitude has been adopted on your part. . . .

We want to remind you of the decisions of the Second Congress of the Communist International on the question of parliamentarism, and we expect you strictly to adhere to them. It is important, above all, that you make concrete plans for parliamentary activity. Discussion on the attitude to be taken by your future representatives in the

Chamber of Deputies and on local government bodies on the various questions on the agenda of the next session, or on the proposals the party will make, must be opened immediately in your meetings and in your Party press, and must be conducted from an exclusively revolutionary point of view. . . .

Among the peasants the struggle must center above all on the control of the "Municipios" and the "Comites Ejectuvos Particulares." Besides the decisions of the national agrarian programme of the Party, you must work out detailed instructions for the activity of the sections depending upon the local conditions prevailing in the various regions concerned. . . .

In the cities the Party will fight for seats in the Ayuntamientos, for representatives in the "Juntas de Cociliacion y Arbitraje," and for the control of the Labor Department by organized workers. On the question of the regulation of Article 123, the Party must work out concrete proposals. This is a question on which you must force the laborites to follow suit. You must call upon Morones and Company to advocate our revolutionary proposals on the subject of labor legislation. Under no circumstances must the Party resort to compromise in this matter. . . .

In conclusion, we want to say a few words about the significance of the nationalist and revolutionary struggle for freedom in the Central American countries. The capitalist development of North America and the backward economic and social development of the countries of Latin America, determine the political attitude of the United States towards the countries of the South. . . . The United States hopes "in time" to parcel out Mexico into single "independent" territories. It is already openly advocating the annexation of fruitful Lower California to the United States as a territory. In Yucatan and in the State of Chiapas, the Americans are fanning the flames of the separatist movements. But times are changing. Even in these backward areas, the proletariat is awakening, is organizing, and is beginning to understand its class condition. In Cuba the revolutionary trade union movement is again raising its head after the defeat it suffered in 1921 at the hands of reaction. In Guatemala a Communist Party of Central America has been founded; in Mexico the revolutionary labor movement has such strong roots that neither the claws of American capital nor of any other capital can tear it to pieces. But the conception is still lacking of the fight for freedom for all the oppressed masses in the West Indies, in Central America and in South America, against the imperialism of the oil magnates and industrial barons of Wall Street. The workers and peasants of Mexico and Central America especially must stand close together. The aim of the common struggle must be to create a League of Central American Workers' and Peasants' Republics. It is the duty of the Communist Party of Mexico to announce this slogan with all revolutionary fervor to the oppressed masses of Central America. The Mexican Party must treat exhaustively the question which we have roughly sketched here. In conjunction with the Communist Party of Central America and the communist group in Cuba, a programme of work and action must be prepared. . . .

B. France

The first citation is from an interview (at a time when the French Communist Party was playing the patriotic game) by M. Thorez, Secretary of the French Communist Party, July 15, 1939, and published in World News and Views. *Thorez called for a policy of collective security and an end of appeasement towards Fascism; he also glorified the ideals of the French Revolution. The second citation is from Thorez's article in* The Communist International, *March, 1940, in which he followed the lead of the Soviet Union in denouncing the war against Hitler and Mussolini as an imperialist war. Thorez himself fled to the Soviet Union.*

—I—

M. THOREZ. The voices of Hitler and Mussolini are the voices of the most reactionary section of big capital. The parasites of society are anxious to prolong the duration of their disastrous rule, which brings nothing but misery and war. They want to destroy democratic liberties solely in order that they may prevent humanity from getting rid of these parasites. Therefore they want to impose by fire and sword a rule of obscurantism—even more barbarous than that of the Middle Ages—of which racialism is the plainest expression. Hitler and Mussolini vilify the principles of 1789, for the reason that the principles of this year, to quote Goethe, mean "more light," whilst big capital, whose agents they are, want more darkness.

. . . The Government of the Republic, after being subjected to considerable pressure by the results of our campaign among every section of the French nation, is only arranging a few official ceremonies from which the people are almost completely excluded. The Government is endeavoring in accordance with the spirit of Munich, to spare the feelings of the dictators, although these for their part will have no hesitation—as the newspaper *Tevere* states, quoting one of Mussolini's spokesmen—spitting in the face of France.

But our government fears above all the anti-fascist mobilisation of the masses of the people, and therefore it prefers to tolerate the action of Nazi agents in France when they slander the French Revolution, following the émigrés of Coblenz.

—II—

In spite of the rigorous censorship, the government broadcasts and the bourgeois press, including the Socialist papers, are beginning to betray unmistakable signs of the rage and fear of France's ruling circles in the face of our Communist Party's fearless and undaunted struggle against the imperialist war.

How has the position changed for the reactionaries since 1914?

During the first imperialist war they found willing servants and accomplices in the treacherous leaders of the Socialist Party. Blum and Jouhaux were already engaged at that time in driving the workers to the slaughter to safeguard the money-bags of the capitalists. The Socialist leaders in Germany, Austria, Great Britain and Belgium were no better, and their concerted betrayal of the working class brought on the shameful collapse of the Second International.

The glorious Bolshevik Party, the Party of Lenin and Stalin, alone was true to the cause of the working class, the cause of proletarian internationalism. Lenin and

Stalin were the leaders of the only party that from the very beginning of the holocaust called on the working people to wage a revolutionary struggle against the imperialist war, called upon them to combat *the enemy at home*. The Bolshevik Party alone, led by Lenin and Stalin, proved capable of organizing and developing this struggle, of leading the working class to victory over tsarism and capitalism, to the conquest of power, which made it possible to build socialism, to lay firm foundations for a new world, for the communist society of labor, prosperity, freedom and peace.

In 1939, on the other hand, we saw the Communists in France and all other countries, modeling themselves on the Bolsheviks and trained in the teaching of Lenin and Stalin, stand true to the cause of the working class, of proletarian internationalism. Our Party holds aloft in steady hands the banner of the Communist International, the standard of revolutionary struggle against the imperialist war. It is calling upon the people to fight the reactionary forces of France and their government, to fight Deladier and his henchmen in order to stop the war and pave the way for peace.

C. India

The policy of the Communist Party of India has ranged from ultra-revolutionary anti-imperialism to collaboration with the British Raj, from condemnation of Ghandi and Nehru as imperialist agents to fawning flattery of the leadership of the first and the neutralism of the second. The first exhibit is extracted from a catechism drawn up by Orgwald in 1933 to instruct Indian Communists on how to operate by the Pan Pacific Trade Union Secretariat, originally set up by the Communist International as its Far Eastern Bureau in 1927. Tactical and Organizational Questions of the Communist Parties of India and Indo-china, *pp. 20 and 29. The second exhibit is extracted from a pamphlet by P. C. Joshi, Secretary of the Indian Communist Party, entitled* The Indian Communist Party (*London, 1942*). *Joshi proclaims an about-face policy for the Communist Party of India from hostility to British imperialism to support of the British Government in India in order to combat Hitler, who had invaded the Soviet Union.*

—I—

Question 10.—If at some town the Communists work legally and are known to the police, how should an illegal organization be formed and generally how should the work be done so that our comrades may not get into the hands of the police? Generally, how should we do our work so as to avoid arrest and keep the leadership intact?

Answer.—As far as I know the conditions in India, it is necessary to build up illegal Communist organizations. For an illegal organization it is easier to work in the prevailing conditions in India, easier to move from one place to another and easier to meet because the police do not know all the comrades. And it is impossible for the police to shadow all the Indians. In so far as the activities of a good many of the comrades will not be known, there will be no very strict watch over them.

If so, is it necessary to throw out the comrades who work legally and are known to the police? Of course not. If in some big town a good Communist is known to the police and he is left unmolested by them, he must leave that town. He should not work in a ward of a town where he is known. He should move in circles where he is unknown. He must go underground. The comrades that are most needed must be transferred to the underground.

If a comrade is not one of those who are needed most, he may remain in his legal position and in this case it is necessary to give him some legal work, such as the publishing of a legal paper, or work in the legally existing trade unions, and so on. It is necessary to watch his work and control him. How is this to be done? It is necessary as far as possible to avoid taking him to meetings of the organization. It is better to instruct some member of the committee to keep in touch with this comrade. Any comrade who knows his bearings more or less could be charged with this task and meet the comrade in such places as would not draw attention. . . .

Question 47.—What are the best methods of working in the mixed army in India? For instance, in some brigade there is a battalion of Punjab-Mussulmans, a battalion of Jats, a battalion of Dogras, and a British battalion. All these battalions are billeted in the provinces, where the population speaks a language different from those of the four battalions. What should be done if there are revolutionary groups in these units, groups that speak a different language from the one spoken by the regional committee, how should the work be co-ordinated, with whom should it be linked up and generally how should the work of agitation and organization be carried on among these soldiers?

Answer.—I will begin with the end. First, they should not be connected with anybody. The army organization must be organized absolutely separately. If they are united, let us say, with the workers' and peasants' organization in the given locality, they will end by both of them falling into the hands of the police. To combine a military organization with a workers' organization is bad for the one and the other. In order to reduce the risk, it is necessary that the organization of the soldiers be kept quite separate from the local organization of workers or peasants. A special representative of the local committee, who is in charge of military work, should be connected with the military organization.

How should the work be carried on here? Obviously the Party organization will have to get comrades from the place where the soldiers come from or find comrades who command the languages spoken by these soldiers, so that connections may be established with them.

I believe this is possible. In Czarist Russia, too, there were 110 nationalities. There, in a like manner, the soldiers who spoke Polish would not be billeted in Poland but somewhere in the Caucasus, while the Caucasians would be transferred to Poland. Still, it was very easy to find people who were able to work among these soldiers. This presented no particular difficulty. Even in the localities where these soldiers are stationed, one may find workingmen who can speak some language spoken by these soldiers.

With a knack for work and a desire to work one could always find some people who will work among these soldiers.

—II—
The Indian Communist Party—Its Work in the War of Liberation

IMPERIALIST WAR INTO PEOPLE'S WAR

The attack on the U.S.S.R. transforms the character of the imperialist war into a people's war. The attack on the U.S.S.R. is a call for people's mobilisation to win the war. The victory of the U.S.S.R. becomes the guarantee of people's liberation all over the world. . . .

On June 22nd, 1942, the peoples of the world ceased being the pawns and victims of the imperialist countries in their struggle for world domination. They now step forward as the main actors, shaping their own destiny, achieving their own liberation by advancing to win the people's war in a people's way. On June 22nd Hitler Fascism rang its own death knell. It was also the death knell of world imperialism as we have known it so far. *The first salvoes fired by the Red Army against the advancing Nazi hordes ushered in the epoch of the struggle for the people's world.*

We opposed the imperialist war for all we were worth —*we must go into the people's war for all we are worth.* We had nothing to gain and everything to lose by supporting the imperialist war. We have nothing to lose and everything to gain by going into the people's war. We can no more fight for our freedom by opposing the war. *We have to realise our freedom by winning this war.*

Anti-Fascism has been the international *policy* of our national movement—today it is to be made the *practice* of our national policy. Fascism is no more the menace to other freedom-loving nations alone, whose cause we support from a distance, with whom we sympathise. Fascism today threatens our own borders. Fascism is no longer the enemy of India's friends, but of India herself. We suffer enslavement under imperialism and are now threatened with intensified enslavement under Fascism—the worst form of imperialism. The world war against Fascism is India's war for national defence.

This war is India's great opportunity to fight for her national liberation, no more in isolation, no more single-handed, but as part of the battle for world liberation. It is the war of the Soviet peoples, whom we pledged support against an imperialist attack. It is the war of the heroic Chinese people, whose five years of lone struggle we have admired with veneration. It is the war of the British people, with whom we have preached friendliness and co-operation despite the British imperial domination over us. It is the war of the enslaved peoples of Europe, for whom our hearts bleed. It is an All-People's war against Fascism and for freedom. It is the Indian people's war no less than the war of all the rest of the peoples of the world. It is war for all that we hold dear, for all that we stood and stand.

The All-People's War is India's War.

The International Front Against Fascism is India's Front for Freedom.

The War of World Liberation is India's War for National Liberation.

— 47 —

COMMUNISM, COLONIALISM, AND THE UNDERDEVELOPED COUNTRIES

"In the last analysis," wrote Lenin in March, 1923, *"the outcome of the struggle [between the Communist and non-Communist world] will be determined by the fact that Russia, India, China, etc., account for the overwhelming majority of the population of the globe."* [1] This assumed two things: that the Asian and African countries, whether colonial or not, would follow the Western path of modernization and industrialization; and secondly, that in their struggles for freedom and national independence the Communists would achieve leadership either openly or

[1] "Better Fewer, but Better," *Selected Works,* Moscow, 1951, Vol. 2, Part II, p. 750.

from behind the scenes. The first is largely true; the second, the Communists have indefatigably sought to make come true. While the non-Communist world watched with puzzled incomprehension, the Communists trained thousands of natives of Asian and African countries in special schools in the role of professional revolutionists. Their first function was to organize local Communist Parties to coöperate with nationalist movements. They were then, if possible, to wrest the leadership from democratic national elements, or to discredit them as "tools of the imperialists" if they refused to turn the nationalist revolution into a social revolutionary one. Once independence was achieved, their task was to exercise unremitting pressure, whether within or without the government, to bring their countries into the Communist camp, or failing that, into a neutralist position which would weaken the democratic West. The following passages are taken from the Theses of the Second Congress of the Third Communist International.

The political situation of the world at the present time has placed the question of the dictatorship of the proletariat in the foreground, and all the events of world politics are inevitably concentrating around one point, namely, the struggle of the bourgeois world against the Russian Soviet Republic, which is grouping around itself the Soviet movements of the vanguard of the workers of all countries, and all national liberation movements of the colonial and subject countries, which have been taught by bitter experience that there can be no salvation for them outside of a union with the revolutionary proletariat, and the triumph of the Soviet power over Imperialism.

Consequently, we must not content ourselves with a mere recognition or declaration concerning the unity of the workers of different nations, but we must carry out a policy of realizing the closest union between all national and colonial liberation movements and Soviet Russia, determining the forms of this union in accordance with the stage of development of the Communist movement among the proletariat of each country, or the revolutionary liberation movement in the subject nations and backward countries. . . .

With regard to those states and nationalities where a backward, mainly feudal, patriarchal, or patriarchal-agrarian regime prevails, the following must be borne in mind: 1) All Communist parties must give active support to the revolutionary movements of liberation, the form of support to be determined by a study of existing conditions, carried on by the party wherever there is one. This duty of rendering active support is to be imposed in the first place on the workers of those countries on whom the subject nation is dependent in a colonial or financial way; 2) Naturally, a struggle must be carried on against the reactionary mediaeval influences of the clergy, the christian missions, and similar elements; 3) It is also necessary to combat the pan-Islam and pan-Asiatic and similar movements, which are endeavoring to utilize the liberation struggle against European and American imperialism for the purpose of strengthening the power of Turkish and Japanese imperialists, of the nobility, of the large land owners, of the clergy, etc.; 4) It is of special importance to support the peasant movements in backward countries against the land owners and all feudal survivals; above all, we must strive as far as possible to give the peasant movement a revolutionary character, to organize the peasants and all the exploited into the Soviets, and thus bring about the closest possible union between the Communist proletariat of Western Europe and the revolutionary peasant movement of the East and of the colonial and subject countries; 5) It is likewise necessary to wage determined war against the attempt of quasi Communist revolutionists to cloak the liberation movement in the backward countries with a Communist garb. It is the duty of the Communist International to support the revolutionary movement in the colonies and in the backward countries, for the exclusive purpose of uniting the various units of the future proletarian parties—such as are Communist not only in name—in all backward countries and educate them to the consciousness of their specific tasks, i.e., to the tasks of the struggle against the bourgeois democratic tendencies within their respective nationalities. The Communist International must establish temporary relations and even unions with the revolutionary movements in the colonies and backward countries, without, however, amalgamating with them, but preserving the independent character of the proletarian movement, even though it be still in its embryonic state. 6) It is essential continually to expose the deception fostered among the masses of the toilers in all, and especially in the backward countries, by the imperialist powers aided by privileged classes of the subject countries, in creating under the mask of political independence various governments and state institutions which are in reality completely dependent upon them economically, financially and in a military sense. As a striking example of the deception practised upon the working class of a subject country through the combined efforts of Allied Imperialism and bourgeoisie of the given nation, we may cite the Palestine affair of the Zionists, where, under the pretext of creating a Jewish state in Palestine, in which the Jews form only an insignificant part of the population, Zionism has delivered the native Arabian working population to the exploitation of England. Only a union of Soviet Republics can bring salvation to the dependent and weak nationalities under present International conditions. . . .

The revolution in the colonies is not going to be a Communist revolution in its first stages. . . . Indeed, it would be extremely erroneous in many of the Oriental countries to try to solve the agrarian problem according to pure Communist principles. In its first stages the revolution in the colonies must be carried on with a programme which will include many petty bourgeois reform clauses, such as division of land, etc. But from this it does not follow at all that the leadership of the revolution will have to be surrendered to the bourgeois democrats. On the contrary, the proletarian parties must carry on vigorous and systematic propaganda of the Soviet idea, and organize the peasants' and workers' Soviets as soon as possible. These Soviets will work in co-operation with the Soviet Republics in the advanced capitalistic countries for the ultimate overthrow of the capitalist order throughout the world.

48

CHINA'S "AGRARIAN REFORMERS"

The victory of the Communist Party of China probably came as a surprise even to Stalin. The Communist Party of China was founded in the Soviet Union in July, 1921. Its program was drawn up in Moscow. It was ordered to support the Chiang Kai-shek nationalist revolution in 1924. This policy ended in disaster in consequence of the Canton uprising expressly commanded by Stalin. Subsequently, the Chinese Communist Party under the leadership of Mao-Tse-tung reconstituted itself and established its headquarters at Yenan in Shensi Province. From there it conducted unremitting guerrilla warfare against the Nationalist regime. After the Japanese invaded China in 1937, Mao followed the Popular Front directives of the 7th Congress of the Comintern. But as the war developed he expanded his power and territory at the expense of the Nationalist regime, which he fought with greater ferocity then he did the Japanese, especially during the period of the Nazi-Soviet Pact. By 1945, when the Second World War ended, Mao became a powerful contender for supremacy in China. It was at this time that a number of influential American scholars and commentators discovered that the Chinese Communists were not really Communists but "agrarian reformers." This conception of Chinese Communism was responsible for the counsel given to Chiang Kai-shek by American advisors that he enter into a coalition regime with Mao Tse-tung.

The Chinese Communists are the most simplistic and orthodox of all contemporary Communists about the ends of Communism. At the same time, they are the most opportunistic about the use of means. They established a Communist "dictatorship of the proletariat" without a proletariat, and on the backs of a peasantry whose entire way of life has been transformed from above. By forced marches and leaps, the Chinese Communists have sought to industrialize China and make her a world-feared power.

These "agrarian reformers" have sought to carry their reforms to Tibet, and even to parts of India, despite the existence of "sacred" treaties and agreements. Since Stalin died, there is some evidence that the Chinese hope the apostolic succession will fall to them.

—A—

China's Revolution Is a Part of the World Revolution

The following passages are from Mao Tse-tung's The Politics and Culture of New Democracy, *which was published in an English translation by the Committee for a Democratic Foreign Policy, New York, 1943, under the title* China's New Democracy. *The nature of Mao's "agrarian reforms," as well as the entire direction of his future policy, are adequately indicated.*

✓   ✓   ✓

The historical characteristic of the Chinese revolution is that it is divided into two steps, that of democracy and that of socialism. The democracy of the first step is not democracy in its general sense, but a new, special type of a Chinese style, the New Democracy. . . .

It is evident that if the present society of China is colonial, semi-colonial and semi-feudal in character, the process of China's revolution must be divided into two steps. The first step is to change the colonial, semi-colonial and semi-feudal form of society into an independent democratic society, while the second step is to push the revolution forward to establish a socialist society. What we are carrying on now is the first step of the Chinese revolution. . . .

The 1911 Revolution in its social character, was a bourgeois-democratic revolution and not a proletarian-socialist revolution. It is not yet consummated, and therefore needs our further effort, because the enemies of this revolution are still extremely strong at present. The word "revolution" in Dr. Sun's famous saying: "The revolution is not yet consummated, and our comrades must still exert their efforts" refers to this bourgeois-democratic revolution.

A change took place in the Chinese bourgeois-democratic revolution after the outbreak of the first imperialist world war and the formation of the socialist state on one-sixth of the earth's surface through the success of the Russian October Revolution in 1917.

Before that, the Chinese bourgeois-democratic revolution belonged to the category of the old bourgeois-democratic revolution of the world, and was a part of it.

Since then, the Chinese bourgeois-democratic revolution has changed its character and belongs to the category of the new bourgeois-democratic revolution. As far as the revolutionary front is concerned, it is a part of the world proletarian-socialist revolution.

Why? Because the first imperialist world war and the victorious socialist October Revolution changed the historical direction of the world, and drew a sharp dividing line between two historical stages. . . .

Although according to social character, the first stage of the first step of this colonial and semi-colonial revolution is still fundamentally bourgeois-democratic, and its objective demands are to clear the obstacles in the way of the development of capitalism, yet this kind of revolution is no longer the old type led solely by the bourgeois class and aiming merely at the establishment of a capitalist society or a country under the dictatorship of the bourgeois class, but a new type led wholly or partially by the proletariat and aiming at the establishment of a New-Democratic society. . . .

Thus, this kind of revolution has become a part of the proletarian-socialist world revolution.

"China's revolution is a part of the world revolution." This correct thesis was proposed as early as 1924-27 during the period of China's Great Revolution. It was advanced by the Communists and was approved by all who participated in the anti-imperialist and anti-feudal struggle of the time. Only the meaning of the theory was not much developed then, and what we mastered was only a dim comprehension of the question. I remember that when Mr. Chiang Kai-shek spoke at Swatow in 1925 during his expedition against Chen Chiung-ming, he also said: "China's revolution is a part of the world revolution."

This "world revolution" is not the old world revolution of the bourgeoisie which has long become a matter of the past, but is the new world revolution, the socialist revolution. In like manner, the "part" means not a part of the old bourgeois revolution but a part of the new socialist revolution. This is an exceedingly great change, a change unprecedented in the world history and the history of China.

It is basing themselves on the correct theory of Stalin that the Chinese Communists advanced this correct thesis.

As early as 1918, Stalin said, in his article commemorating the first anniversary of the October Revolution:

"The following are the three most important points out of the great world significance of the October Revolution. First, it enlarges the scope of the national problem, from the partial problem of opposing national oppression to the general problem of the liberation of oppressed peoples, colonies and semi-colonies from the yoke of imperialism. Secondly, it widens the possibility and opens the true road for this liberation, greatly promotes the liberation work of the Western and Eastern oppressed peoples, and attracts them into the common, victorious anti-imperialist course. Thirdly, it forms a bridge between the socialist West and the enslaved East, *i.e.,* it establishes a new anti-imperialist revolutionary front connecting the Western proletariat and the Eastern oppressed peoples through the Russian Revolution." (Stalin: "The October Revolution and the National Question," *Pravda,* Nov. 6 and 19, 1918.)

The significance of China's revolution is greatly magnified today, because it is happening at a time when the political and economic crises of capitalism have brought the world step by step toward the second imperialist war; when the Soviet Union has reached the transitional period from Socialism to Communism and has the ability to lead and to assist the proletariat, the oppressed peoples and all the revolutionary peoples of the world; when the proletarian forces of the various capitalist countries are growing stronger and stronger; and when the Communist Party, the proletariat, the peasantry, the intelligentsia and the petit-bourgeoisie become a mighty, independent political power. At such a time, should we not estimate that the

world significance of China's revolution has been greatly
magnified? We should. China's revolution is a magnificent
part of the world revolution!

—B—

"Let a Hundred Flowers Blossom"

*After the Hungarian Revolution of workers and stu-
dents was suppressed by Soviet soldiers in 1956, Mao Tse-
tung delivered a famous speech on February 27, 1957.
"On the Correct Handling of Contradictions Among the
People," in which he seemed to be advocating a more
liberal attitude towards discussion and inquiry. Newspapers were permitted to publish views dissenting from
the reigning Communist orthodoxy. A great surge of
criticism manifested itself in every field. Dissenters were
urged to come out into the open. Many did. Thereupon
the Communist Party loosed another fierce campaign of
purge and suppression, branding these flowers of doctrine
as poisonous weeds which must be chopped down. The
critics were compelled to recant under the most humiliat-
ing circumstances and many sent "to camps for reform
through labor."*

*The tactic behind this deceptive move towards liberal-
ism was clearly revealed in an editorial in the Communist
People's Daily (Peking) editorial of July 1, 1957:*

For a time, in order to let the bourgeoisie and the bourgeois intellectuals wage this battle, we . . . did not counter
the frantic attacks made by the reactionary bourgeois Right-
ists. The reason was to enable the masses to distinguish
clearly between those whose criticism was well-intentioned
and those who were inspired by ill will. In this way the
forces for an opportune counter-blow amassed strength.
Some people call this scheming, but we say it was quite
open. We told the enemy in advance that before monsters
and serpents can be wiped out, they must first be brought
into the open, and only by letting poisonous weeds show
themselves above ground can they be uprooted. . . . Why
have our reactionary class enemies enmeshed themselves in
the net that was spread for them?

*The term "contradiction" in Mao's speech may be
rendered as "conflict of interest." Mao admits that conflicts of interest (e.g. strikes) may occur in a Communist
China, but maintains that such conflicts are "non-an-*

*tagonistic." When they occur in non-Communistic socie-
ties, "they are antagonistic."*

*Throughout his speech Mao distinguishes between ideas
and policies which are good for the "people" and those
which aid the "enemy." But in every case the Communist
Party leadership alone is the judge of which is which.
Among the criteria for distinguishing between a blossom
and poisonous weed of thought, Mao lists whether they
help to consolidate the Communist dictatorship and the
leadership of the Communist Party.*

*These extracts are from the speech published in its
entirety in* The New Leader *of September 9, 1957, with
an Introduction by Geoffrey Hudson. The quotation from
the editorial in the Communist* People's Daily *is from Mr.
Hudson's Introduction.*

↗   ↗   ↗

What should our policy be toward non-Marxist ideas?
As far as unmistakable counter-revolutionaries and wreck-
ers of the socialist cause are concerned, the matter is easy;
we simply deprive them of their freedom of speech. But
it is quite a different matter when we are faced with
incorrect ideas among the people. Will it do to ban such
ideas and give them no opportunity to express themselves?
Certainly not. It is not only futile but very harmful to
use crude and summary methods to deal with ideological
questions among the people, with questions relating to the
spiritual life of man. You may ban the expression of
wrong ideas, but the ideas will still be there. On the other
hand, correct ideas, if pampered in hot-houses without
being exposed to the elements or immunized against
disease, will not win out against wrong ones. That is why
it is only by employing methods of discussion, criticism
and reasoning that we can really foster correct ideas,
overcome wrong ideas and really settle issues.

While criticizing doctrinairism, we should at the same
time direct our attention to criticizing revisionism. Revisionism, or rightist opportunism, is a bourgeois trend of
thought which is even more dangerous than doctrinairism.
The revisionists or right opportunists pay lip-service to
Marxism and also attack "doctrinairism." But the real
target of their attack is actually the most fundamental
elements of Marxism. They oppose or distort materialism

and dialectics, oppose or try to weaken the people's democratic dictatorship and the leading role of the Communist party, oppose or try to weaken socialist transformation and socialist construction. Even after the basic victory of the socialist revolution in our country, there are still a number of people who vainly hope for a restoration of the capitalist system. They wage a struggle against the working class on every front, including the ideological front. In this struggle, their right-hand men are the revisionists.

On the surface, these two slogans—let a hundred flowers blossom and a hundred schools of thought contend—have no class character; the proletariat can turn them to account, and so can the bourgeoisie and other people. But different classes, strata and social groups each have their own views on what are fragrant flowers and what are poisonous weeds. So what, from the point of view of the broad masses of the people, should be a criterion today for distinguishing between fragrant flowers and poisonous weeds?

In the political life of our country, how are our people to determine what is right and what is wrong in our words and actions? Basing ourselves on the principles of our constitution, the will of the overwhelming majority of our people and the political programs jointly proclaimed on various occasions by our political parties and groups, we believe that, broadly speaking, words and actions can be judged right if they:

1. Help to unite the people of our various nationalities, and do not divide them.

2. Are beneficial, not harmful, to socialist transformation and socialist construction.

3. Help to consolidate, not undermine or weaken, the people's democratic dictatorship.

4. Help to consolidate, not undermine or weaken, democratic centralism.

5. Tend to strengthen, not to cast off or weaken, the leadership of the Communist party.

6. Are beneficial, not harmful, to international socialist solidarity and the solidarity of the peace-loving peoples of the world.

Of these six criteria, the most important are the socialist path and the leadership of the Party. These criteria are put forward in order to foster, and not hinder, the free discussion of various questions among the people. Those who do not approve of these criteria can still put forward their own views and argue their cases. When the majority of the people have clear-cut criteria to go by, criticism and self-criticism can be conducted along proper lines, and these criteria can be applied to people's words and actions to determine whether they are fragrant flowers or poisonous weeds. These are political criteria. Naturally, in judging the truthfulness of scientific theories or assessing the esthetic value of works of art, other pertinent criteria are needed, but these six political criteria are also applicable to all activities in the arts or sciences. In a socialist country like ours, can there possibly be any useful scientific or artistic activity which runs counter to these political criteria?

"Let a hundred flowers blossom" and "let a hundred schools of thought contend," "long-term coexistence and mutual supervision"—how did these slogans come to be put forward?

They were put forward in the light of the specific conditions existing in China, on the basis of the recognition that various kinds of contradictions still exist in a socialist society, and in response to the country's urgent need to speed up its economic and cultural development. . . .

We are confronted by two types of social contradictions —contradictions between ourselves and the enemy and contradictions among the people. These two types of contradictions are totally different in nature. . . .

The contradictions between ourselves and our enemies are antagonistic ones. Within the ranks of the people, contradictions among the working people are non-antagonistic, while those between the exploiters and the exploited classes have, apart from their antagonistic aspect, a non-antagonistic aspect. Contradictions among the people have always existed, but their content differs in each period of the revolution and during the building of socialism.

In the conditions existing in China today, what we call contradictions among the people include the following:

Contradictions within the working class, contradictions within the peasantry, contradictions within the intelligentsia, contradictions between the working class and the peasantry, contradictions between the working class and peasantry on the one hand and the intelligentsia on the other, contradictions between the working class and other sections of the working people on the one hand and the national bourgeoisie on the other, contradictions within the national bourgeoisie, and so forth. Our People's Government is a government that truly represents the interests of the people and serves the people, yet certain contradictions do exist between the Government and the masses. These include contradictions between the interests of the state, collective interests and individual interests; between democracy and centralism; between those in positions of leadership and the led, and contradictions arising from the bureaucratic practices of certain state functionaries in their relations with the masses. All these are contradictions among the people; generally speaking, underlying the contradictions among the people is the basic identity of the interests of the people.

It will take a considerable time to decide the issue in the ideological struggle between socialism and capitalism in our country. This is because the influence of the bourgeoisie and of the intellectuals who come from the old society will remain in our country as the ideology of a class for a long time to come. Failure to grasp this or, still worse, failure to understand it at all can lead to the gravest mistakes—to ignoring the necessity of waging the struggle in the ideological field. Ideological struggle is not like other forms of struggle. Crude, coervice methods should not be used in this struggle, but only the method of painstaking reasoning. Today, socialism enjoys favorable conditions in the ideological struggle. The main power of the state is in the hands of the working people led by the proletariat. The Communist party is strong and its prestige stands high.

—C—

Love, Literature, and Politics

Before the advent of the Chinese Communists to power all aspects of their theory crudely reflected the dogmas of Soviet Bolshevik-Leninism in its Stalinist form. Mao-Tse-tung here speaks on Problems of Art and Literature, *the substance of a speech delivered at a Conference in Yenan in May, 1942.*

Anyone who considers himself a Marxist-Leninist revolutionary writer, especially a writer who belongs to the Communist Party, must have a general knowledge of Marxism-Leninism. At present, however, many of our comrades fail to understand even the most fundamental concepts of Marxism-Leninism. It is, for example, a fundamental concept that objective conditions determine the subjective, that the objective conditions of class struggle and national struggle determine our thinking and our sentiments. In fact, these comrades reverse this principle. They say that everything begins with "love." Speaking of love, there can be only love of a class, or class-love, in a class society. Yet these comrades seek a love that stands above all class distinctions; they seek abstract love, abstract freedom, abstract truth, abstract human nature, etc., and thereby prove how deeply they have been influenced by the bourgeoisie. We must uproot this influence and bring an open mind to the study of Marxism-Leninism. . . .

Since we realize that our literature and art must serve the masses, then we can go a step further and discuss (1) the inner-party problem of the relation between the literature and art work of the party and party work as a whole; and (2) the problem of our relations with those outside the party, *i.e.,* the relation between party writers and artists and non-party writers and artists; in other words, the problem of a united front in literature and art.

Let us consider the first problem. All culture or all present-day literature and art belong to a certain class, to a certain party or to a certain political line. There is no such thing as art for art's sake, or literature and art that lie above class distinctions or above partisan interests. There is no such thing as literature and art running parallel to politics or being independent of politics. They are in reality nonexistent.

In a society with class and party distinctions, literature and art belong to a class or party, which means that they respond to the political demands of a class or party as well as to the revolutionary task of a given revolutionary period. When literature and art deviate from this principle, they divorce themselves from the basic needs of the people.

The literature and art of the proletariat are part of the revolutionary program of the proletariat. As Lenin pointed out, they are "a screw in the machine." Thus the role of the party's work in literature and art is determined by the over-all revolutionary program of the party. Deviation from this principle inevitably leads to dualism and pluralism, and eventually to such views as Trotsky advocated: Marxist politics but bourgeois art.

We are not in favor of overemphasizing the importance of literature and art but neither must we underestimate it. Although literature and art are subordinate to politics, they in turn exert a tremendous influence upon politics. Revolutionary literature and art are part of a revolutionary program. They are like the aforementioned screws. They may be of greater or lesser importance, of primary or secondary value when compared with other parts of the machine, but they are nevertheless indispensable to the machine; they are indispensable parts of the entire revolutionary movement. If we had no literature and art, even of the most general kind, we should not be able to carry on the revolution or to achieve victory. It would be a mistake not to recognize this fact.

49

YUGOSLAVIA

Until 1948 the Communist Party of Yugoslavia was the most militant as well as the most orthodox of the Communist Parties in the satellite countries of the Soviet Union. Belgrade was the headquarters of the Cominform (The Communist Information Bureau) which in 1947 was organized to function in place of the Comintern. Suddenly on June 28, 1948, a communique appeared in the official organ of the Czechoslovak Communist Party announcing the expulsion of the Communist Party of Yugoslavia on grounds that Tito and his group were pursuing an unfriendly policy towards the Soviet Union and its Communist Party leadership.

To the Western world this came as a complete and stunning surprise.

Subsequently the correspondence between the Central Committee of the Yugoslav and Soviet Union's Communist Parties was published. It revealed that Tito had adopted measures to prevent Stalin's representatives from building up a pro-Soviet faction to take over the Yugoslav Communist Party and imposing the Kremlin's line on all its domestic policies. Stalin withdrew his military and civilian specialists and accused Tito of slandering the Soviet Union and lapsing into Menshevik revisionism and counter-revolutionary Trotskyism. Tito protested his undying loyalty to Marx, Lenin and Stalin, but insisted on keeping the reins of power in his own hands. He was able to follow this course because, unlike other satellite regimes, he controlled military forces independent of the Soviet Red Army.

No fundamental ideological difference separated Tito and Stalin except Tito's refusal to accept his own liquidation at the hands of those more subservient to Stalin than himself.

With the help of the West, Tito managed to remain in power. After Stalin's death, a near-reconciliation between

Tito and Khrushchev took place. But having tasted independence, Tito has been loath to surrender it. He has sought to make the best of both worlds. He halted agricultural collectivization in his own country and permitted a limited autonomy to peasants to market their products. He moderated his terroristic measures after liquidating some weak and quiescent remnants of former Social-Democratic groups. His most dramatic acts of repression have been directed against those individuals who refuse to be silent and who criticize the oppressive and anti-democratic character of his regime. Milovan Djilas, *a former high-ranking Yugoslav Communist, was jailed for having written, and published abroad,* The New Class, *a critique of Yugoslav Communism as a new system of class exploitation. (See some extracts published below.) Djilas was subsequently released on parole, then rearrested and sentenced to a longer term in jail for publishing his* Conversations with Stalin.

In foreign affairs, despite the receipt by the Yugoslav regime of massive aid, without any strings, running to billions of dollars from the United States government, Tito has consistently supported the Kremlin on main issues in dispute between the democratic and Communist worlds. He has sought to align the so-called neutralist nations in a campaign which considers the defensive, nuclear strategy of the West against threatened Communist aggression as a provocation to the Kremlin, whose peaceful intentions are taken for granted despite Yugoslavia's own experience with the Kremlin. Thus the resumption of nuclear testing by the United States was condemned at the instigation of Tito, at the meeting of neutral nations held in Belgrade in 1962, but no criticism was made of the violation in September, 1961, of the Soviet pledge not to resume nuclear testing—the action which led to the reluctant decision by the United States.

There is no reason to doubt Tito's commitment to Bolshevik-Leninism even though this by itself is not sufficient to predict the specificities of his political behavior.

The following readings consist of (A) extracts from the text of the published correspondence between the Communist Parties of the U.S.S.R. and Yugoslavia as translated by the Royal Institute of International Affairs, London, 1948; (B) some extracts from the program of

the League of Communists of Yugoslavia together with
other observations from leading Yugoslav Communists;
(C) excerpts from official documents and speeches during
the period of reconciliation between the U.S.S.R. and
Yugoslavia following Stalin's death, and (D) excerpts
from Djilas' The New Class.

—A—

The Soviet-Yugoslav Dispute

I. STALIN'S CHARGES

. . . The Yugoslav military leaders have begun to abuse
the Soviet military advisors and to discredit the Soviet
army. . . .

Yugoslav security organs controlled and supervised the
Soviet Representatives in Yugoslavia. . . . They not only
follow representatives of the Soviet government but also
the representative of the Communist Party of the Soviet
Union in the Cominform. . . . It would be ridiculous to
think that the Soviet government would agree to keep its
civilian specialists in Yugoslavia in such circumstances. . . .

We know that these anti-Soviet rumors circulating
among the leading comrades in Yugoslavia, for instance
that "the Communist Party of the S.U. is degenerate,"
"great power chauvinism is rampant in the U.S.S.R.,"
"the U.S.S.R. is trying to dominate Yugoslavia economically," "the Cominform is a means of controlling the
other Parties by the C.P.S.U.," etc. These anti-Soviet allegations are usually camouflaged by left phrases such as
"socialism in the Soviet Union has ceased to be revolutionary" and that "Yugoslavia alone is the exponent of
revolutionary socialism." . . .

We are disturbed by the present condition of the Communist Party of Yugoslavia. . . . Decisions of the Party
organs are never published in the press, neither are reports
of Party assemblies. Democracy is not evident within the
C.P.Y. itself. . . . Criticism and self-criticism within the
Party does not exist or barely exists. . . . The Party
cadres are under the supervision of the Minister of State
Security. . . . The Party should control all the State organs in the country including the Ministry of States Security . . . in Yugoslavia we have just the opposite. It is

understandable that we cannot consider such an organization of a Communist Party as Marxist-Leninist, Bolshevik.

The spirit of the policy of the class struggle is not felt in the C.P.Y. The increase in the capitalist elements in the villages is in full swing, and the leadership of the Party is taking no measures to check these capitalist elements. . . .

In Yugoslavia . . . the People's Front is considered the chief leading force and there was an attempt to get the Party submerged within the Front. In his speech at the Second Congress of the People's Front, Comrade Tito said: "Does the C.P.Y. have any other program but that of the People's Front? No, the C.P.Y. has no other program. The program of the People's Front is its program." (This is the theory of the Mensheviks.) As is known, Lenin described these Mensheviks as malicious opportunists, and liquidators of the Party.

We cannot understand why the English spy, Velebit, still remains in the Ministry of Foreign Affairs of Yugoslavia as the first Assistant Minister. . . . The Soviet government cannot place its correspondence with the Yugoslav government under the censorship of an English spy.

The Yugoslav leaders put the foreign policy of the U.S.S.R. on a par with the foreign policy of the English and Americans and feel they should follow the same policy toward the Soviet Union as towards the imperialist States, Great Britain and the United States. In this respect, the speech by Comrade Tito in Ljubljana in May, 1945 is very characteristic. He said: "We seek also a just end; we demand that every one shall be master in his own house; we do not want to pay for others; we do not want to be used as a bribe in international bargaining; we do not want to get involved in any policy of spheres of interest."

This was said in connection with the question of Trieste. As is well known, after a series of territorial concessions for the benefit of Yugoslavia, which the Soviet Union extracted from the Anglo-Americans, the latter, together with the French, rejected the Soviet proposal to hand Trieste over to Yugoslavia and occupied Trieste with their own forces, which were then in Italy. Since all other means were exhausted, the Soviet Union had only one other method left for gaining Trieste for Yugoslavia—to start war with the Anglo-Americans over Trieste and take it by force. The Yugoslav comrades could not fail to realize that after such a hard war the U.S.S.R. could not enter another. However, this fact caused dissatisfaction among the Yugoslav leaders, whose attitude was described by Comrade Tito. The statements by Tito in Ljubljana were not directed only against the imperialist states but also against the U.S.S.R. . . .

II. TITO'S REPLIES

We must first of all emphasize that we were terribly surprised by the contents (of your letters). We feel that the reason for its contents, that is, for the accusations and attitudes towards individual questions, is insufficient knowledge of the situation here. . . .

As for the withdrawal of Soviet military experts, we see no other reason for it than that we decided to reduce their number to the necessary minimum because of financial difficulties. . . .

We think that if there were some irregularities on the part of our trade organs . . . then some means could have been found to agree on and eliminate all that interferes with the proper development of trade relations between our two countries.

The allegations that the Yugoslav State Security Department follows Soviet specialists and other Soviet people are not true. . . .

Your letter states that we are making anti-Soviet criticisms and criticisms of the C.P.S.U. . . . It is very difficult for us to understand how such serious accusations can be advanced without mentioning their sources. . . . We feel that on the basis of unidentified persons and suspicious information, it is incorrect to draw conclusions and make accusations like those brought in the letter, against men who have performed invaluable services in popularizing the U.S.S.R. in Yugoslavia. . . . Among many Soviet people there exists the mistaken idea that the sympathy of the broad masses in Yugoslavia towards the U.S.S.R. came of itself, on the basis of some traditions which go back to the time of Czarist Russia. This is not so. Love of the U.S.S.R. did not come of itself. It was stubbornly inculcated into the masses of the Party and the people in general by the present leaders of the new Yugoslavia, including in the first rank, those so seriously accused in the letter. . . .

As regards the questions of the internal life of the C.P.Y. which is mentioned in your letter, it can be seen that you have received completely inaccurate information and have formed an erroneous picture. Accordingly we cannot agree with your evaluation of our Party. . . .

The allegation that the policy of the class struggle is not realized in the C.P.Y., and that capitalist elements in the villages and cities are being strengthened, etc., is completely inaccurate. . . .

The C.P.Y. has a completely assured leadership in the People's Front because the C.P.Y. is the nucleus of the People's Front. Therefore there is no danger of its dissolving into the People's Front—as is said in the letter. . . . We study and take as an example the Soviet system, but we are developing socialism in our country in somewhat different forms. . . .

As to Velebit and why he still remains in the Ministry of Foreign Affairs. The matter stands thus. Kardelj and Djilas once told Molotov that we are not at all clear about Velebit, we never had any proof then and we have none today. The matter is still under investigation and we would not care to remove and destroy a man on the basis of suspicion. . . .

If you were to ask us if there were anything with which we were not satisfied on your part then we should openly say there are many reasons why we are dissatisfied. . . . We will mention a few. First, we regard it as improper for the agents of the Soviet Intelligence Service to recruit in our country, which is going towards socialism, our citizens for their intelligence service. . . .

We have proof that certain agents of the Soviet Intelligence Service in recruiting our Party members cast doubts on our leaders, sought to ruin their reputation, showed them as inefficient and unreliable. . . . We cannot allow the Soviet Intelligence Service to spread its net in our country. . . .

These and similar matters with which we are not satisfied are numerous. However, can this be the reason for the straining of our mutual relations? No. These are questions which can be eliminated and explained. . . .

Our only desire is to eliminate every doubt and dis-

belief in the purity of the comradely and brotherly feeling
of loyalty of our C.C. of the C.P.Y. to the C.P.S.U. . . .

We desire that the matter be liquidated in such manner
as we prove, by deeds, that the accusations against us are
unjust. That is, we will resolutely construct socialism and
remain loyal to the Soviet Union; remain loyal to the doctrines of Marx, Engels, Lenin, and Stalin. The future will
show, as did the past, that we will realize all that we promise you. . . .

By order of the C.C. of the C.P.Y.

J. B. Tito

E. Kardelj

—B—

Yugoslavia's Way

*The Program of the League
of the Communists of Yugoslavia
(Translated by Stoyan Pribechevich—
New York, 1958)*

Successful development of socialist relations in our
country also depends on the development of socialism in
the world, for our socialist development is a part of the
world-wide socialist transformation. Successes achieved
along this path by the world socialist forces facilitate our
own development, just as the accomplishments of our own
country contribute to the general revolutionary experience
of the labor movement and to the development of socialism as a whole. . . . [*p. xix*]

Resistance to improper practices in relations among
socialist countries—resistance which in various ways has
taken place more than once—has revealed the progressive
aspirations of the peoples of the socialist countries: to
build socialism in accordance with their specific conditions,
having in mind the interests of socialism as a whole. To
label this policy "national communism" can only be the
result of dogmatic or great-power conceptions or of bourgeois ideological influence and intrigue. [*p. 73*]

Peace in contemporary conditions primarily means
peaceful coexistence of peoples and states with different
social systems. This coexistence must not be passive, en-

trenched in bloc positions. It must be active, aiming at a constant widening of cooperation among peoples. [*p. 76*]

The policy of active coexistence inevitably leads in every capitalist country to the checking and weakening of the forces which act as brakes on progress and which, at the same time, harbor the potential danger of provoking a new world war. This policy broadens the basis of the struggle against imperialism and colonialism. [*p. 78*]

The class-political essence of the people's government in Yugoslavia is the dictatorship of the proletariat, that is, government by the specific alliance of the working class, as the leading social force, with other working people. [*p. 111*]

Simultaneously, the Communists will continue the struggle for keeping key positions of state authority in firm revolutionary hands. [*p. 122*]

In everyday practice, these tendencies also appear in irresponsible use of social funds; exaggerated differences in salaries and rewards; fighting for material privileges connected with certain positions; creation of small cliques in the managements of enterprises and economic and administrative institutions; arbitrariness of persons in charge, and so on.

In everyday practice, the tendencies of bureaucratism are most frequently shown in an "office approach" to social problems, such as red-tape and formalistic handling of affairs, callous behavior toward people, lack of feeling of responsibility toward burning issues, and so on. [*p. 146*]

The present social plan of Yugoslavia establishes the basic proportions in social production and distribution, assuming, within these proportions, free initiative of economic enterprises under market conditions and some regulative measures of the state. [*p. 154*]

The social-political basis of socialist democracy in Yugoslavia consists of workers' self-management, represented in Workers' Councils and other self-governing organs of producers; self-management of the working people in the basic cells of society—the Communes; and in the most varied forms of social self-management through organs in which interested citizens and organizations take part. [*p. 168*]

The Communists will pay particular attention to the development of Workers' Councils. Workers' Councils are democratic economic-political organs of social self-management through which direct producers independently manage enterprises and take a decisive part in the development of the forces of production—within a single coordinated social economic plan and in accordance with the general interests of the community, expressed in a single coordinated economic system. [*p. 173*]

The Commune is the basic political-territorial organization of self-management of the working people and the basic social-economic community of the population within its territory. The Communists should pay great attention to the development of the Commune. [*p. 175*]

As long as our society is exposed to the pressures of antisocialist forces, organs of internal security will be an important and indispensable weapon of socialism. [*p. 185*]

Excerpt from Edward Kardelj's speech at the Federal Assembly on April 1, 1952 (from Kardelj's Socijalistička Demokratija—*Belgrade, 1952*)

. . . If anyone were to engage in planning a multiparty system in our country, it would either prove him to be not only an opponent of socialism but above all an enemy of the independence and freedom of our peoples, or else that he understood nothing of what is happening in the world today.

Excerpt from Jugoslovenski Ekonomski Sistem 1954 (*Belgrade, 1954*)

The Yugoslav economy is a planned economy. As distinguished from the usual conceptions of a planned economy, the plan, or better said, the plans . . . are not central and rigid plans. The plans of the Yugoslav economy are different from the plans of the USSR and the countries under its domination. They do not prescribe compulsory tasks for the enterprises in regard to production, prices, quality, etc. All these elements are left to the action of the free market, to the action of supply and demand. Plans in the Yugoslav economy are in their essence only aimed at channeling and coordinating the trends of general development.

—C—

Period of Reconciliation

*Excerpt from a Statement by Soviet First Party Secretary
Nikita S. Khrushchev on arrival at Belgrade Airport, May
26, 1955* [1]

We sincerely regret what happened and resolutely reject
the things that occurred, one after the other, during that
period. On our part, we ascribe without hesitation the ag-
gravations to the provocative role that Beria, Abakumov
and others—recently exposed enemies of the people—
played in the relations between Yugoslavia and the USSR.

*Excerpt from the Joint Soviet-Yugoslav
Declaration, Belgrade, June 2, 1955* [2]

Compliance with the principle of mutual respect for,
and non-interference in, internal affairs for any reason
whatsoever, whether of an economic, political or ideological nature, because questions of internal organization,
or difference in social systems and of different forms of
Socialist development are solely the concern of the individual countries.

Tito, *Govori i Članci* (*Speeches and Articles*), Vol. XI
Zagreb, 1959, (Translated from Serbo-Croatian).

Excerpt from Tito's Speech in Stalingrad, June 11, 1956 [3]

Yugoslavia, in time of war as well as in time of peace,
marches shoulder to shoulder with the Soviet people toward the same goal—victory of socialism.

[1] Bass, Robert, and Marbury, Elizabeth, eds. *The Soviet-Yogo-
slav Controversy, 1948-58: A Documentary Record* (New
York: The East Europe Institute, 1959), p. 53.

[2] *Ibid.*, p. 57.

[3] Tito, *Govori i Članci* (*Speeches and Articles*) (Zagreb, 1959;
translated from Serbo-Croatian), Vol. XI, p. 111.

Excerpts from Marshal Tito's Speech at Pula, November 11, 1956 [4]

. . . It was a fatal error to call the Soviet army at a time when the demonstrations were still taking place. It was a great mistake to call the army of another country to give a lesson to the people of the country, even if there had been some shooting. . . .

Now, what is the lesser evil: chaos, a civil war, a counter-revolution and a new world war, or the intervention of the Soviet troops which were there? The first would have been a catastrophe, and the second was a mistake. Of course, if this saves Socialism in Hungary, then we will be able to say, comrades, that—despite our objections to interference—Soviet intervention was necessary.

—D—

A Critical Voice

Excerpts from Milovan Djilas,
The New Class: An Analysis of the Communist System
(New York: Frederick A. Praeger, 1957)

Although the Communist revolution may start with the most idealistic concepts, calling for wonderful heroism and gigantic effort, it sows the greatest and the most permanent illusions. [*p. 30*]

In contrast to earlier revolutions, the Communist revolution, conducted in the name of doing away with classes, has resulted in the most complete authority of any single new class. Everything else is sham and an illusion. [*p. 36*]

. . . The new class may be said to be made up of those who have special privileges and economic preference because of the administrative monopoly they hold. [*p. 39*]

. . . The new class is voracious and insatiable, just as the bourgeoisie was. But it does not have the virtues of frugality and economy that the bourgeoisie had. The new class is as exclusive as the aristocracy but without aristocracy's refinement and proud chivalry. [*p. 60*]

The party is the main force of the Communist state and government. It is the motive force of everything. It unites within itself the new class, the government, ownership, and ideas. [*p. 78*]

[4] Bass and Marbury, *op. cit.*, p. 57.

Communist regimes are a form of latent civil war between the government and the people. [*p. 87*]

. . . The Communist leaders handle national property as their own, but at the same time they waste it as if it were somebody else's. Such is the nature of ownership and government of the system. [*p. 120*]

. . . This is how it is with these high priests who are simultaneously policemen and owners of all the media which the human intellect can use to communicate its thoughts—press, movies, radio, television, books, and the like—as well as of all substance that keeps a human being alive—food and a roof over his head. [*p. 134*]

Contemporary Communism is that type of totalitarianism which consists of three basic factors for controlling the people. The first is power; the second, ownership; the third, ideology. [*p. 166*]

Ideas, philosophical principles and moral considerations, the nation and the people, their history, in part even ownership—all can be changed and sacrificed. But not power. Because this would signify Communism's renunciation of itself, of its own essence. Individuals can do this. But the class, the party, the oligarchy cannot. This is the purpose and the meaning of its existence. [*p. 170*]

— 50 —

HUNGARY

Hugh Seton-Watson, Professor of Russian History at the University of London, has succinctly and correctly described the Hungarian Revolution of 1956 as "a rising of the workers against exploitation, of the intellectuals against thought-control, and of the whole nation against the Soviet imperialists." Section A below is devoted to a series of broadcasts from Free Radio Kossuth and Free Radio Petofi on the day of the attack, November 4, 1956. Section B reprints Premier Nagy's last statement to the Hungarian nation and to the West. Section C gives the

resolutions adopted by the United Nations General Assembly branding the aggression of the Soviet regime as a
violation of the basic freedom of the Hungarian people.
These resolutions, which still stand, illumine the Soviet
conception of "peaceful coexistence." Section D reprints
several broadcasts from Moscow on "crushing the conspiracy." The final sections, E and F, record an exchange
between French and Russian intellectuals on the Hungarian uprising.

✓   ✓   ✓

—A—

The Attack at Daybreak
4 NOVEMBER[1]

Budapest

Attention! Attention!
Attention! Attention!
Now Imry Nagy, President of the Council of Ministers
of the Hungarian People's Republic is going to address
you! [*05:19*]
This is Imry Nagy speaking, the President of the Coun-
cil of Ministers of the Hungarian People's Republic.
Today at daybreak Soviet forces started an attack against
our capital, obviously with the intention to overthrow the
legal Hungarian democratic Government.
Our troops are fighting.
The Government is in its place.
I notify the people of our country and the entire world
of this fact.
[*The announcement was followed by the National
anthem, and then repeated in English, Russian, and
French, and German.*]

Free Radio Kossuth

Attention! Attention! Attention! [*05:56*]
Premier Imry Nagy calls Minister of Home Defence,
Pal Maleter, the chief of our General Staff, Istvan Kovacs,
and the other members of the military delegation who
went yesterday at 22:00 hrs. to the headquarters of the
Soviet Supreme Command and who have not returned

[1] From: *The Hungarian Revolution: A White Book*, ed. by
Melvin Lasky (New York, 1957), pp. 228-229, 239.

until now, to come back without further delay in order to take over their respective offices.

Free Radio Kossuth

Attention! We read now an important announcement! [07:14]

The Hungarian Government requests officers and soldiers of the Soviet army not to shoot. Avoid bloodshed! The Russians are our friends and will remain our friends in the future!

Free Radio Kossuth

This is the Association of Hungarian Writers speaking to all writers, scientists, all writers' associations, academies, and scientific unions of the world. We turn to leaders of intellectual life in all countries. Our time is limited. You know all the facts. There is no need to expand on them. Help Hungary! Help the Hungarian writers, scientists, workers, peasants and intelligentsia. Help! Help! Help!

Free Radio Kossuth [07:56]

[*The message was repeated in German and Russian. After the writers' appeal, music was played until 08:10. Then the signal was discontinued, although a silent carrier wave could still be detected until 09:45. . . .*]

SOS! SOS! SOS!

Free Radio Kossuth [08:24]

Civilized people of the world, listen and come to our aid. Not with declarations, but with force, with soldiers, with arms. Do not forget that there is no stopping the wild onslaught of Bolshevism. Your turn will also come, if we perish. Save our souls! Save our souls! . . .

Civilized peoples of the world! We implore you in the name of justice, freedom and the binding moral principle of active solidarity to help us. Our ship is sinking. Light is failing. The shadows grow darker every hour over the soil of Hungary. Listen to our cry, civilized peoples of the world, and act. Extend to us your fraternal aid.

SOS! SOS!—May God be with you!

Free Radio Petofi [14:34]

—B—

Premier Nagy's Last Message to the Hungarian Nation and the West[2]

This fight is the fight for freedom by the Hungarian people against the Russian intervention, and it is possible that I shall only be able to stay at my post for one or two hours. The whole world will see how the Russian armed forces, contrary to all treaties and conventions, are crushing the resistance of the Hungarian people. They will also see how they are kidnapping the Prime Minister of a country which is a Member of the United Nations, taking him from the capital, and therefore it cannot be doubted at all that this is the most brutal form of intervention. I should like in these last moments to ask the leaders of the revolution, if they can, to leave the country. I ask that all that I have said in my broadcast, and what we have agreed on with the revolutionary leaders during meetings in Parliament, should be put in a memorandum, and the leaders should turn to all the peoples of the world for help and explain that today it is Hungary and tomorrow, or the day after tomorrow, it will be the turn of other countries because the imperialism of Moscow does not know borders, and is only trying to play for time.

—C—

Resolutions Adopted by the United Nations General Assembly with Reference to Hungary

RESOLUTION 1004 (ES-II)

The General Assembly,

Considering that the United Nations is based on the principle of the sovereign equality of all its Members,

Recalling that the enjoyment of human rights and of fundamental freedom in Hungary was specifically guaranteed by the Peace Treaty between Hungary and the Allied and Associated Powers signed at Paris on 10

---

[2] From Paragraph 291 of the *United Nations Report of the Special Committee on the Problem of Hungary* (General Assembly Official Records, 11th Session Supplement #18 A/3592).

February 1947 and that the general principle of these rights and this freedom is affirmed for all peoples in the Charter of the United Nations,

Convinced that recent events in Hungary manifest clearly the desire of the Hungarian people to exercise and to enjoy fully their fundamental rights, freedom and independence,

Condemning the use of Soviet military forces to suppress the efforts of the Hungarian people to reassert their rights,

Noting moreover the declaration of 30 October 1956 by the Government of the Union of Soviet Socialist Republics of its avowed policy of non-intervention in the internal affairs of other States,

Noting the communication of 1 November 1956 (A/3251) of the Government of Hungary to the Secretary-General regarding demands made by that Government to the Government of the Union of Soviet Socialist Republics for the instant and immediate withdrawal of Soviet forces,

Noting further the communication of 2 November 1956 (S/3726) from the Government of Hungary to the Secretary-General asking the Security Council to instruct the Government of the Union of Soviet Socialist Republics and the Government of Hungary to start the negotiations immediately on withdrawal of Soviet forces,

Noting that the intervention of Soviet military forces in Hungary has resulted in grave loss of life and widespread bloodshed among the Hungarian people,

Taking note of the radio appeal of Prime Minister Imre Nagy of 4 November 1956,

1. *Calls upon* the Government of the Union of Soviet Socialist Republics to desist forthwith from all attack on the people of Hungary and from any form of intervention, in particular armed intervention, in the internal affairs of Hungary;

2. *Calls upon* the Union of Soviet Socialist Republics to cease the introduction of additional armed forces into Hungary and to withdraw all of its forces without delay from Hungarian territory;

3. *Affirms* the rights of the Hungarian people to a government responsive to its national aspirations and dedicated to its independence and well-being;

4. *Requests* the Secretary-General to investigate the situation caused by foreign intervention in Hungary, to observe the situation directly through representatives named by him, and to report thereon to the General Assembly at the earliest moment, and as soon as possible suggest methods to bring an end to the foreign intervention in Hungary in accordance with the principles of the Charter of the United Nations;

5. *Calls upon* the Government of Hungary and the Government of the Union of Soviet Socialist Republics to permit observers designated by the Secretary-General to enter the territory of Hungary, to travel freely therein, and to report their findings to the Secretary-General;

6. *Calls upon* all Members of the United Nations to co-operate with the Secretary-General and his representatives in the execution of his functions;

7. *Requests* the Secretary-General in consultation with the heads of appropriate specialized agencies to inquire, on an urgent basis, into the needs of the Hungarian people for food, medicine and other similar supplies, and to report to the General Assembly as soon as possible;

8. *Requests* all Members of the United Nations, and invites national and international humanitarian organizations to co-operate in making available such supplies as may be required by the Hungarian people.

564th Plenary Meeting
4 November 1956.

RESOLUTION 1005 (ES-II)

The General Assembly,

Noting with deep concern that the provisions of its resolution 1004 (ES-II) of 4 November 1956 have not yet been carried out and that the violent repression by the Soviet forces of the efforts of the Hungarian people to achieve freedom and independence continues,

Convinced that the recent events in Hungary manifest clearly the desire of the Hungarian people to exercise and to enjoy fully their fundamental rights, freedom and independence,

Considering that foreign intervention in Hungary is an intolerable attempt to deny to the Hungarian people the exercise and the enjoyment of such rights, freedom and independence, and in particular to deny to the Hungarian people the right to a government freely elected and representing their national aspirations,

Considering that the repression undertaken by the Soviet forces in Hungary constitutes a violation of the Charter of the United Nations and of the Peace Treaty between Hungary and the Allied and Associated Powers,

Considering that the immediate withdrawal of the Soviet forces from Hungarian territory is necessary,

1. *Calls again* upon the Government of the Union of Soviet Socialist Republics to withdraw its forces from Hungary without any further delay;

2. *Considering* that free elections should be held in Hungary under United Nations auspices, as soon as law and order have been restored, to enable the people of Hungary to determine for themselves the form of government they wish to establish in their country;

3. *Reaffirms* its request to the Secretary-General to continue to investigate, through representatives named by him, the situation caused by foreign intervention in Hungary and to report at the earliest possible moment to the General Assembly;

4. *Requests* the Secretary-General to report in the shortest possible time to the General Assembly on compliance herewith.

571st Plenary Meeting
9 November 1956.

—D—

Radio Moscow: "Crushing the Conspiracy. . . ." [3]

NOVEMBER 4, 1956

Moscow

This morning the forces of the reactionary conspiracy against the Hungarian people were crushed. A new Hungarian Revolutionary Worker-Peasant Government, headed by the Prime Minister Janos Kadar, has been formed. The Government has appealed to the Hungarian people to ally its forces in defence of the victories of the people's democratic system and for a final rout of the reactionary conspirators headed by Horthy officers who served in the Hitlerite army.

[3] From: Radio Moscow, quoted in Lasky, *op. cit.*, p. 240.

The Revolutionary Worker-Peasant Government has appealed to the Command of the Soviet troops for assistance in the suppression of the insurgents who were recently protected by the remnants of the Imre Nagy Government, which has disintegrated as a result of the resignation from it of honest Hungarian patriots.

The counter-revolutionary bands nesting in public buildings are being successfully smashed and are capitulating. . . . [21:05 GMT]

. . . Many Hungarian workers who were deceived by the insurgents' propaganda have had their eyes opened. They have seen how the enemies of the people's regime, who tortured and hanged the finest representatives of the Hungarian people, tried to re-establish the authority of the capitalists and landowners of Hungary. In Budapest and other Hungarian towns order is being restored, the resistance of negligible troops of insurgents in Budapest is being crushed with the active participation of the Hungarian population. . . . [15:10 GMT]

During 4 November events have led to a complete defeat of the forces of counter-revolution. . . . The proclamation of the new Revolutionary Government in Hungary has found a lively response among genuine patriots. [21:10 GMT]

—E—

To the Soviet Government [4]

Paris

The undersigned, who never harbored unfriendly feelings to the U.S.S.R. and socialism, today consider themselves justified in protesting to the Soviet Government against the use of guns and tanks to suppress the uprising of the Hungarian people and its striving to independence, even taking into account the fact that some reactionary elements, which made appeals on the rebel radio, were involved.

We consider and always will consider that socialism, like freedom, cannot be carried on the point of a bayonet. We fear that a government, imposed by force, will soon be compelled, in order to stand its ground, to resort to

[4] From: *France-Observateur* (*Paris*), November 15, 1956. Quoted in Lasky, *op. cit.*, p. 278.

force itself and to the injustices against its own people which ensue from this. . . .

We are equally opposed to the hypocrites. . . . We deny the right of protest against Soviet intervention in Hungary to those who kept silent, or even expressed approval, when the U.S. drowned in blood the freedom won by Guatemala. . . .

The first and principal demand which we address to the Soviet Government . . . is the demand for truth. Where truth triumphs, crime becomes impossible; where it is suppressed, there can be neither justice, nor peace, nor freedom.

JEAN-PAUL SARTRE	VERCORS
CLAUDE ROY	ROGER VAILLANT
CLAUDE MORGAN	SIMON DE BEAUVOIR

(Among Others)

—F—

Reply From Russian Intellectuals[5]

Moscow

Yes, what has taken place in Hungary is grave and tragic. But you see only one side in this. . . . You are mistaken! You do not see the whole truth!

The people of Hungary was dissatisfied with the situation in the country. . . . We think that a share of responsibility is ours. . . . We know that our country adopted measures [to help Hungarian leaders correct "grave mistakes"], but what has happened forces us to think that these measures were inadequate. . . . Are there no other paths for correcting mistakes except the unleashing of counter-revolutionary fascist forces seeking the liquidation of the people's democratic order and the formation in Hungary of the centre for a new war? . . .

Many of us met you, Vercors, Roger Vaillant, Jean-Paul Sartre, Simone de Beauvoir, Claude Morgan, in Paris, in Moscow, and in other cities of the world. Many of you showed courage in difficult times, took part in the armed resistance to fascism. Then you saw the truth. Look it in the face now too. . . . We do not wish the black

[5] From: *Literary Gazette*, Moscow, November 22, 1956. Quoted in Lasky, *op. cit.*, p. 278.

memory of 1933, the year of the coming-to-power of
fascism, to be repeated again in history. Not in Hungary,
nor anywhere else!

And we want you to know about this and to think
about it.

M. SHOLOKHOV   K. SIMONOV
K. FEDIN   B. SMIRNOV
V. KATAYEV   A. KORNEICHUK
V. PANOVA

(Among Others)

— 51 —

POLAND

*Knowledge of the geography and history of a nation is
always relevant in understanding the culture of a country.
But in understanding the nature of Poland as a Communist nation, geography and history are of preeminent
importance. For Poland's greatest national liability has
been her geography, bordered on one side by a mammoth
empire, and on the other by one of the most aggressive
nations of Western Europe. During the last few centuries,
Poland has been periodically ravaged by the Prussian
eagle and the Russian bear, irrespective of the dynastic or
ideological standards under which the predatory attack
was carried out. Its wounds fed strong sentiments of
patriotism and nationalism, leaving a permanent legacy
of anti-German and anti-Russian feeling among the
population—except for a handful of internationalists who,
inspired by Western ideals of social reform, organized
socialist and then Communist parties.*

*History also explains the paradox that in contemporary
Poland today even Polish Communists, who are few in
number, strongly fear and distrust Russian Communists,
whose armed support enables them to retain power. For
Stalin liquidated the Polish Communist Party completely*

in 1938, ruthlessly purging almost every leading Communist by execution or concentration-camp exile. After the war Gomulka accepted Stalin's aid, program and terror in destroying every vestige of legal non-Communist opposition. However, he was reluctant to adopt the same pattern of terror to settle differences among the new Polish Communist Party which had come into being, or to accept the Soviet pattern of forced collectivization of Polish agriculture. He was removed from power at the Kremlin's command, imprisoned and tortured. After Stalin's death, Gomulka came back to power during the year when Poland trembled on the brink of an Anti-Communist Revolution. Cast, despite himself, in the role of a national symbol of resistance to Stalinism, Gomulka was able to divert Polish restlessness away from the violent path of the Hungarian Revolution.

Gomulka today enjoys reluctant support by an overwhelmingly anti-Communist population because, given present Western policy, the only alternative the Poles see to him is the restoration of Stalinist patterns. At the same time, to insure popular suffrance without organized opposition, Gomulka has decollectivized agriculture, permitted the free market to some extent to reappear, entered into an uneasy truce with the Church, substituted economic coercion for execution and imprisonment to deal with critics of Communism, and enlarged the area of scientific and cultural autonomy for those who are willing to abstain from direct or indirect political criticism of the basic assumptions of Communist society. Speech in cafés still remains relatively free; but control over the press is being reintroduced, probably in part because of Soviet pressure.

The clue to Poland today is to be found in the fact that Gomulka, still a principled Communist, believes that— given a continued monopoly of political power—he can eventually lead the Polish population to accept Communism. He must resist those Poles who truly wish to liberalize Poland and who look back with nostalgia to the years 1955-56, when Poland was on the eve of an anti-Communist revolution. At the same time he must appease the Kremlin, which fears that Gomulka's milder and more gradual measures will increase the appetite for political freedom among the Poles, and thus generate another dangerous political crisis. The Kremlin still holds the lash in the event that the Polish people balk at taking Gomulka's bit and unhorse him.

The following excerpts consist of (A) an important political poem by a Communist poet, Adam Wazyk, symptomatic of the dissatisfaction of Polish Communists with the Stalinist regime of Boleslaw Berut, the Kremlin's Polish puppet (Polish literary men as well as Polish workers sparked the opposition to Polish Stalinism which soon took on proportions of a national movement); (B) an editorial comment from Free Europe *magazine concerning the reaction to Wazyk's poem; (C) excerpts from Gomulka's speech when he was first restored to power in 1956; (D) excerpts from an influential series of articles on humanism and Communism ("Konflikt humanizmow") from the Communist periodical,* Przeglad kuturalny, *Warsaw, Nos. 37-41, September and October, 1961, by Adam Schaff, a Communist philosopher who acts as a liaison man between the Polish Communist Party and the Polish intellectuals. Schaff's function is to try to contain revisionist and critical tendencies among intellectuals by promising them a limited autonomy in their professional disciplines (providing they do not offend political orthodoxy, especially the monopoly of all political power by the Communist Party as the agent of the proletarian dictatorship). The evils of the past, particularly the intellectual terror of the party line in science, are laid at the door of Stalin, during whose days Schaff ventured no public criticism of Stalinist "mistakes and deviations." This indicates that the Polish Communist Party has reaffirmed the Leninist view which makes the Party the sole judge both of the flexible limits of intellectual freedom and of what offends Marxist orthodoxy. Because science and technology are so important for the construction of the Polish economy, scientific tendencies previously viewed with suspicion—e.g., relativity theory, cybernetics, mathematical economics—are no longer denounced by the watch-dogs of doctrinal orthodoxy. On the other hand, literature and the drama, whose remarkable efflorescence helped produce the conditions that enabled Gomulka to make his way from prison to the pinnacle of power, are now being progressively leashed by administrative measures.*

—A—

A Poem for Adults[1]

By Adam Wazyk

1.

When, by error, I jumped on a wrong bus
people in it, as usual, were returning from work.
The bus rushed down an unknown street,
O Holy Cross Street, no longer Holy Cross,
where are your antique shops, book-stores, students?
Where are you, the dead?
The memory of you peters out.
Then the bus stopped
on a dug-up square.
Old skeleton of a four-storey house
anticipated the verdict of fate.
I got off in the square
in a working district,
where grey walls become silver, reminiscing.
People were hurrying home
and I did not dare ask them the way.
In my childhood, had I not come to this house?
I returned like a man
who had gone for medicine
and come home twenty years later.
My wife asked me where I'd been.
My children asked me where I'd been.
I said nothing and sweated like a mouse.

2.

Squares turn like cobras,
houses stand like peacocks,
give me any old stone
and I'll be back in my city.
Standing, a thoughtless pillar,
under the candelabrum,
I praise, admire and curse
on abra- and abracadabra.
Heroically, I venture
under the splendid columns

[1] Reprinted, with permission, from *News From Behind the Iron Curtain,* Vol. 5, No. 1, January, 1956.

and pay no heed to the puppets
of Gallux,† painted for coffins.
Here youngsters come for ice cream!
All of them are young and yet
their memories reach the ruins;
girls will soon have babies.
What's in the stone endures,
pathos and rubbish together,
here, future poets of Warsaw,
you'll learn your A's B's and C's.
Love all this most naturally,
I loved, I loved other stones,
grey and really magnificent,
sounding of reminiscence.
Squares turn like cobras,
houses stand like peacocks,
give me any old stone
and I'll be back in my city.

3.

"Today our sky is not empty."
(from a political speech)

It was dawn and at dawn I heard the sound of
jets,
very expensive, no doubt, expensive, but still we
must. . . .
When we don't want to speak about our earth simply,
we say, then we say: our sky's not empty.
People walk here anyhow and dress in denim,
women grow old here early, very early. . . .
When we don't want to speak about our earth simply,
we say, then we say: our sky's not empty.
Beyond the ocean an apocalypse curls in clouds
and here a passerby, a passerby kneels down. . . .
When we don't want to speak about the earth simply,
the kneeling man says: the sky's not empty.
Here a legion of boys lets out a cloud of pigeons
and a girl is tying a sky-blue kerchief. . . .
When we don't want to speak about the earth simply,
we say, then we say: the sky's not empty.

† Department store in which so-called luxury articles are sold.

4.

From villages and little towns they come in carts
to build a foundry and dream out a city, dig out of the
    earth a new Eldorado.
with an army of pioneers, a gathered crowd,
they jam in barns, barracks and hostels,
walk heavily and whistle loudly in the muddy streets:
the great migration, the twisted ambition,
with a string on their necks—the Czestochowa cross,
three floors of swear-words, a feather pillow,
a gallon of vodka and the lust for girls.
Distrustful soul, torn out of the village soil,
half-awakened and already half-mad,
in words silent, but singing, singing songs,
the huge mob, pushed suddenly
out of medieval darkness: un-human Poland,
howling with boredom on December nights. . . .
In garbage baskets and on hanging ropes
boys fly like cats on night walls,
girls' hostels, the secular nunneries,
burst with rutting—and then the "Duchesses"
ditch the foetus—the Vistula flows here. . . .
The great migration building industry,
unknown to Poland, but known to history,
fed with big empty words, and living
wildly from day to day despite the preachers,
in coal gas and in slow, continuous suffering
the working class is shaped out of it.
There is a lot of refuse. So far there are grits.

5.

This also happens: a brown cloud of smoke
rises above the mine that's been set afire,
the shaft's been cut off, the subterranean suffering
never will be told, the dark shaft now a coffin,
the saboteur has blood and bones and hands,
one hundred families cry, two hundred,
they write in papers or they do not write,
and only broken smoke stays in the air.

6.

At a railway station
Miss Jadzia's at the counter

she's so nice when she yawns
she's so nice when she pours. . . .
ATTENTION! THE ENEMY PLIES YOU WITH VODKA
You'll be poisoned here for sure
Miss Jadzia'll pull off your boots
she's so nice when she yawns
she's so nice when she pours. . . .
ATTENTION! THE ENEMY PLIES YOU WITH VODKA
Do not go, my boy, to Nowa Huta
or you'll be poisoned on the way,
take warning from the treacherous poster
and the national fish in your stomach. . . .
ATTENTION! THE ENEMY PLIES YOU WITH VODKA

7.

I'll not believe, my friend, that lions are calves,
I'll not believe, my friend, that calves are lions,
I'll not believe, my friend, in magic curses
or in reasons kept under glass,
but I believe that the table has four legs,
but I believe that the fifth leg is a chimera,
and when chimeras come together, my friend,
one dies slowly of heart disease.

8.

It's true,
when the brass trumpets of boredom
jam the great educational aim,
when vultures of abstraction eat out of our brains,
when students are shut off in textbooks without windows,
when our language is reduced to thirty magic formulas,
when the lamp of imagination dies out,
when the good people from the moon
refuse us the right to have taste,
it's true,
then we are in danger of becoming ignorant and dull.

9.

They fished the drowned man out of the Vistula.
They found a piece of paper in his pocket:
"My sleeve is right,
my button is wrong,
my collar is wrong,

but my strap is right."
They buried him under a willow tree.

10.

In a freshly plastered street of new buildings
lime dust circles and a cloud rushes through the sky.
Pulverizers, rolling in the street, press the surface,
transplanted chestnut-trees bloom and sing in twilight.
Little and big children scatter under the chestnut-trees,
dragging wood for fuel from half-pulled-down scaffolds.
The staircase is full of names, melodious, feminine names,
fifteen-year-old whores walk down the planks to the base-
    ment,
their smiles seem made of lime, they smell of lime,
in the neighborhood the radio plays darkly for magical
    dances,
the night comes, hooligans play hooligans. How difficult
it is to sleep in childhood among the singing chestnut
    trees. . . .
Disappear into darkness, dissonances! I wanted so much
    to be glad
of novelty, tell you about the young street, but not this
    one!
Was I deprived of the gift to see, or the gift of convenient
    blindness?
All I have is a short note, the poems of a new sorrow.

11.

Speculators took her to a quiet hell
in an isolated villa—she escaped.
She wandered drunk all night,
slept on cement till light.
They threw her out of art school
for lack of socialist morality.
She poisoned herself once—they saved her.
She poisoned herself again—they buried her.

12.

All this is not new. Old is the Cerberus of socialist mo-
    rality.
Fourier, the dreamer, charmingly foretold
that lemonade would flow in seas.

Does it not flow?
They drink sea-water,
crying:
"lemonade!"
returning home secretly
to vomit.

13.

They came and said:
"a Communist does not die."
No man has lived forever.
Only the memory of him is to remain.
The more valuable the man,
the greater the pain.
They came and cried:
under socialism
a hurt finger does not hurt.
They hurt their fingers.
They felt the pain.
They began to doubt.

14.

They shouted at the ritualists,
they instructed,
enlightened and
shamed the ritualists.
They sought the aid of literature,
that five-year-old youngster,
which should be educated
and which should educate.
Is a ritualist an enemy?
A ritualist is not an enemy,
a ritualist must be instructed,
he must be enlightened,
he must be shamed,
he must be convinced.
We must educate.
They have changed people into preachers.
I have heard a wise lecture:
"Without properly distributed economic incentives
we'll not make technical progress."
These are the words of a Marxist.
This is the knowledge of real laws,

the end of utopia.
There will be no novels about ritualists,
but there will be novels about the troubles of inventors,
about anxieties which move all of us.
This is my naked poem
before it matures
into troubles, colors and odors of the earth.

15.

There are people tired of work,
there are people from Nowa Huta
who have never been in a theater,
there are Polish apples unobtainable by Polish children,
there are children scorned by criminal doctors,
there are boys forced to lie,
there are girls forced to lie,
there are old wives thrown out of homes by their husbands,
there are exhausted people, suffering from angina pectoris,
there are people who are blackened and spat at,
there are people who are robbed in the streets
by thugs for whom legal definitions are sought,
there are people waiting for papers,
there are people waiting for justice,
there are people who have been waiting for a long time.
On this earth we appeal on behalf of people
who are exhausted from work,
we appeal for locks that fit the door,
for rooms with windows,
for walls which do not rot,
for contempt for papers,
for a holy human time,
for a safe return home,
for a simple distinction between words and deeds.
We appeal for this on the earth,
for which we did not gamble with dice,
for which a million people died in battles,
we appeal for bright truth and the corn of freedom,
for a flaming reason,
for a flaming reason,
we appeal daily,
we appeal through our Party.

Nowa Kultura (Warsaw),
August 21, 1955.

—B—
Party Attacks Wazyk's Poem[2]

Why did *A Poem for Adults* create such a sensation in Poland? The question cannot be fully answered merely by stating that a Communist poet has written a verse critical of the Communist reality around him. In spite of the narrow margin of freedom in Communist-dominated countries, some critical prose and poetry has appeared. The significance of the Wazyk poem lies in its tone, its perceptiveness, and the degree of condemnation in it. With its intensity of despair, disgust and rebellion, the poem is the most sincere, bitter and spontaneous cry of man's disillusionment with Communism that has so far appeared behind the Iron Curtain. That this cry was written by a Communist poet only adds to its irony and drama.

Wazyk not only refuses to accept present day Polish reality as he sees it, but he condemns it. He cannot, as the Party would have him do, project into a misty future, because today is drab, hateful and without hope or promise. He commits the sin of escaping into the past, that same past which Communist propaganda has for the past ten years condemned to perdition. However evil the past may have been, Wazyk says, he prefers it to the present and even to the Communist version of the future. He can no longer reconcile that promise-dream with the picture of "fifteen-year-old whores whose smiles seem made of lime," or the image of the man who has lost his mind, because he no longer is permitted to use it, or the women who grow old too early.

Wazyk sees all this and more, and he does not treat these things gingerly. His bitterness and disillusionment take him across the border of caution, and out of his anger and despair, he makes a truly meaningful arraignment of that system for which he had once declared himself.

Wazyk's *A Poem for Adults* did not have to wait for attack: *Trybuna Wolnosci*, organ of the Central Committee of the Polish Communist Party, and *Poprostu*,

[2] Reprinted, with permission, from *News From Behind the Iron Curtain*, Vol. 5, No. 1, January, 1956.

the cultural weekly of the Polish Communist Youth League (ZMP) attacked the poem and Wazyk in their respective issues of September 21-27 and September 4.

"How does it happen that a Party poet in our country writes about our life a poem full of bitter disillusionment, if not of outright contempt. Wazyk weights the lying phraseology, the ideological emptiness and hypocrisy, the empty declamation and cold dogmas, which in reality is emptiness of heart and mind. These things are known and we do not hide them, nor seek to hide them. . . .

"Wazyk indulges in a cold passion of generalization in such a way that he could expose himself to the accusation of irresponsibility in matters of much less importance. This poem is a bad and cruel half-truth. . . .

Poprostu was even more bitter and its article was titled "On the Gift of Convenient Blindness—in Prose." It wrote:

"What Wazyk said is true about 'The big migration building industry.' It does not consist of angels who will be taken alive to the Communist heaven. The life of the people is often difficult, dirty, tragic and boring. This is true of what Wazyk said of the nights of girls in the working hostels, 'those temporary nunneries,' about what he said of the emptiness of big phrases, of lies, routine thinking, about bandits who are tried for 'bikinism,' about people who wait too long for justice. All this is. But despite it, I think that *A Poem for Adults* is wrong from beginning to end. . . .

"I think that the poet who has lived ten years in Poland and writes poetry in Poland should not be allowed to 'go out for a walk and return' as a man who went out to bring medicine and returned after twenty years to cry with bewilderment: 'Oh, oh, how many bad things, how much evil!' . . ."

—C—

Gomulka's Keynote Speech[3]

Following are major excerpts from the new First Secretary's speech, which was released by the official Polish press service on October 21, 1956.

When I addressed the November Plenum of the Party

[3] Reprinted, with permission, from *News From Behind the Iron Curtain*, Vol. 5, No. 11, November, 1956.

Central Committee seven years ago, it was my last speech to the members of the Central Committee. . . . these years constitute a closed historical period. I am deeply convinced that those years belong to the irrevocable past. There has been much evil in those years. The legacy that the period left the Party, the working class and the nation is more than alarming in certain spheres of life. . . .

ATTACKS WRONG INVESTMENT POLICY

Generally speaking, after the conclusion of the Six Year Plan, which according to its premises was meant to raise the standard of living of the working class and of the entire nation, we are faced today in the first year of the Five Year Plan with immense economic difficulties which are growing from day to day. We contracted important investment credits for the expansion of industry and when the time came for the payment of the first installments we found ourselves in the situation of an insolvent bankrupt. We had to ask our creditors for a moratorium. In the meantime a considerable part of these credits in the shape of machines and installations has so far found no application in production and will not find any such application for long years to come; a part of these funds has to be considered irrevocably lost. The balance of payments in the Five Year Plan shows a considerable deficit despite the moratorium. . . . In this situation the reality of the Five Year Plan . . . is greatly impaired. . . .

. . . Such facts as have been cited can in no way be passed over in silence. For it should be said clearly that the whole nation has to pay for the bad economic policy, and the working class is more affected than others. The CC of the Party has failed to draw, to say the very least, the necessary Party consequences with regard to the people who bear the results of this state of affairs.

STRESSES AGRICULTURAL CRISIS

[In 1955], 78.8 percent of farmland was in individual farms; kolkhozes owned 8.6 percent and State farms 12.6 of total area owned by these three types of farm. The percentage produced by these three types was: individual farms—83.9 percent, kolkhozes including household plots —7.7 percent, and State farms including auxiliary holdings of agricultural workers—8.4 percent. When estimating the value of overall production per hectare of arable land we arrive at the following figures: individual farms, 621.1 *zloty;* kolkhozes, 517.3 *zloty;* State farms, 393.7 *zloty* at constant prices. . . . This is, in brief outline, the economic picture of collective farms. It is a sad picture. In spite of great outlays they had smaller results and greater production costs. I need not mention the political aspects of the problem.

DESCRIBES BAD LIVING CONDITIONS

Particular concern must be aroused by the housing problem in the countryside. . . . Every year we should build 150,000 rooms in the countryside in order to maintain the number of rooms at the 1950 level. This amounts to some 900,000 rooms for the Six Year Plan; only some 370,000 were built. It must be concluded that during the Six Year Plan about 600,000 rooms turned into dust. . . . The situation is not much better in the field of public services, health resorts or sanatoria. . . .

The working class recently gave a painful lesson to the Party leadership and the government, when it seized the weapon of strike and went out to demonstrate in the streets on Black Thursday, last June. The Poznan workers shouted in a powerful voice: Enough! This cannot go on any longer! Turn back from the wrong road! . . . The Poznan workers did not protest against People's Poland, against Socialism. . . . They protested against the evil which was widespread in our social system . . . against the distortion of the fundamental principles of Socialism. . . . The clumsy attempt to present the painful Poznan tragedy as the work of imperialist agents and provocateurs was politically very naïve. . . . The causes of the Poznan tragedy and of the profound dissatisfaction of the entire working class are to be found in ourselves, in the leadership of the Party, in the government. . . . The juggling with figures which showed a 27 percent rise in living standard during the Six Year Plan proved a failure. It only exasperated people more. . . .

OUTLINES NEW POLICIES

The 20th CPSU Congress stimulated a turn in the political life of the country. . . . People began to straighten their backs. Silent, enslaved minds began to shake off the poison of mendacity, falsehood and hypocrisy. The rigid cliches, previously predominant on Party platforms and at public meetings, as well as in the press, began to give place to creative, living words. . . . Above all, the working people wanted to know all the truth, without any embellishments, any omissions. In the situation which arose following the 20th Congress, when it was necessary to act quickly and consistently, to draw conclusions from the past, to go to the masses with all frankness and to tell them the truth . . . the Party leadership failed to work out quickly a line of concrete action. . . . It is necessary to change a great deal in our people's government, in the organization of our industry, in the methods of work of the State and Party apparatus. It is necessary, in short, to replace all the bad parts of our model of Socialism. . . . We must tell the hard truth to the working class: We cannot afford any more serious wage increases, for the string has been strained to such a degree that it can break. . . .

With regard to collective farms, the basically sound ones should be assisted by repayable investment credits, and all forms of State grants should be abolished. Collectives which have poor chances of development and which bring only economic loss should not be granted credits, but rather the members of such cooperatives should be confronted with the problem of dissolving the collective. . . . The joining of collective farms is voluntary. This excludes not only threats or psychological compulsion, but also economic compulsion. Tax assessments and the establishment of quota deliveries can also be instruments of economic compulsion. . . . Why should not, for instance, the Catholic Progressive Movement compete with us in the search for and the realization of forms of cooperative farming? It is a poor idea to maintain that only Communists can build Socialism, only people holding materialist social views. . . . I have in mind the abolition of quota deliveries which cannot be . . . an economic feature of our system. . . .

ADVOCATES DIFFERENT ROADS TO SOCIALISM

How did it happen that our Party . . . permitted the many distortions of the recent past to arise? We shall look for a long time to find the answer. It is contained in the problem of the roads leading to the construction of Socialism, as well as in the shaping of a model for Socialism. What is constant in Socialism boils down to the abolition of the exploitation of man by man. The roads of achieving this goal can be and are different. . . . The model of Socialism can also vary. It can be like that of the Soviet Union. It can be shaped in a manner seen in Yugoslavia. It can be different still. . . . After the Second World War the Soviet Union ceased to be the only country building Socialism. People's China and a number of the People's Democracies, including Poland . . . entered the world arena. . . . The mutual relations between the Parties and States of the Socialist camp do not and should not give any cause for complications. . . . These relations should be built on the principles of international working class solidarity, on mutual confidence and equality of rights, mutual granting of assistance, mutual, friendly criticism. Within the framework of such relations each country should have full independence, and the rights of each nation to a sovereign government in an independent country should be fully and mutually respected. This is how it should be and I would say that this is how it is beginning to be.

REINTERPRETS "CULT OF INDIVIDUAL"

Stalin, as the leader of the Party and the Soviet Union, formally recognized all the above principles. . . . He not only recognized them, he proclaimed them. In fact, however, these principles could not fit within the framework of what makes up the cult of the individual. The cult of the individual was not confined solely to Stalin. It is a certain system which prevailed in the Soviet Union and which was grafted on to probably all Communist Parties, as well as to a number of countries of the Socialist camp, including Poland. The essence of the system was the creation of an individual hierarchic ladder of cults. . . . In the block of Socialist States Stalin stood at the top of this hierarchic ladder. All those who stood on lower rungs of the ladder bowed their heads before him. Those who bowed their heads were not only the other leaders of the CPSU and the leaders of the Soviet Union, but also the leaders of the Communist and Workers' Parties of the countries of the Socialist camp. The latter, that is, the

First Secretaries of the Central Committees of the Parties of the various countries, who sat on the second rung of the ladder of the cult of the individual, donned in turn the robes of infallibility and wisdom. But their cults radiated only on the territory of their own countries where they stood at the top of the national cult ladder. This national cult could be called only a reflected brilliance, a borrowed light. It shone as the moon does. Nonetheless it was all powerful in the sphere of its action.

The bearer of the cult of the individual was omniscient, knew how to do everything, solved everything, directed everything and decided everything within the sphere of his activity. He was the most intelligent man, regardless of his personal knowledge, capacity, or other personal qualities. . . .

Under the system of the cult of the individual the Party as a whole could act independently only within the framework of subordination to the chief cult. If someone attempted to transgress these limits he was threatened with excommunication by his comrades. If the matter concerned a whole Party, it was excommunicated by the remaining Communist Parties. Under such conditions, could the mutual Party and State relations of the Parties and countries of the People's Democracies on the one hand and the CPSU and the Soviet Union on the other hand be shaped on principles of equality? Clearly not. It was prevented by the system of the cult of the individual, a system organized with precision, crushing every independent Socialist thought. . . .

LASHES OUT AT "BESTIAL TORTURES"

In Poland, too, tragedy occurred when innocent people were sent to their deaths. Many others, including Communists, were imprisoned, often for many years, despite their innocence. Many people were submitted to bestial tortures. Terror and demoralization were widespread. On the soil of the cult of the individual phenomena arose which violated and even nullified the most profound meaning of the people's power. We have put an end to this system, rather, we are putting an end to it once and for all. Great appreciation should be expressed to the 20th Congress of the CPSU which so greatly helped us in the liquidation of this system. Although the system of the cult of the individual was born in the Soviet Union, this does not mean that blame for all the evil which happened in Poland can be put on Stalin, on the CPSU or the Soviet Union. We also had our own domestic variety of Beriaism. These are matters . . . which require more thorough investigation and clarification. The leadership of the Party should set up a commission to inquire whether in the cases of people who are now being rehabilitated and who were arrested in the past on the instruction or with the agreement of the Politburo or part of the Politburo, there were no instances of deliberate provocation, of deliberately accusing people of deeds they had not committed. . . . Clarification of this matter is essential and should be undertaken by a commission of completely impartial people.

All the opponents of Socialism, all the enemies of People's Poland, cannot fail to take advantage of the present situation. The greater activity shown by these elements . . . has also caused certain waverings among Comrades in the Party leadership and in the provinces. . . . That is why it is necessary firmly to tell . . . the entire nation: the road of democratization is the only road. . . . We shall not deviate from this road and we shall defend ourselves with all our might against being pushed off this road. And we shall not allow anyone to use the process of democratization to undermine Socialism. . . . And if there is anyone who thinks that it is possible to kindle an anti-Soviet mood in Poland then he is deeply mistaken. . . . Polish-Soviet relations based on the principle of equality and independence will create among the Polish people such a profound feeling of friendship for the Soviet Union that no attempt to sow distrust for the Soviet Union will find a response among the Polish people. Such relations are guarded first of all by our Party and together with it by the entire nation. . . .

—D—

Communism and Humanism[4]

By Adam Schaff

Communist ideology is certainly not dead. It acts, and it acts powerfully. But it is worth asking how it can be made even more effective, how to remove obstacles (if such exist) to its influence over people. Now certainly one of the means will be increasing and extending the humanist contents of socialism, strengthening the ideological offensive of socialist humanism. The strongest card used in propaganda against Communism and Marxism today is in the capitalist world the problem of liberty of the individual, the problem of democracy under a socialist system. This is the strongest card because it really reaches people and frightens them away from socialism. They believe most often that they have democracy and we have dictatorship, and therefore, that they respect the right of the individual and we slight him. This view often builds a wall between them and socialism, it constitutes a real political and ideological fact which we must appreciate for what it is worth. What makes up such a belief? Many factors: beginning with conscious hostility to socialism, through yielding to hostile propaganda, to the effects of our own mistakes and clumsiness. We have neglected for years in our theoretical thinking the question of the individual and his problems. And this fact was adequately exploited by hostile propaganda. It is not so easy to guess that when we say "dictatorship" we mean "the highest form of democracy" and we make no mistake. Finally the facts from life, facts taken from the history of the building of socialism, facts which we have called "mistakes and deviations." We try to explain the social genesis of these facts, but we do not try to justify them. And we should not, we must not. Yet these are also elements eagerly exploded by the enemy and his propaganda.

Dialectics of freedom and its limitations constitutes a

[4] English translation by the Polish Press service (CFE). A German translation will be found in *Ost-Probleme,* February 9, 1962.

further consequence of this basic fact, namely of the class struggle in contemporary society. Under conditions of struggle AGAINST the ideals of humanism, and thereby AGAINST freedom, the demand for absolute freedom is absurd if not criminal. As long as there are enemies of freedom, as long as they are capable of effective fight, so long must various limitations of their freedom be accepted of necessity by socialist humanism, because it is a fighting humanism.

Unlimited freedom for the enemies of freedom as long as they are effectively capable of fighting means more than a danger of deviation and excess—it means the CERTAINTY of defeat of the cause of freedom. For that reason socialist humanism in the name of the freedom of the individual proclaims the necessity of limiting this freedom under special conditions.

The dialectics of democracy and dictatorship is another social expression of the above-mentioned conflict. Only against this background can one understand the Marxist theory of the state which must go to democracy through dictatorship and holds the dictatorship of the proletariat as a higher form of democracy than the bourgeois democracy. Those two last problems not only appear jointly, but constitute at the same time the most difficult point of socialist humanism. . . .

. . . If people in many cases follow the voice of anti-Communist propaganda, it is because they fail to understand the real situation and are deceived by appearances. It is more difficult to understand—especially when the public opinion is shaped by bourgeois propaganda—that a monoparty system, violently combatting the opposition to its views, forbidding opposition political activities, etc., is a democracy of a higher order. The mistakes of our propaganda, variations of terminology and, most important, mistakes in implementing the ideas of the dictatorship of the proletariat, eagerly exploited by the enemy—have made the dialectics of the road, which through Draconian restrictions leads to the fullest freedom of man, harder to understand. . . .

My thesis runs as follows—educating members of a socialist society in the spirit of socialist humanism, making them understand the humanist and freedom aims of ours, is the more necessary, the greater is the practical need to apply coercion and limitation of civic freedom, if only to a certain extent and under certain circumstances. Socialist democracy, like other democracies, does not shirk from applying coercion—it is in this form of state power, a dictatorship of a definite class directed against another class. The danger here lies in the alienation of the function of coercion. The history of the French revolution teaches us the dangers of this alienation of functions and apparatus of coercion, it is also shown by our own experiences of the so-called past period of mistakes and deviations. It is a question of recent and painful problems. . . .

In certain areas at least, scientific and artistic creation is directly connected to politics, it expresses progressive or reactionary social trends and may influence the society in the spirit of progress or in that of reaction.

But, starting with socialist humanism and its ideas on the development of human personality, one may reach a conclusion of great practical importance: political interference in scientific and artistic creation should be an exception, reduced to cases of a clearly political character. The principle of the freedom of thought is fully maintained, although a certain element of subjectivism in choice and evaluation is inevitable. Creators must be offered subjects of special social value, they should be ideologically influenced in their outlook, especially in the field of social problems, etc. It is the basic meaning of Party guidance of science and art, apart from the organizational forms of their development which lies in the area of politics and cannot be identified with freedom of creative thought. The aims of socialism here are also a full and unrestricted freedom and the limitations are of a temporary character and are caused by a periodical and painful political necessity.

A scientist or an artist standing on Marxist ground can develop science and culture only under conditions when there is a freedom of discussion and research, when there is a possibility of a clash of views. This obviously creates additional political difficulties and dangers, but without this risk any progress of science and culture would be slowed down, and this in turn would reflect in politics; if only in the sense of weakening the possibility of correcting mistakes which might be committed in political practice. . . .

Part VI
FACTS AND ILLUSIONS

52

THE CANADIAN ESPIONAGE OPERATION

Volumes have been written about the espionage activities of the Soviet Union in foreign countries. The magnitude and effectiveness of this activity surpasses anything known in recorded history. One of the chief functions of Communist Parties throughout the world is to recruit operatives for the Soviet espionage apparatus.

The character of the Soviet espionage system was dramatically revealed by Igor Gouzenko, a clerk in the Soviet Embassy in Canada, who fled with a mass of documents whose genuineness even the Soviet regime admitted. At the very time when Canada, Britain and the United States were aiding the Soviet Union to withstand the assault of Hitler, the Kremlin was making a massive effort to ferret out all possible information bearing on the postwar defenses of these countries. Even more numerous rings existed in the United States—one of which is described in Whittaker Chambers' Witness. *Further information on the activities and techniques of Soviet espionage rings is contained in the writings of many other Soviet defectors who were principals in these operations, e.g., W. Krivitsky,* In Stalin's Secret Service; *A. Foote,* Handbook for Spies; *and works by Petrov and Orloff. These may be supplemented by D. Dallin's* Soviet Espionage; *Willoughby's* Shanghai Conspiracy; *and Pilot's* Atomic Spies. *The chapter on "Ideological Espionage" and its appendix in my* Political Power and Personal Freedom *(New York, 1959) summarizes some of the material.*

The following brief extracts are from The Report of the Royal Commission, *Ottawa, 1946, which was set up by the Canadian Parliament to investigate the documents of Gouzenko and to interrogate witnesses.*

✓   ✓   ✓

Authenticity and Accuracy of the Russian Documents

Gouzenko carried away with him on the night of the 5th September, 1945, when he permanently severed his connection with the Soviet Embassy, the documents which have already been referred to in this Report.

No occasion was neglected throughout the inquiry to test their authenticity and accuracy. We were, however, steadily and increasingly impressed by the evidence as it developed during these numerous and lengthy sessions. It brought to light an unhappy but unfaded picture of organized and progressing spying activities in Canada.

We have before us certain admissions made by the Soviet Government; admission by conduct of certain members of the Soviet Embassy at Ottawa; and express admissions by certain persons in the service of the Canadian Government. We have before us other relevent evidence which we shall also discuss. . . .

Conclusion

As to the information sought by the networks, we are unable to report with any degree of conclusiveness. We have seen only the small selection of Zabotin's espionage documents which Gouzenko was able to collect immediately before he left the Embassy; among these the telegrams, in which *The Director* listed his instructions, were all dated within the last week in July and the month of August 1945. The Military Intelligence network had been functioning at least since mid-1942.

Moreover the documents outline only the work of the espionage system headed in Canada by Colonel Zabotin, although the evidence discloses the existence of other parallel networks, some at least of which have been functioning for many years.

The evidence we have shows that Zabotin's organization was particularly anxious to obtain technical information regarding devices which would be used in the post-war defences of Canada, the United Kingdom and the United States; secret information regarding political plans and policies of these countries; economic information which would be useful in assessing the economic and military potential of Canada; details regarding the location of Canadian defence industries; information on certain telephone land-lines and tapping devices; and documents which could be used by Russian agents "planted" in Canada or elsewhere, plus information whereby such agents could enter Canada and acquire a base of operations here.

The following selection of extracts from the documents illustrates the variety of subjects on which material was sought:—

Supplement to No. 11923

N 11931
22.8.45

To Grant

Take measures to organize acquisition of documentary materials on the atomic bomb!

The technical processes, drawings, calculations.

Director,
Grant   22.8.45.
22.8.45.

. . . Try to get from him before departure detailed information on the progress of the work on Uranium. . . .

. . . Badeau asks for permission to change to work on Uranium. There is a possibility either by being invited or by applying himself, but he warned that they are very careful in the selection of workers and that they are under strict observation. . . .

ASSIGNMENT No. . . . . . .

Assigned personally 25.8.45

1. Answer last letter regarding the new radio tubes, radio-locators (both for $\Lambda = 1, 2, 3$ cm) and the other questions indicated in that letter.
2. Try to find out any particulars about the "Electron Shells."
3. For the next time bring the following books: LG 13853; GL 14017 and P(RAD) 13920. P.S.—burn after reading.

ASSIGNMENT No. 2

Assigned 6.7.45 directly : : :

1. To give the basic description of the features of the contrivance transmitting and receiving radio tubes for $\Lambda = 3$ and $\Lambda = 1$ cm. and their technical manufacture.
2. The same with respect to tube "4j-33."
3. New work in the field of radio locators for antiaircraft artillery and aeroplanes with $\Lambda = 3$ and $\Lambda = 1$ cm.
4. What are the features of the "T-R Switch" on wave $\Lambda = 3$ cm and $\Lambda = 1$ cm.
5. The types of radio antennae for $\Lambda = 3$ and $\Lambda = 1$ cm.
6. What are they engaged in on the second floor at the "Boyd Station," there is a supposition that they study infra-red rays and develop cm. radio installations.
7. To give a more detailed technical description of "an/aps-10."
8. According to the latest literature indicate each graph (?) in it.

Remarks:

1. As the opportunity arises, to obtain samples of the radio tubes.
2. Also to give us documentary material for photographing.
3. If there is no opportunity in fulfilling certain requests, no special activity to be displayed.
4. After reading this material burn it.

TASK No. 1

Badeau: 1. In the month of June 1945 the Military Air Force of Canada jointly with the Photographic Research Committee and also with the Optics Section of National Research Council, conducted tests of the new photo bomb (photo flash bombs bursting) of 750 million candle power, and of special lenses for aerial-photography by night.

It is desired to have on these questions the following information:—

Assigned
on 5.7.45

    a. What is the composition with which the photo bomb is filled and as much as possible write out its formula.

    c. What is the surface area lit up by the flare of this bomb and the duration of its flare.

    d. The maximum height from which it is possible to carry out practical photographing by means of this bomb.

    e. What are the features of the new photo-lenses and what are their basic technical data (focus, light power, etc.).

    f. [What is the organization of the Photographic Research Committee and who are its directors.]

2. What new jobs are being conducted by the Photographic Research Committee in the sphere of altitude aerial-photography and in colour aerial photography and photographing through the clouds by means of infra-red rays.

    Give the newest types of aerial-photo apparatuses used by the R.C.A.F. and by the R.A.F. and their basic data:—

    a. The type of the apparatus (the brand).

    b. The maximum height of photographing.

    c. The number of adapters and the size of the photographs.

    d. [The methods of itinerary and level photographing.]

    e. The types of lenses, their light power and the focal distances.

1. Tactical and technical facts of the naval and coastal hydro[-phonic] acoustic stations working in ultra-sound diapason. Common review on the "Caproni"'s stability of the U.S.A. and Great Britain.

2. Stability, type of "Asdic" which is used in new submarines and other ships.

3. Sets of the "Sonra"'s type, working on the radio direction finding principle so-called hydro [direction] location finding sets.

4. Situation of hydrophonic sets in the ships of different classes.

5. Plants, workshops, Scientific Research Institutes and laboratories in England and in the U.S.A. which are making and planning the hydrophonic apparatus.

6. Passing of the planning and the test of examples of new types of the hydrophonic apparatus.

7. Knowledge of the battle utilization of the hydrophonic means.

266

To the Director,

We have received from Badeau 17 top secret and secret documents (English, American and Canadian) on the question of magnicoustics, radio-locators for field artillery; three secret scientific-research journals of the year 1945. Altogether about 700 pages. In the course of the day we were able to photograph all the documents with the help of the Leica and the photofilter. In the next few days we will receive almost the same amount of documents for 3 to 5 hours and with one film we will not be able to cope with it. I consider it essential to examine the whole library of the scientific Research Council.

Your silence on my No. 256 may disrupt our work on photographing the materials. All the materials I am sending by regular courier.

Grant

27.8.45

N 11273
11.8.45.

To Grant.

It is very important to receive information on the following questions:—

(a) To confirm the official data about the transfer of American troops from Europe to the USA and to the Pacific, also the headquarters of the 9th army, 3, 5, 7, 13 armoured Corps, 18 ADK, 2, 4, 8, 28, 30, 44, 45, 104th Infantry Divisions and 13th Tank Division. To establish the dates of transfer.

    (b) Dislocation of the headquarters of the 8, 16 Armoured Corps, 29, (75), 89th Infantry Divisions, 10th Tank Divisions, 13th and 17th ADD. Also about the dislocation of the Brazilian Infantry Division.

    (c) Are the 6th and 12th Army Groups in Europe, what is their composition and their dislocation, the dates and direction of their transfer.

    (d) Has there been organized a headquarters of the American occupation forces in Germany, its location, who was appointed as its Commander.

    (e) The dislocation of the First Air Borne Army, the plans for its future use.
    Hurry.

8.8. The Director.

Grant
11.8.45
To make known to Brent

This list is not exhaustive, and other aims of Zabotin's network appear in various Sections of this Report.

Some of the objectives disclosed by the documents, such as lists of names, such as psychological and "political" reports, on the personnel of various sections of the Canadian Armed Forces Headquarters or of various Government Departments and Agencies, obviously refer to plans for further recruiting of agents. This subject is discussed in Section II. 5, above.

This report shows that Zabotin successfully fulfilled many of the tasks assigned to him. His superiors in Moscow were obviously satisfied with his work in Canada, for in August, 1954, he was awarded two Orders or Decorations, the Order of the RED BANNER, and the Order of the RED STAR, which, as Gouzenko said, "are given for good organization work." The Chief of General Intelligence telegraphed Zabotin to congratulate him on these awards and added: "I wish you further success in your honourable work." Gouzenko said that when this message arrived Zabotin said to Rogov: "I have nothing to be afraid now to go to Moscow."

53

IDEOLOGICAL ESPIONAGE: HARRY GOLD'S CONFESSION [1]

The case of Klaus Fuchs, the Soviet atomic spy, as well as the arrest and conviction of a half dozen of his American confederates, revealed a facet of the Communist movement which those who had judged it only by its ideas had until then largely ignored. It was a peculiar mixture of idealism and treason which led to the fall of Harry Gold and others. On July 27, 1957, from his jail cell, Gold, Prisoner No. 19312, wrote a moving statement in which he described "Soviet techniques for influencing sincere people." He detailed certain incidents which occurred during his personal association with Soviet agents and in the course of carrying out espionage for the Russians, and then showed how these incidents fitted into an overall pattern. The final section of Gold's statement, "The summing up," is reprinted here.

✦   ✦   ✦

. . . The overall pattern is the deceptively simple one of, "Tell 'em what they want to hear"—but because of its obviousness, it disarms and thereby becomes tremendously effective. The simplest and most used idea is to espouse an incontrovertibly decent cause, one really of solid worth and undeniably correct. In my case, the ready-made one of anti-Semitism. Did I have a horror of anti-Semitism? So did the Soviet Union—actively so (as far as the face was presented to me). And, as with a symphony, there are minor themes, all building up to the crescendo of the coda. Such are:

(*1*) Let's start them [the gulls] in a small way, any way at all, but let's start. Have them get the habit of working for the Soviet Union.

[1] From: *From Hearing Before the Internal Security Subcommittee,* August 15, 1957.

(2) Bolster up the [*phantom*] of the courageous individual who dares disagree, the man of true moral fiber . . . and from there one can easily go on to a lack of respect for the properly established procedures and authority . . . and then, inevitably, to take matters into one's own hands.

(3) Feeding the individual's self-esteem: This appears so plainly a sucker play, that it doesn't ever seem likely to succeed. But see how nicely it was accomplished. Me and my lofty idealism and let's not forget the neat backspin on the item of contempt for the Communist Party of the United States.

(4) Reaction to kindness: This doesn't have to be anything big or of great moment and, preferably, little, if any, monetary value should be involved. We humans seem to most appreciate the small, considerate, selfless gestures and such an event binds one even closer to the donor.

(5) Where the Russians positively wanted to make certain, they just crashed ahead with blunt, out-and-out flattery. This works too, because a person won't believe that anyone would try such a brash approach. It's as if a man's closest friend were to say (for no apparent reason), "I'm going to kill you," and forthwith does so—the victim would probably laugh and turn his back at just the moment before the tragic event.

The last element in the Soviet structure requires a place by itself, right along with the overall pattern given earlier (it's too important, especially right now, to be relegated to a minor theme status). I refer to the Russians dwelling on the prospect that all nations would live in peace. It's sort of, "Look, Mom, no brass knuckles," gambit. Plus, "See, I smile and make jokes— Ergo, I'm no monster; I'm human." This is the deadliest of all.

But remember: "Tell 'em what they want to hear."

With this goes also the decision that I was always to regard myself as an American citizen, working under cover for the Soviet Union solely because of the obstructive tactics of industrialists and politicians. Even that much-belabored trip to Moscow carried with it the explicit understanding that I was to return to the United States. The Russians nurtured this idea most carefully: Harry Gold—loyal American. To me the true horror underneath "buying" the Soviet way of life resides in the inevitable, completely inexorable demand for a payment —but the currency in use is the human soul and there is the awful corollary, that fact that a man becomes willing, even eager, to do any bidding, no matter how loathsome.

I am aware that the portrait given here of my reactions to the Soviets' maneuvering of my personality is delineated in harsh strokes. Looking back, as I said before, it does seem as if it were another day, another age, almost another world. Yet I know what occurred and what I did.

HARRY GOLD, *No. 19312.*
Lewisburg, Pa., July 27, 1957.

— 54 —

A POLITICAL TRIPTYCH OF COMRADE KHRUSHCHEV *

The following quotations present in brief but striking form the essence of a political biography. Further comment is unnecessary.

✓ ✓ ✓

—A—
"Stalin is our banner!"

KHRUSHCHEV, JANUARY 30, 1937 (*Pravda*, JANUARY 31)

Comrade workers, men and women, engineers, employees, men of science and art, and all working people of our country! We are gathered here on Red Square, to raise our proletarian voice in complete support of the sentence passed by the Military Collegium of the Supreme Court against the enemies of the people, the traitors of

* From: *Problems of Communism*, Vol. X, No. 6, November-December, 1961. The reference here is to the second of the Great Purge Trials, held January 23-30, 1937.

the Motherland, the betrayers of the workers' cause, the spies, the diversionists, agents of fascism, the vile, despicable Trotskyites. . . . These murderers aimed at the heart and brain of our party. They have lifted their villainous hands against Comrade Stalin. By lifting their hands against Comrade Stalin they lifted them against all the best that humanity possesses. For Stalin is hope; he is expectation; he is the beacon that guides all progressive mankind. Stalin is our banner! Stalin is our will! Stalin is our victory!

—B—

"Stalin . . . committed arbitrary actions and abuses of power."

KHRUSHCHEV AT THE 22ND CONGRESS, OCTOBER 27, 1961

Stalin elevated certain curtailments of intraparty and Soviet democracy, inevitable under conditions of an acute struggle against internal and external enemies, to the levels of standards of intraparty and state affairs. He flagrantly flouted the Leninist principles of leadership and committed arbitrary actions and abuses of power. . . . Thousands of absolutely innocent people perished, and each person is a whole story. Many party leaders, statesmen, and military leaders lost their lives. . . . When we investigated [*some of these cases*] . . . , we asked Molotov, Kaganovich, and Voroshilov: Are you in favor of rehabilitating them? Yes, we are in favor, they replied. But it was you who executed these people, we said with indignation. So when did you act according to your conscience—then or now? But they gave no reply to this question, they will not give one.

—C—

"Comrade Khrushchev did that excellently. . . ."

A. SHELEPIN AT THE 22ND CONGRESS, OCTOBER 26, 1961

The routing of the antiparty group is a major victory of our party and its Leninist Central Committee, a victory whose significance for the entire cause of Communist construction is difficult to overestimate. Today we all have a more accurate picture of the disaster from which the party, the people, and the country were saved by the resolute actions of the Central Committee and personally of Nikita Sergeyevich Khrushchev, who played an outstanding part in the unmasking and routing of the factionaries. Comrade Khrushchev did that excellently and in a Leninist manner.

VAN NOSTRAND ANVIL BOOKS already published

1 *MAKING OF MODERN FRENCH MIND*—H. Kohn
2 *THE AMERICAN REVOLUTION*—R. B. Morris
3 *THE LATE VICTORIANS*—H. Ausubel
4 *WORLD IN THE 20th CENTURY*—L. L. Snyder
5 *50 DOCUMENTS OF THE 20th CENTURY*—
    L. L. Snyder
6 *THE AGE OF REASON*—L. L. Snyder
7 *MARX AND THE MARXISTS*—S. Hook
8 *NATIONALISM*—H. Kohn
9 *MODERN JAPAN*—A. Tiedemann
10 *50 DOCUMENTS OF THE 19th CENTURY*—
    L. L. Snyder
11 *CONSERVATISM*—P. Viereck
12 *THE PAPACY*—J. A. Corbett
13 *AGE OF THE REFORMATION*—R. H. Bainton
14 *DOCUMENTS IN AMERICAN HISTORY*—
    R. B. Morris
15 *CONTEMPORARY AFRICA*—T. W. Wallbank
16 *THE RUSSIAN REVOLUTIONS OF 1917*—J. S. Curtiss
17 *THE GREEK MIND*—W. R. Agard
18 *BRITISH CONSTITUTIONAL HISTORY SINCE 1832*
    —R. L. Schuyler and C. C. Weston
19 *THE NEGRO IN THE U.S.*—R. W. Logan
20 *AMERICAN CAPITALISM*—L. M. Hacker
21 *LIBERALISM*—J. S. Schapiro
22 *ERA OF THE FRENCH REVOLUTION, 1789-1799*—
    L. Gershoy
23 *HISTORY OF MODERN GERMANY*—L. L. Snyder
24 *HISTORY OF MODERN RUSSIA*—H. Kohn
25 *NORTH ATLANTIC CIVILIZATION*—M. Kraus
26 *NATO*—M. Salvadori
27 *DOCUMENTS IN U.S. FOREIGN POLICY*—
    T. P. Brockway
28 *AMERICAN FARMERS' MOVEMENTS*—
    F. A. Shannon
29 *HISTORIC DECISIONS OF SUPREME COURT*—
    C. B. Swisher
30 *MEDIEVAL TOWN*—J. H. Mundy and P. Riesenberg
31 *REVOLUTION AND REACTION 1848-1852*—
    G. Bruun
32 *SOUTHEAST ASIA AND WORLD TODAY*—
    C. A. Buss
33 *HISTORIC DOCUMENTS OF W. W. I*—L. L. Snyder
34 *HISTORIC DOCUMENTS OF W. W. II*—
    W. C. Langsam
35 *ROMAN MIND AT WORK*—P. MacKendrick